THE SCIENCE OF RELATIONSHIPS

Answers to Your Questions about Dating, Marriage, and Family

Gary W. Lewandowski Jr.
Timothy J. Loving

Benjamin Le
Marci E. J. Gleason

Contributors

Jennifer J. Harman
Jody L. Davis
Lorne Campbell

Robin S. Edelstein
Nancy E. Frye
Lisa A. Neff

M. Minda Oriña
Debra Mashek
Eshkol Rafaeli

Kendall Hunt
publishing company

Kendall Hunt
publishing company

www.kendallhunt.com
Send all inquiries to:
4050 Westmark Drive
Dubuque, IA 52004-1840

ISBN 978-1-4652-0140-9

Printed in the United States of America
10 9 8 7 6 5 4 3

CONTENTS

PREFACE

You might be wondering, "Why do we need another book on relationships?" Well, if the book in question is like all of the existing books out there, in that it offers the opinion of a single author, the answer is we don't need another book on relationships—at least like that. What we do need is a book on relationships that takes a new approach. Thankfully, this book represents a new way of writing about relationships. Until now, if you wanted to learn about relationships, the most common way to do so was to read a traditional self-help or advice book, read an advice page on the Internet, or pick up a magazine from the check-out line at the store. Other options, though largely underutilized, would be to take a college course on relationships or read the hundreds of scientific articles that relationship scholars publish annually in academic journals. These approaches each have their pros and cons. This book offers a new option, representing a hybrid that capitalizes on the positive features of both popular *and* academic sources.

This new approach presents the leading research on romantic relationships in a way that is informative, engaging, and fun. The contributors of this book, all of whom are experts in the scientific study of interpersonal relationships, collectively felt that the relationship books currently lining bookshelves were too heavy on opinion and too light on quality, fact-based information. So, on a snowy June night in Breckenridge, Colorado, as over a dozen of us crammed into a hot tub, the idea for this book was born. Now you might be wondering if that was too many people. For a six-person hot tub, perhaps; but for a book on relationships that seeks to provide expert information, the more the merrier. In fact, the scope of relationships is so broad that it is nearly impossible for any one person to be an expert on the entire field.

Having so many experts ensures that someone with a deep knowledge of that area delivers the information. All of the contributors to this book hold a Ph.D.

in the study of relationships. Our specialties cover the spectrum of relationship experiences, including dating, attraction, passion, making love last, and breaking up. Collectively, we have been studying relationships for 200 years! Not only are we relationship scientists, but a majority of us are also college professors who routinely teach classes on relationships. As a group we have also dated, divorced, been engaged, been dumped, cheated, been cheated on, fallen in love, gotten into fights, made-up, hooked-up, had kids, and avoided having kids, although not necessarily in that order. So we don't just study relationships—we have lived them as well! Our combined personal experiences and doctoral training make this type of book, where research findings are applied to everyday contexts, possible.

We all have relationships, so aren't we all experts? Not exactly. Just because people prepare their own dinner every night, it doesn't make them all Jamie Oliver, Rachel Ray, or Wolfgang Puck. When it comes to relationships, an expert is someone who has extensive knowledge of the scientific research. But why is research important? A fundamental human motivation involves trying to understand the world. Often we seek understanding by gathering information about our lives through comparisons to others. In the context of relationships, it is not uncommon to ask friends what their relationships are like as a way of better understanding our own. Other times you might go to the bookstore to pick up a book about relationships or simply go Googling for the answers.

Although these sources may provide information about your relationships, they are limited in a very important way. They represent the opinions of only of only a few people (e.g., your friend, the author of the book). If you had a chance to ask hundreds or thousands of people about their relationships, how their partners treat them, if they ever experience feelings of doubt, and so on, would you? In essence, this is what we do as researchers. We pose questions and have hundreds of people provide responses so that we can more accurately capture what relationships are generally like. This way we are sure to get a better feel for what most people's experiences are like, rather than the potentially idiosyncratic or biased viewpoints of a few individuals who happen to write relationship books. Similarly, if you want to know what most people watch on TV, you would look at the Nielsen ratings, not what your next-door neighbor watches.

Some people might think that no one knows their relationships better than they do, so it doesn't matter what other people have to say. Unfortunately, we are often inaccurate in our perceptions and evaluations of ourselves. People who want to believe their relationships are perfect may seek out information that confirms these beliefs, and when confronted with evidence that their relationships aren't perfect, they tend to find fault with the evidence. Because of these biases, it is important to use scientific information that arrives at objective conclusions that are untainted by personal beliefs. This way, you can focus on how things *really* are, and less on how you *hope* things are.

One of the complaints people often have about science and scientific writing is that it is often not very definitive and instead provides lots of "It depends" types of answers. Although it is true that no conclusion is 100% certain, general conclusions can still be made. Throughout this book, we have tried to provide you with the take-home points that have emerged from research, while also discussing the many details and caveats that characterize complex social relationships. Thus, in some cases, our characterization of an original study may be somewhat of a departure from the original author's intended conclusion. Much like you can drive a car or use your iPad without fully understanding how it works, we believe that you can benefit from the scientific study of relationships without knowing all of the details. However, we do hope that a byproduct of your interest in this book will be an enhanced curiosity into the methods scientists use to uncover this information.

Still skeptical about the need for experts and science in living your own individual life? Consider the case of the weather. On a daily basis, we often benefit from being informed about what the conditions outside will be like. Is it going to rain? Will it be cold? To find out this information, we don't call our friend to see what they think. Instead, we rely on the weather forecast based on the collection of large amounts of data, which is then interpreted by experts. If scientific data are good enough to dictate your wardrobe, shouldn't they be good enough to help with other areas of your life? We think so.

We have gathered a collection of the most commonly asked questions about relationships and families to help provide you with the information that will be most useful to your relationship. Each question is followed by an answer based in science, presented in a way that is easy to understand and apply to your relationships. We have organized the book and partitioned the questions around the most common themes relationship scientists tend to focus their attention (e.g., attraction, love, commitment). Each theme serves as its own chapter, with two or more questions covered as part of each chapter. As a whole, the book contains the most up-to-date scientific findings on attraction, finding a partner, dating, flirting, whether love lasts forever, why people break up, getting over a break up, whether some people are more ready for relationships than others, what makes us become close to another, the experience of love, the role of sex in relationships, knowing if you have a good partner/relationship, why people stay in a bad relationship, the role of counseling, how relationships change over time, cheating, jealousy, conflict, improving communication, good and bad fighting, cohabitation, having kids, and parenting. You might think that's a lot of information. In fact, this is only the tip of the iceberg.

CHAPTER 1

Attraction & Relationship Initiation

Take a second to look up from your book and quickly glance at the person nearest to you (take a peek at a picture if you're reading alone). In the blink of an eye, you have registered that person's physical attractiveness. Are they closer to a perfect 10 or a perfect zero? Every enduring romance has to start somewhere, and that place is often a spark of physical attraction. However, deciding someone is attractive is just the first step. Next, you must assess whether there is mutual interest before you go and make a fool of yourself. Often, the key to starting a relationship is being at the right place at the right time. So, the question becomes: Where is the right place to maximize your opportunities to meet Mr. or Ms. Right?

Q1: WHAT MAKES SOMEONE HOT, AND OTHERS NOT?

Gary W. Lewandowski Jr.

Let's face it. Some people are more physically attractive than others. How else do you explain Brad Pitt? Virtually everyone that looks at him says, "That guy is HOT!" In fact, he is so hot that even straight guys will begrudgingly admit, "Not that I go that way, but if I did… okay, he's sort of attractive." So what makes Brad Pitt attractive, and the guy behind the counter at your local convenience store unattractive (not to mention a bit creepy)?

A person's overall physical attractiveness is a combination of many things, but derives mostly from facial attractiveness and body attractiveness. We know a pretty face when we see it, and there is widespread agreement about facial attractiveness across cultures and ages.[1] Pinpointing what makes a face appear attractive is a bit more complicated (especially because we make our judgments so quickly). However, a few general characteristics of attractive faces have been identified.

What determines the attractiveness of women's and men's faces?

First, attractive faces tend to be symmetrical.[2] Specifically, if you were to draw an imaginary line down the middle of your face from your hairline to your chin, symmetrical faces tend to have features that are mirror images of one another. Of course, most faces match up to some degree (two eyes, two ears, etc.), but attractive faces are more perfect mirror images than less-attractive faces. Still not convinced? Think of Halloween masks of witches, monsters, and so on. To make the masks scarier, designers make them uglier. One of the ways they do that is by making the faces asymmetrical—a droopy eye, a crooked nose, a giant wart on one cheek; you get the picture.

Attractive faces, especially in females, also tend to have baby-like features.[3] Not so much the baldness, drool, and toothless smile, but the stuff that make babies cute, such as large prominent eyes, full lips, a small chin, and a small nose. To get an idea of what we mean, think of Reese Witherspoon or Jessica Alba: Large eyes, pouting full lips, along with a delicate nose and chin. In fact, women who have these features are considered attractive across many cultures. Take a look at the list of features again. It's hardly coincidental that women's make-up is designed to highlight the eyes and lips, making both seem larger and more appealing.

It's also not a coincidence that men generally don't apply make-up to these areas. (For a notable exception, please see Russell Brand or any guy in an emo band.) The features that generally make women attractive aren't the same as those that make men attractive. For men, masculinity is key.[4] These include things such as a strong jaw line, prominent cheekbones, and broad foreheads. Although it may sound like we are describing a gorilla, good examples of these features in humans are Mathew McConaughey (naked bongos and all) and George Clooney. Both are easily more attractive than a gorilla!

What about men who are generally considered attractive, but don't possess these traits, such as Leonardo DiCaprio or Justin

Timberlake? Well, don't kick poor Leo or Justin to the curb just yet. It turns out that women's preference for males may vary depending on how fertile they are.[5] When women are most fertile (i.e., around the time they are ovulating), they prefer more masculine men, such as Colin Farrell, Russell Crowe, or perhaps a stunning vampire like Edward Cullen (especially, apparently, very sullen and pale women). However, during other times, Leo is still king of the world; women prefer men with more youthful, feminine features because guys like this are seen as more nurturing.

What determines the attractiveness of women's and men's bodies?

Okay, now let's assume that you're at a costume party and everybody is wearing one of those costume masks like you see in old movies. So much for facial symmetry! However, when it comes to what makes some people hot and others not so hot, facial attractiveness is only part of the story. Even though you might not admit it, you probably check out the body of your target of lust shortly after or just before looking at his or her face. (You know, that quick up and down scan you do with your eyes.) Well, what's going to get you to nudge your friend to check out that hottie in the corner? Just like with faces, men and women are looking at (drooling over) different things.

In women's bodies, there's a universal formula that seems to be related to how hot she is—it's known as the *waist-to-hip ratio*.[6] We'll avoid asking you to do any unnecessary math, but it might be helpful to illustrate with some numbers. Let's assume that a woman like Scarlett Johansson has "34–23–35" proportions. First, if you can manage to do it, ignore her bust size. The second two numbers refer to her waist size and hip size. The optimal ratio appears to be about .70, or the width of the waist is about 70% of the width of the hips (think of your typical hourglass figure). What's interesting is that this ratio works for different-size bodies. Anna Nicole Smith was considerably heavier than Scarlett Johansson, but she still conformed to the magic .70. It also works cross-culturally—the same ratio is preferred around the world, although the average overall body size may vary considerably.

Researchers have actually studied this phenomenon by analyzing the waist-to-hip ratio of *Playboy* centerfolds and Miss America winners (gotta love science!).[7] Their results strongly demonstrated the consistency in preference for this ratio dating back to the 1920s. Whereas they found that overall body size of these beauties decreased over time, the waist-to-hip ratio remained remarkably consistent. In other words, although the centerfolds ranged from Marilyn Monroe (who would be relatively heavy-set by Playboy's current standards) to Twiggy (the Kate Moss of the 1970s), they all had similar waist-to-hip proportions. Similarly, women find a high shoulder to waist ratio, which equates to broad shoulders and a robust upper body (i.e., the "V-back"), to be attractive in the men they are ogling.[8] Lanky men like Daniel Tosh aren't hunks—but Ryan Reynolds is (in the case of Tosh, humor matters, but that's another topic altogether). These ratios relate to sexual behavior such that males and females with more desirable ratios have a greater number of sexual partners, have intercourse at an earlier age, and are more likely to have sex outside of their primary relationship.

How can I improve the attractiveness of my figure?

Now, you might be thinking that there's not much you can do to change your waist-to-hip ratio or shoulder broadness, but people try; ever notice how men at the gym are obsessed with building huge lats and pecs, while ignoring their chicken legs? And how many of the women *aren't* concerned with building huge shoulder and back muscles? Instead, they are focusing on glutes and abs. In addition to trying, mostly in vain, to sculpt their bodies, both men and women can create the illusion of these desirable physical characteristics. Just like how women use make-up to enhance facial features, the clothing that you choose can accentuate these key attributes. An Armani suit is cut to create the illusion of a man's broad shoulders that tapers towards his waist. And without a doubt, women's fashion certainly focuses on creating and showing off her perfect .70. Tight jeans, spandex, and even leggings are not coincidental fashion choices. Of course, we are also all aware that men and women are increasingly turning to plastic surgery in an attempt to obtain that "perfect" figure.

Where did these preferences in face and body shapes come from?

Some researchers argue that they evolved over the course of human history as a way of finding a good mate.[9] For men, this would be a young and fertile woman (which might be identified through big eyes and wide hips); for women—a strong man with the ability to nurture and protect (which might be identified through big shoulders and strong cheekbones). Regardless of why these preferences started, many claim that the media and commercial industries perpetuate and add to these ideals through imagery in television shows, magazines advertisements, and music videos as a way of creating demand for their products. What is obvious is that these preferences clearly exist—making some people hot, and others not.

TAKE-HOME POINTS

- ♡ Both men and women prefer individuals who have symmetrical facial features and a general appearance of health.
- ♡ Men are attracted to women with youthful facial features and a waist-to-hip ratio of .70. This is consistent across both time and culture.
- ♡ Women are generally more attracted to men who have prominent cheekbones, square chins, and broad shoulders.
- ♡ Researchers believe these preferences evolved because they were suggestive of good genes and, therefore, good mates.

References

1. Langlois, J. H., L. Kalakanis, A. J. Rubenstein, A. Larson, M. Hallam, and M. Smoot. 2000. "Maxims or Myths of Beauty? A Meta-Analytic and Theoretical Review." *Psychological Bulletin* 126 (3): 390–423.
2. Thornhill, R., and S. W. Gangestad. 1994. "Human Fluctuating Asymmetry and Sexual Behavior." *Psychological Science* 5 (5): 297–302.
3. Berry, D. S., and L. Z. McArthur. 1985. "Some Components and Consequences of a Babyface." *Journal of Personality and Social Psychology* 48 (2): 312–23.
4. Cunningham, M. R., A. P. Barbee, and C. L. Pike. 1990. "What Do Women Want? Facial Metric Assessment of Multiple Motives in the Perception of Male Facial Physical Attractiveness." *Journal of Personality and Social Psychology* 59: 61–72.
5. Penton-Voak, I. S., D. I. Perrett, and D. L. Castles. 1999. "Menstrual Cycle Alters Face Preference." *Nature* 399: 741–42.
6. Singh, D., B. J. Dixson, T. S. Jessop, B. B. Morgan, and A. F. Dixson. 2010. "Cross-Cultural Consensus for Waist–Hip Ratio and Women's Attractiveness." *Evolution and Human Behavior* 31 (3): 176–81.

7. Singh, D. 1993. "Adaptive Significance of Female Physical Attractiveness: Role of Waist-to-Hip Ratio." *Journal of Personality and Social Psychology* 65 (2): 293–307.
8. Hughes, S. M., and G. R. Gallup. 2003. "Sex Differences in Morphological Predictors of Sexual Behavior: Shoulder to Hip and Waist to Hip Ratios." *Evolution and Human Behavior* 24 (3): 173–78.
9. Buss, D. M., and M. Barnes. 1986. "Preferences in Human Mate Selection." *Journal of Personality and Social Psychology* 50: 559–70.

Dig Deeper

Orbuch, T. L., and S. Sprecher. 2003. "Attraction and Interpersonal Relationships." In *Handbook of Social Psychology,* edited by J. Delamater and J. Delamater, 339–62. New York: Kluwer Academic/Plenum Publishers.
Sprecher, S., and D. Felmlee. 2008. "Insider Perspectives on Attraction." In *Handbook of Relationship Initiation,* edited by S. Sprecher, A. Wenzel, J. Harvey, S. Sprecher, A. Wenzel, and J. Harvey, 297–313. New York: Psychology Press.

Q2: How Can I Tell If Someone Is Interested in Me?

Debra Mashek

Imagine that you're out at a café enjoying your latte, muffin, and free WiFi when you notice a hottie across the room staring at you and unsuccessfully stifling a smile. Sweet! Your new haircut is already paying off! That was a smile—he's obviously into you, right? Or maybe he's into that episode of *The Family Guy* playing on the TV mounted directly above your booth and is simply fighting the urge to laugh out loud (at the cartoon, not at you).

People don't typically go around flashing a Derek Zoolander-esque "Blue Steel" look, so deciphering romantic interest is a difficult endeavor. On the one hand, if you fail to notice someone's interest in you, you miss out on the high of realizing someone thinks you're "All that!" not to mention the missed opportunity to form a relationship with that person. On the other hand, if you incorrectly think someone is interested in you (what researchers refer to as a *false positive*), you risk wasting valuable time and effort flashing your proverbial peacock feathers. You also open yourself up to the sting of rejection and embarrassment you might feel on getting shot down after making your approach. "Hello…oh, you weren't really giving me a flirty face? Good talk." Ouch. Worse, misperceiving romantic or sexual interest plays a role in sexual harassment[1] and sexual assault.[2] That's a definite—and potentially illegal—ouch.

Is a smile just a smile?

At least three factors complicate our ability to detect romantic interest. First, some situations are more ambiguous than others. If you go to a singles' event and someone smiles at you while making eye contact, chances are good that person is at least a little interested in you. However, that same eye contact and smile on the face of a waiter more likely signals, "May I take your order, please?" (and "Please don't be stingy when tipping"). If you're trying to figure out whether someone is interested in you, take a moment or two to think through alternative explanations for the way the other person is behaving. As any social psychologist will tell you, people fundamentally underestimate the influence of the situation and overestimate the person's role. It's possible that the situation, not their hidden longing for you, is driving their behavior.

Second, some people are easier to "read" than others. Some display their romantic intentions like a billboard with flashing neon lights (think Snooki on the Jersey Shore); others are much more subtle. In a clever test of individuals' abilities to judge the romantic interest of others, Place and colleagues[3] showed English-speaking participants short video clips of German-speaking speed-daters. Study participants judged whether each person in the video was interested in his or her speed-dating partner. (By using German-speaking "targets," the study participants couldn't use what the daters were actually saying to determine level of interest.) Importantly, the speed-daters had already provided information about their actual level of interest, which made it possible for the researchers to know how accurate the study participants were in predicting which of the speed-daters had expressed interest in their "date."

Based on data from this study, men are more transparent with their romantic intentions than women (the drooling is a sure giveaway). Observers more accurately predicted male interest in female interaction partners than they predicted female interest in male interaction partners. But—and this is important—observers were still far from perfect at predicting men's romantic interest. They predicted interest 61% of the time (remember, a chimp flipping a coin should be correct 50% of the time). Thus, even though we're social animals who are wired to make sense of social situations, our romantic detection systems are imperfect at best. And, of course, there's an important caveat with the Place and colleagues' study: The outside observers made their evaluations of other people's videotaped dating interactions while sitting in the relatively quiet confines of a research lab. That's a different sort of task than trying to figure out, in the heat of the moment with the noise and distraction of other people, whether that hottie on the other side of the café is interested in you. That said, if you think a guy is expressing interest in you, you can trust your hunch a bit more than if you think a gal is expressing interest in you. (See question 4 for insight into why men may be more transparent in signaling interest than are women.)

A third factor complicating our ability to know when others are interested in us is that some of us are better "people readers" than others. For example, in the speed-dating study, it turns out that study participants who were already in a romantic relationship made more accurate predictions about the actual interests of the speed-daters than did people who were single. That doesn't necessarily mean dating causes us to be more accurate perceivers, but it's perfectly reasonable to think that, given their clear ability to pair up with someone, those in relationships are better at identifying romantic interest. If you're trying to figure out if someone is checking you out, it might be a good idea to ask your friends—especially friends who are already in relationships. If they're picking up on the same vibe you are, then squirt some of your Listerine PocketMist and make your move.

Are there any clear-cut signs of romantic interest?

Altogether, then, when trying to gauge someone's romantic interest, we know there are costs associated with guessing wrong, and we know a number of factors muddle the task of guessing correctly. So what's a guy or gal to do? Well, on the upside, research suggests some behaviors really do signal romantic interest. In one study, a bunch of guys were asked to evaluate photos of women who were displaying a range of different facial expressions, some that were meant to signal flirtation and others that were meant to be neutral.[4] More than 70% of the guys recognized a specific facial expression as signaling flirtation. The photos perceived as most flirtatious showed a woman with "head turned to one side, head tilted down slightly, a slight smile, and eyes turned forward (toward the implied target)." However, keep in mind that these were images of women posing, not photos of women out in the "wild" (or out in a social situation) actually trying to signal "Come hither." This is important: Just because a bunch of men think a particular face means "Let's get it on" doesn't mean that's the message intended every time that look flashes across someone's face. It also points out something to keep in mind about flirtation more generally. People flirt to create a sense of sexual interest in the target, but don't always have any intention of acting on that increased interest. Sometimes it's to see if you're interested, sometimes it's to toy with you, and sometimes it is just a way for the person doing the flirting to pass the time.

In a nifty study evaluating the extent to which participants' self-ratings of interest in an interaction partner corresponded with their actual behaviors, Grammer and colleagues[5] videotaped and then *coded* (i.e., observed, analyzed, and categorized) the behaviors an individual displayed during an interaction, and later asked that individual to indicate their degree of actual interest in the interaction partner. In other words, the researchers recorded individuals while they had an opportunity to flirt, and then asked them to watch the recording and indicate when they were flirting. This method allowed the researchers to determine whether certain observable behaviors—like a smile or a hair flip—map onto people's actual interest. Although the behaviors that took place during the first few minutes of the 10-minute interaction didn't correlate with professed romantic interest, some behaviors observed *later* in the interaction did. For example, women who fussed with their clothing, tilted their head, smiled coyly, and used a lot of hand motions when speaking later reported being interested in the guy with whom they had interacted. The men who spent more time talking during the latter half of the interaction period reported greater romantic interest with their interaction partner.

So, yes, body language can signal important information—but, again, body language is ambiguous. In fact, scholars hypothesize this ambiguity serves a self-protective factor in that it allows people to venture out in public again when an object of interest does not reciprocate that interest.[6] Basically you are putting yourself out there, but not all the way out there. If the target of your affection doesn't reciprocate, you can easily play it off as them misperceiving your intentions. The take home point—we can rarely know for sure that someone is interested in us unless they walk up and say, "I'm interested in you."

"How you doing?" Are opening lines effective?

That said, all is not lost: *You* can opt to signal loud and clear that you are interested in someone else. How? Well, holding in mind the imperfections of the nonverbal mode of communication, give *words* a try (augmented with some batting eyelashes and asymmetrical grins, as you see fit). In one study, participants read stories about men approaching women and evaluated the likely effectiveness of the different "chat-up lines" the men used.[7] Male and female participants thought the most successful lines would be those that demonstrated personal qualities (e.g., generosity, helpfulness) and cultural competence (e.g., discussing paintings or music). Participants predicted that the men would fail miserably when directly requesting sex or attempting to use sexual humor. So, guys, skip the Flintstones jokes about "making your bed rock," and try, instead, to show your sweet and sophisticated side.

In a similar study, Wade and colleagues[8] asked men to evaluate the effectiveness of a bunch of opening lines women had said they might use to indicate interest. According to the men in the study, there are several opening lines women can use that would be particularly effective: directly asking a man on a date, hinting at a date, giving a man her phone number/requesting a call, or trying to find out what things they may share in common. So, gals, here are some lines you can try: "Want to hang out this weekend?"; "You should come down to the bar with us"; "Call me: 867-5309, the name's Jenny"; and "You're a Gleek, too?! We should watch next week's episode together." In a nutshell, women are looking for signs of a good partner; men are looking for someone interested.

Conclusions

Unfortunately, we can't mate with everyone (oh, how exhausting that would be!) and thus must spend our valuable—and limited—mating resources on partners who are most likely to be receptive to our efforts. We figure out who those others are by paying attention to their displays of interest and being accurate in our interpretations of those displays. And, of course, potential partners are paying attention to us and the vibe or flirty faces we are putting out there. So, although we can gain useful information by monitoring nonverbal signals, there's a lot to be said for directly saying what's on your mind.

TAKE-HOME POINTS

♡ At least three factors complicate the task of figuring out whether others are romantically interested in us: some situations call for behavior that, in other situations, might be considered flirtations; some people are easier to read than others; and some of us are just better than others at reading other people.

♡ Although some nonverbal signals are clearly interpreted as flirtatious, it is not clear whether every time someone gives "the look" if she or he is asking you to come hither.

♡ Rather than trying to rely on nonverbal communication as the sole tool for deciphering or signaling romantic interest, use your words.

References

1. Johnson, C. B., M. S. Stockdale, and F. E. Saal. 1991. "Persistence of Men's Misperceptions of Friendly Cues across a Variety of Interpersonal Encounters." *Psychology of Women Quarterly* 15: 463–475.
2. Abbey, A., P. McAuslan, and L. T. Ross. 1998. "Sexual Assault Perpetration by College Men: The Role of Alcohol, Misperception of Sexual Intent, and Sexual Beliefs and Experiences." *Journal of Social and Clinical Psychology* 17: 167–195.
3. Place, S. S., P. M. Todd, L. Penke, and J. B. Askenforpf. 2009. "The Ability to Judge the Romantic Interest of Others." *Psychological Science* 20: 22–26.
4. Canterberry, M., O. Gillath, and E. L. Rosenberg. 2011. *The FACS of flirting: Evidence for a specific female flirting expression.* In M. Canterberry (Chair), Cues and strategies for communicating interest in romantic relationship initiation. Symposium conducted at Society for Personality and Social Psychology, San Antonio, TX.
5. Grammer, K., K. Kruck, A. Juette, and B. Fink. 2000. "Non-Verbal Behavior as Courtship Signals: The Role of Control and Choice in Selecting Partners." *Evolution and Human Behavior* 21: 371–390.
6. Whitty, M. T. 2004. "Cyber-Flirting: An Examination of Men's and Women's Flirting Behaviour Both Offline and on the Internet." *Behaviour Change* 21: 115–126.
7. Bale, C., Morrison, R., and P. G. Caryl. 2006. "Chat-Up Lines as Male Sexual Displays." *Personality and Individual Differences* 40(4): 655–664.
8. Wade, T., L. K. Butrie, and K. M. Hoffman. 2009. "Women's Direct Opening Lines Are Perceived as Most Effective." *Personality and Individual Differences* 47: 145–149.

Dig Deeper

Johnson, C. B., Stockdale, M. S., and Saal, F. E. 1991. "Persistence of Men's Misperceptions of Friendly Cues across a Variety of Interpersonal Encounters." *Psychology of Women Quarterly* 15: 463–475.

Q3: WHAT'S THE BEST WAY TO MEET SOMEONE?

Benjamin Le

The majority of this book focuses on things that happen after you've paired off with someone. However, the fact of the matter is that you need to actually meet one or more potential romantic partners before a relationship can develop. So where and *how* do people tend to meet their future mates? Rather than simply provide a top-10 list of the general locations where individuals meet others (e.g., at the library, through friends, on a runaway bus), let's discuss the basic psychological principles that are at play during initial encounters. Understanding these principles allows you to understand the best places to find a partner with whom you will be compatible (i.e., someone you will find attractive for the long haul).

They're right under your nose

You might think that you need to travel the globe, searching high and low for your true love. Although that would be fun, and we don't want to discourage any potential globe-trotting, chances are that your soul mate (or evening-mate, as the case may be) is right under your nose. At the most basic level, *physical* closeness leads to *psychological* closeness. You have to interact with a person to have a relationship with him or her, and being in each other's space ups the chances of having an interaction. As a result, potential partners are really all around you—in your neighborhood, in one of your classes, in your church, or in a cubical down the hall. And not surprisingly, the less distant they are from you, the more you interact with them (it's no wonder that couples move in together).

Not only does physical proximity increase the odds of meeting and interacting with someone, but just seeing a person a lot can lead you to like them more. Ever notice how ubiquitous Coke and Pepsi signs are? Advertisers try to increase liking for their products simply by having people see them more. This is a well-known phenomenon in psychology known as the *mere exposure effect;*[1] in other words, merely being exposed to something can make you like it more. Interestingly, the mere exposure effect is especially powerful when you are not actually aware that a particular person or object is in fact more frequently seen. One study demonstrated this by having four women (who were *confederates,* or accomplices of the experimenters, and were pretested to be of similar attractiveness) sit in on a college course that was held in a large lecture hall.[2] Each of the women attended the class a different number of times (0, 5, 10, or 15 visits). At the end of the semester, the students in the class were shown pictures of the four women and asked to make several judgments about them. Even though members of the class did not necessarily recognize one woman more than another, the students thought the women who were in the class more frequently were more attractive (even though they didn't necessarily remember seeing them!). In short, the girl (or guy) next door has a competitive advantage in winning your heart because you are likely to see that person more often. Like a fungus, she (or he) is going to grow on you whether you realize it or not.

Go to the places you typically go

Physical proximity doesn't just promote attraction; we also happen to share characteristics with people who are in our vicinity. This *similarity* is also very important.[3] Think of it this way: You probably chose your particular college, job, or place to live for the same reason that others did. Generally speaking, "Birds of a feather flock together," and the bulk of the research on this topic indicates that individuals are attracted to those who are similar in beliefs, personality, and demographic characteristics such as family background.[4] Collectively, these two factors (proximity and similarity) explain why so many celebrities date each other: they are in the same place (e.g., movie sets, studios, eating at The Ivy) and they have a lot in common (e.g., money, good looks, narcissism, paparazzi-induced rage).

So what does this have to do with where you are likely to meet potential mates? Clearly, to meet a similar partner, you must frequent those places where those similar to you congregate. If you are into GTL (gym, tanning, and laundry), perhaps you should spend your summers at the Jersey Shore where others share similar priorities. Likewise, clubs or groups that support the things about which you are passionate, as well as church or other community organizations, would be a good starting place.

Your friends and family know best

Also, don't overlook the importance of the role that friends and family play during the early stages of relationships. The connections you have with others through your "social network" (a la the "Six Degrees of Kevin Bacon" game) refers to *social proximity*—people who are not necessarily physically close to you, but are close to you through connections (think two degrees of separation rather than six).[5] In fact, roughly half of all relationships begin when individuals are introduced to each other by a mutual acquaintance, and two out of three people know members of their partner's social networks prior to meeting their partner.[6] Furthermore, these proportions are similar for both males and females, which means that both sexes rely on their social networks as a means of initiating their romantic relationships. (Maybe Mark Zuckerberg is on to something...)

Friendship and family networks serve as an important source of potential mates for a variety of reasons. Mathematically, the *field of eligibles* grows exponentially when considering those individuals that are known by friends and family (remember the saying, "When you sleep with someone, you sleep with everyone that person has slept with too"—the field of eligibles is sort of the same thing, but in a good way). In addition, beyond the power of increased numbers, social networks may take an active role in selecting particularly suitable mates. They encourage partnerships that they see as good matches, and may filter out poor mate choices. This obviously works when you and your matchmakers want similar things in a mate, but is more problematic when your mom or friends want you to date only lawyers whereas you prefer struggling musicians. Luckily, there is an added bonus if you do meet someone through your social networks: the support for relationships provided by social networks may be crucial for relationship development and success[7] (see also question 24). In short, odds are that your next relationship partner is a friend of a friend or knows a member of your family. Your social network is an invaluable resource in introducing you to potential mates and for screening that pool of individuals to exclude undesirable or incompatible partners. The moral of this story: If you don't like your current pool of dating partners, it might be time to get some new friends. It may be their fault you're single.

* * *

So far, the answer to the question, "Where's the best place to meet someone?" might seem somewhat obvious. Potential partners are in close proximity, within the same social circles that you travel, and they are out there doing the same activities as you. Next, we highlight something that's a bit less obvious, and has to do with the particular places that one might look for partners (e.g., at dance clubs versus libraries): How does the energy level, or psychological and physical arousal, of a particular situation impact attraction and relationship initiation?

Arousal, eh? Now get your mind out of the gutter, what scientists mean by *arousal* is somewhat different than the sexual arousal you may be thinking about, although, as you'll see, the two are linked in interesting ways. When we say *arousal*, we are referring to general things like alertness, engagement, and a heightened level of physical activity, such as an elevated heart rate. For example, you experienced arousal if you were cowering in your seat while watching *Paranormal Activity* compared to watching "Hannah Montana" (please tell us you were not watching a lot of "Hannah Montana"—that may be why you're single). The cowering is the result of arousal. It turns out that you are primed to be attracted to people you meet when you are experiencing higher levels of arousal, especially when you don't even know it.

Love on a bridge

Imagine that you're out hiking in beautiful Vancouver, British Columbia, and you come to a bridge that you must cross to reach the other side of the canyon. But this isn't just any bridge. This particular bridge is straight out of an Indiana Jones movie: it is shaky and wobbly, longer than a football field, and is swaying 20 stories high in the air over a river chock-full of jagged rocks and anacondas (okay, we made up that last part about the snakes). As you cross the bridge, you meet an experimenter who shows you an ambiguous picture and asks you to tell a story about what might be taking place in that scene. As you finish your response, the experimenter gives you his/her phone number in case you "have any questions about the study" and you continue on your way. Meanwhile, further down the river, other participants did the same thing and talked to the same experimenter while crossing a sturdy and wide bridge that was only 10 feet above the water.

The psychologists who conducted this experiment, Donald Dutton and Arthur Aron,[8] wanted to see if the shaky bridge led the males in their study to express greater attraction to the female experimenter. Before we get to the findings, really imagine yourself crossing the shaky bridge—you feel a bit nervous and unsure of yourself, your heart is beating, your stomach feels a bit queasy, and you are sweating just a bit—the fear of plunging to your death has a way of doing that. This physiological response is likely a reasonable reaction for a dangerous bridge crossing, but it also sounds an awful lot like a first date. Dutton and Aron speculated that walking across the bridge created a sense of arousal that participants would mistakenly believe was caused by the experimenter, rather than the physical environment ("Why is my heart racing? I must love you!"). Sure enough, they discovered that males who crossed the shaky bridge were actually more likely to call the experimenter (ostensibly because they were attracted to her) than the males who crossed the sturdy bridge. Moreover, those same shaky-bridge guys wrote stories that contained more sexual content than those who crossed the sturdy bridge. They interpreted these findings as evidence that the guys on the shaky bridge *misattributed* the arousal caused by the shaky bridge to the experimenter, putting their minds in the gutter and making them more likely to pursue her.

So, what does this have to do with where you should meet partners? Clearly, you should stalk the nearest old bridge and wait until a viable partner meanders across. Or, more broadly, you may want to seek out situations that have an element of physical and psychological arousal compared to less active, yet fun activities. The "chemistry" you feel with your rock-climbing partner will certainly be more intense than with members of your book club. Activities such as dancing, sports, and outdoor adventures, especially those where you have to work closely and cooperatively with the potential partner, have a much better chance of yielding attraction, and would be a great place to spark a relationship.

* * *

Finally, we can't talk about places to meet others without addressing how recent technological advancements have affected relationship initiation. Does speed dating work? What about meeting with online matchmaking services? The best way to answer these questions is to consider the extent to which proximity, similarity, social networks, and arousal are represented in these methods of meeting others.

In terms of proximity, speed dating does bring potential partners into physical proximity with each other, if only for a very brief and isolated time period. Likewise, Internet dating sites forego physical proximity for virtual proximity. Neither of these avenues seems to harness the power of the mere exposure effect, which require *repeated* contact. Although perhaps Facebook's insistence that you friend your friend's friend (two other people you know are friends with him/her!) could work in a mere exposure type of way.

As far as similarity, it's unclear that speed dating betters one's chances of meeting similar others, except that the sheer number of people one meets while speed dating might create a better chance of stumbling across similar others (at least similar others who will try meeting others through speed dating!). Of course, speed dating or dating sites can use particular criteria as a way of narrowing the field to only those with a certain interest or demographic, such as http://www.JDate.com (a dating service for Jewish singles) and http://www.Cupidtino.com (a site for enthusiasts of Macs and other Apple products). Likewise, more sophisticated dating sites use demographic and psychological dimensions (e.g., personality) as criteria for suggesting partners; similarity is likely to be a key factor in these equations.

At one level, dating sites and speed dating both offer an alternative to traditional social networks as a means of introducing you to potential partners. If social networks are important for simply broadening your field of possible mates, Internet or speed dating likely can accomplish the same thing. However, these alternate methods may lack the "personal touch" that facilitates existing social network's insight into your relationships. Friends, roommates, and family are still likely to know you better than do online matchmaking and speed-dating services. Furthermore, they provide support for those relationships they approve of, which is associated with relationship longevity. However, as these technologies evolve, they may begin to be as well informed and develop mechanisms to provide relationship support.

Finally, is speed dating exciting and arousing? It likely is, with the movement around the room, time constraints on the interactions, and the overall atmosphere created at these events. However, it is not clear that sitting on your sofa using your laptop to surf for potential mates is that exciting, but those cat videos your mom keeps sending to you are pretty cute, so at least there is that.

Conclusion

Hopefully, this chapter has helped you augment your "Meet-a-Mate" toolbox with several strategies that have empirical support. The implementation is up to you. Will you take advantage of arousal by looking to strike up conversations with sweaty potential partners at the gym? Will you consider similarity more heavily when looking for matches on your online dating site? Will you use the powers of Facebook to poke a friend of a friend? Or will you merely expose yourself (in a socially acceptable, non–Pee-Wee Herman, way) to a field of eligibles? In any case, meeting someone is a crucial first step toward establishing a happy and meaningful relationship.

TAKE-HOME POINTS

- ♡ We tend to like people/things that we see often; this is known as the *mere exposure effect.*
- ♡ Similarity is associated with liking; there is much empirical support for the saying, "Birds of a feather flock together."
- ♡ A large number of people are introduced to their mates through friends and family, and social networks are a powerful way of increasing the range of people you meet.
- ♡ The psychological arousal caused by fear and physical activity (e.g., heart racing, sweaty palms) can be misattributed as attraction for other people; meeting people in locations that promote arousal leads to greater interpersonal "chemistry."

References

1. Zajonc, R. B. 1968. "Attitudinal Effects of Mere Exposure." *Journal of Personality and Social Psychology* 9: 1–27.
2. Moreland, R. L., and S. R. Beach. 1992. "Exposure Effects in the Classroom: The Development of Affinity among Students." *Journal of Experimental Social Psychology, 28*, 255–276.
3. Byrne, D. 1971. *The Attraction Paradigm.* New York: Academic Press.
4. Surra, C. A., C. R. Gray, T. M. L. Boettcher, N. R. Cottle, and A. R. West. 2006. "From Courtship to Universal Properties: Research on Dating and Mate Selection, 1950 to 2003." In *The Cambridge Handbook of Personal Relationships,* edited by A. L. Vangelisti and D. Perlman, 113–130. Cambridge: Cambridge University Press.
5. Parks, M. R. 2007. *Personal Relationships and Personal Networks.* Mahwah, NJ: Lawrence Erlbaum Associates.
6. Parks, M. R., and L. L. Eggert. 1991. "The Role of Social Context in the Dynamics of Personal Relationships." In *Advances in Personal Relationships,* Vol. 2, edited by W. H. Jones and D. W. Perlman, 1–34. London: Jessica Kingsley.
7. Etcheverry, P. E., and C. R. Agnew. 2004. "Subjective Norms and the Prediction of Romantic Relationship State and Fate." *Personal Relationships* 11: 409–428.
8. Dutton, D. G., and A. P. Aron. 1974. "Some Evidence for Heightened Sexual Attraction under Conditions of High Anxiety." *Journal of Personality and Social Psychology* 30: 510–517.

Dig Deeper

Sprecher, S., A. Wenzel, and J. Harvey, Eds. 2008. *Handbook of the Initiation of Relationships.* New York: Psychology Press of Taylor and Francis.

CHAPTER 2

Love

"I Love You". . . few combinations of words carry as much weight and significance. Simply put, they can make or break a relationship. Mutual proclamations can be a glorious, life-changing event, but nothing is as awkward (or potentially devastating) as an unreciprocated "I love you." Yet, for all of its significance in romantic relationships, love remains a very vague concept. Type in the word love in any internet search engine and you'll be provided with a list of more than 4.3 billion hits, with very few of those providing the same definition. A regular topic of poems, songs, movies, gossip, and so on, we are a species fascinated by the idea and importance of love. In this chapter, we explore if we are really meant to love just one person, the purpose of love, whether love blinds us to reality, and whether love lasts forever.

Q4: ARE WE MEANT TO BE MONOGAMOUS?

Lorne Campbell

It feels like almost every day we hear about famous celebrities, politicians, and athletes who have been caught having sex with someone other than their spouses or dating partners. These people are generally criticized for their questionable, even immoral, behavior, but rarely are we shocked to hear that people cheat. Okay, that Hugh Grant incident back in 1995 was a bit surprising. But was anyone surprised that Jude Law was being less than faithful? Or that Tiger Woods was prowling around with women who weren't his wife? Or that Jessica Simpson was rumored to enjoy the company of other men when married to Nick Lachey? Or that Kobe

Bryant was playing forward for the adultery all-stars? In light of this evidence, the title of this chapter asks a very important question: Are humans meant to be monogamous? Or, to paraphrase Will Smith in his song *Chasing Forever*, "Is monogamy a monoga-must?"

The answer to this question is not straightforward. Research does suggest that although a lot of people are not monogamous, the majority of people do remain faithful to their partners. Any answer to the question, therefore, must address the conditions that make it more likely for some people to cheat on their partners but others to keep their zippers securely fastened. In fact, *monogamy*, or the practice of having a single mate during a period of time, seems to be a dying trend in modern American society. In many surveys, around 30% of both men and women in committed long-term relationships report that they have cheated on their partners at least once.[1] Perhaps more surprisingly, between 2% and 10% of males are being cuckolded. That's not nearly as fun or funny as it sounds. Being *cuckolded* basically means that these men are unknowingly raising children they believe to be their own genetic offspring, but are not.[2] On a global scale, infidelity is the most frequently cited reason for divorce across cultures.[3]

Is monogamy the best strategy?

Recent theorizing and research in evolutionary psychology—a field of psychology that believes that (1) our most basic instinct is to pass on our genes, and (2) much of the stuff we do today is a result of what made us best able to pass on our genes in our distant human past—provides one possible answer. According to Robert Trivers' parental investment theory,[4] differences in how much time and effort men and women invest in the production of children can explain the types of mating strategies that men and women are more likely to use. When it comes to procreation, a male's minimal contribution can take as little as a few minutes and a teaspoon of sperm. Women, however, at the very least must invest more than nine months of gestation and experience the pain and potential medical complications associated with childbirth. What's more, while a woman is spending nine months carrying her child, the father still has the capacity to share his teaspoon and few quality minutes with other women. Based on these differences in minimal parental investment, Trivers suggested that women should prefer long-term committed relationships and be fairly choosy when selecting mates because of the high costs involved in becoming pregnant (and even higher costs if she raises the child herself). According to the theory, men, however, should look for multiple mating opportunities and be less choosy when seeking mates (i.e., have lower standards), because mating opportunities usually have fewer costs associated with them.

Gender differences in monogamy

This theory partly answers the question, "Are we meant to be monogamous?" For men, maybe not. According to parental investment theory, men should be expected to cheat more often than women because seeking multiple sexual partners should result in more children. This simple answer, however, is somewhat insufficient when considering heterosexual relationships. It takes two to tango: When a man cheats on his partner, it means a woman has agreed to have sex with him. A "choosy" female looking for a long-term relationship should not be having sex with a man committed to another woman. Unless there are only a handful of women sating the sexual desires of a large pool of men (e.g., prostitutes), it is obvious that women cheat as well. But why would women forego monogamy? Recent work by Steven Gangestad and Jeffry Simpson addresses this conundrum.[5] They rightly point out that not all men have the looks and buying power of Brad Pitt or Johnny Depp—meaning that a lot of men would be hard-pressed to find a lot of women willing to have sex with them. They also point out that not all women are looking for a guy with lots of money to settle down with, and that some women may be more interested in the quality of the men's genes inside his jeans. Specifically, some women may forgo the long-term security provided by a relationship with an average partner and take advantage of short-term opportunities to be with especially high-quality men with good genes. This interesting idea allows us to predict with greater certainty *when* women will stray and when they will stay faithful.

A lot of recent research shows that men with good genes (i.e., they're attractive and healthy) tend to be highly desired by women as sexual partners. These men tend to have more symmetrical physical features, meaning the left side of their body more closely mirrors the right side of their body. No need to worry, however; you can leave your protractor and calipers safely at home. Although you may not notice a person's symmetry, your perceptions of their physical attractiveness are closely related to perceptions of symmetry. Women have even rated the scent of more symmetrical men as more appealing than the scent of less symmetrical men, highlighting another way to tell the difference between men with "good genes" and "OK genes." Symmetrical men are more self-confident and compete more directly with other men to win the affections of women.[5] More symmetrical men are also more likely to have sex with women who are already in long-term relationships, meaning that some women satisfy their sexual desires outside of their relationships with men that have good genes. There is a twist to these findings that is particularly fascinating—women are only more attracted to more symmetrical men when they are ovulating, or when sexual encounters have a greater likelihood of resulting in pregnancy. If women are primarily attracted to the quality of the genes these men possess, then it makes sense for them to be aroused by more symmetrical men when they can best take advantage of these good genes (i.e., during peak fertility) and pass them on to their children.

Conclusion

It is possible to conclude, therefore, that some people are destined to be monogamous, if not by their own choice, then by the choices of others. Men with good genes are simply more desirable as sexual partners, and thus are more likely to be successful at locating multiple partners over time than other men. Men with OK genes or bad genes will be more successful when directing their energies toward creating and maintaining monogamous relationships. Whereas most women may be more comfortable seeking long-term romantic bonds, there are women who find the allure of men with good genes too irresistible, particularly when they are ovulating.[6] Mind you, psychologists don't think that people go out and cheat because they think to themselves, "This is going to help me maximize the number and quality of my offspring" (not to mention that this makes for an awkwardly worded online dating profile). Rather, the instinct to pass on our genes has evolved into certain tendencies—namely our tendency to engage in a mating strategy that is best given who we have to compete against and who is available to us as partners. Ultimately, this suggests that we all have the capacity to be monogamous, or not.

TAKE-HOME POINTS

♡ There is a lot of cheating going on, but still most people are faithful to their spouses.

♡ Evolutionary psychology suggests that men may be able to maximize the number of children they have (genes they pass on) by having sex with lots of people.

♡ Women may find certain men (the good-looking ones) even more attractive when they are ovulating—perhaps because they want the good-looking genes to pass on to potential offspring.

♡ It seems there may be some incentive for humans to mate with different (attractive) people.

References

1. Thompson, A. P. 1983. "Extramarital Sex: A Review of Literature." *Journal of Sex Research* 19: 1–22.
2. Baker, R. R., and M. A. Bellis. 1995. *Human Sperm Competition.* London: Chapman and Hall.
3. Betzig, L. 1989. "Causes of Conjugal Dissolution: A Cross-Cultural Study." *Current Anthropology* 30: 654–676.
4. Trivers, R. L. 1972. "Parental Investment and Sexual Selection." In *Sexual Selection and the Descent of Man,* 136–179, edited by B. Campbell, 136–179. New York: Aldine de Gruyter.
5. Gangestad, S. W., and J. A. Simpson. 2000. "The Evolution of Human Mating: Trade-Offs and Strategic Pluralism." *Behavior and Brain Sciences* 23: 573–587.
6. Gangestad, S. W., R. Thornhill, and C. Garver-Apgar. 2005. "Adaptations to Ovulation." In *The Handbook of Evolutionary Psychology,* edited by D. Buss, 344–371. Hoboken, NJ: John Wiley and Sons.

Dig Deep

Baker, R. 1996. *Sperm Wars: The Evolutionary Logic of Love and Lust.* New York: BasicBooks.

Birkhead, T. 2000. *Promiscuity: An Evolutionary History of Sperm Competition.* London: Faber and Faber Limited.

Fisher, H. 1992. *Anatomy of Love: A Natural History of Mating, Marriage, and Why We Stray.* New York: Ballantine Books.

Q5: WHAT IS THE PURPOSE OF LOVE?

Lorne Campbell

According to ancient Greek philosophers, including Socrates, the world would descend into chaos if it were not for *love*. Modern-day philosophers such as the Beatles are in complete agreement, singing that *All You Need Is Love*. Love is what motivated Romeo Montague and Juliet Capulet to stay together despite the fact that their families were sworn enemies. If you have not read Shakespeare (or seen the movie), this is a spoiler alert: The love Romeo and Juliet shared ultimately resulted in their deaths because their families resolutely forbade them to be with each other, and Romeo and Juliet chose death over not being with the person they loved! Clearly, love is very important and powerful—powerful enough to make lovers sacrifice their own lives.

Scientists agree that love is important in our lives as well as an incredible motivator of behavior. Indeed, an analysis of 166 societies by Jankowiak and Fischer[1] concludes that romantic love is found worldwide, and, interestingly, more than 90% of *everyone in the world* will marry at least once during their lives.[2] Yet, despite its prevalence and importance, scientists have rarely agreed on exactly what love *is*. Ellen Berscheid, one of the most prominent researchers to investigate love, lamented this fact when she asked and answered a simple yet important question: "How many meanings does the word 'love' have? Legion."[3] Legion (adjective): many, numerous (www.merriam-webster.com). On a philosophical level, this is problematic: If love truly has an infinite number of meanings, then it ceases to be meaningful. If it is everything, then it runs the risk of being nothing. Yet, we know, and relationship science knows, that it is more than nothing. Romeo and Juliet didn't commit double-suicide for nothing! Which brings us back to the original question...

What Is the Purpose of Love?

There is a growing consensus among researchers from different academic disciplines that love, at least *romantic* love (see question 7), evolved in humans to help keep parents together, which increases the chances that any children they had would survive.[4] In this scenario, one parent can feed the kid while the other fights the sabre-tooth tigers. Think about it: human babies have very large but underdeveloped brains and small, relatively weak bodies, meaning that they are completely dependent on caregivers for their survival. A baby abandoned in the woods would not survive despite being cared for by wolves (Mowgli from *The Jungle Book* being the rare fictional exception). Two parents, at least in ancestral times, were in a better position to keep their kids alive. Even today, when infants receive care from both parents over their childhood, they tend to have better health, are less likely to die in childhood, and have a higher standard of living in their adult years compared to when they receive care from only one parent.[5] Thus, the survival of our species relied on our ancestors falling in love and forming relatively long-term committed relationships. Put another way, love appears to be the fuel that motivates us to maintain our relationships.

Nonverbal Signals Make Us Feel Loved

Building on the idea that love is a commitment device, Gian Gonzaga and his colleagues[6] suggest that love promotes commitment to *one* person in the presence of many possible alternative partners. Expressing love in various ways (e.g., telling your partner you love her or him, providing help and support for your partner, gazing into your partner's eyes and smiling), communicates to your partner that you are committed to your relationship. This is a good thing; we all need a little reassurance every now and then.

If you are in love right now, try this thought experiment. Sit back, close your eyes, and think of your partner. Think of when you met your partner, the excitement you felt as you fell in love, and the comfort you feel when in his or her arms. When researchers asked women in love to do a similar visualization task, the women displayed head nods and what are called *Duchenne smiles,* or smiles that cannot be faked because they involve the cooperation of many muscles.[7] Interestingly, people can determine how much love their partners feel for them based on how often their partners display behaviors such as Duchenne smiles and head nods. When we are in love we spontaneously, and often unconsciously, express our feelings to our partners in very subtle ways, and they in turn feel loved. Another fascinating result of this study was that the oxytocin levels (what some call the *love hormone*) in the women's blood increased after thinking of their partner. Oxytocin is a hormone that evokes feelings of contentment, reductions in anxiety, and feelings of calmness and security when we are around a mate. Simply thinking of the person you love can have a calming effect, making you feel committed for the long haul.

Love Means I Have Eyes for You Only

We may communicate our love to our partners, and they may be the source of oxytocin spikes that make us feel warm and fuzzy, but does love prevent the eyes from wandering to check out other attractive people? Sunglasses were invented for a reason! We are exposed to many, many beautiful and successful people every day, whether it be in person, on television, the Internet, or in print media. Being reminded of all these possible alternatives to our current partner can have a negative effect on our feelings toward our partners. For example, men feel less love for their partners after looking at pictures of *Playboy* models,[8] and women are less enchanted with their partners after viewing pictures of successful and ambitious men.[9] Maybe you shouldn't have your boyfriend watch *America's Next Top Model* with you, or have your girlfriend watch sports with all of those rich and successful athletes. So how do people in relationships focus their attention away from these potential alternatives?

Love also motivates individuals to approach their intimate partner and move *away* from tempting alternative partners—a very good thing (your future children think so, at least). First, individuals in love seem to perceive the physical beauty of people other than their partners less positively than do single individuals. If you show pictures of attractive men and women to a group of your friends, odds are your single friends will think the opposite-sex people (if they are heterosexual) in the pictures are hot. Your partnered friends, however, will likely be less smitten. Being in a loving and committed relationship seems to make people distort perceptions of physical reality, helping them think their partners are so much better looking than everyone else's partners.[10] Love seems to make you think your partner is better looking, increasing your commitment levels.

When in love, individuals are able to quickly shift their attention away from attractive opposite-sex others to focus on something else. Imagine that you are viewing a lot of pictures of attractive opposite-sex people on the Internet, and you control how fast you click through the images. If you are in love, you will most likely spend less time looking at each picture than you would if you are single.[11] Recent research even suggests that people in relationships can automatically shift their attention away from attractive opposite-sex others presented on a computer screen so that they can engage in a very boring, but not relationship-threatening, decision-making task ("Is this a circle or square?").[12] When in love, you have eyes only for your partner.

Conclusion

Research is consistent with the idea that love is a type of commitment device. When in love, we are drawn to our partners and show our affections, often in very subtle ways. Importantly, when you express your love to your partner, they feel loved in return. People in love also *derogate*, or put down, the appeal of opposite-sex people who are not their partners, and do not spend as much time checking out alternative partners. Love has a way of keeping people focused on each other, which keeps them together longer. As the Beatles said, "All you need is love, love. Love is all you need."

TAKE-HOME POINTS

♡ Scientists do not agree on what love is, but do agree that it is a powerful motivator that exists in all known cultures.
♡ We express our love of our partners both intentionally (saying "I love you") and unintentionally (smiling when we think about our partners).
♡ Love increases our feelings of commitment to our partners.

References

1. Jankowiak, W. R., and E. F. Fischer. 1992. "A Cross-Cultural Perspective on Romantic Love." *Ethnology* 21: 149–155.
2. Buss, D. M. 1985. "Human Mate Selection." *American Scientist* 73: 47–51.
3. Berscheid, E. 2010. "Love in the Fourth Dimension." *Annual Review of Psychology* 61: 1–25.
4. Mellen, S. L. W. 1981. *The Evolution of Love*. Oxford: Freeman.

5. Geary, D. C. 2000. "Evolution and Proximate Expression of Human Paternal Investment." *Psychological Bulletin* 126: 55–77.

6. Gonzaga, G. C., D. Keltner, E. A. Londahl, and M. D. Smith. 2001. "Love and the Commitment Problem in Romantic Relations and Friendships." *Journal of Personality and Social Psychology* 81: 247–262.

7. Gonzaga, G. C., R. A. Turner, D. Keltner, B. Campos, and M. Altemus. 2006. "Romantic Love and Sexual Desire in Close Relationships." *Emotion* 6: 163–179.

8. Kenrick, D. T., S. E. Gutierres, and L. L. Goldberg. 1989. "Influence of Popular Erotica on Judgment of Strangers and Mates." *Journal of Experimental Social Psychology* 25: 159–167.

9. Kenrick, D. T., S. L. Neuberg, K. L. Zierk, and J. M. Krones. 1994. "Evolution and Social Cognition: Contrast Effects as a Function of Sex, Dominance, and Physical Attractiveness." *Personality and Social Psychology Bulletin* 20: 210–217.

10. Simpson, J. A., S. W. Gangestad, and M. Lerma. 1990. "Perceptions of Physical Attractiveness: Mechanisms Involved in the Maintenance of Romantic Relationships." *Journal of Personality and Social Psychology* 59: 1192–1201.

11. Miller, R. S. 1997. "Inattentive and Contented: Relationship Commitment and Attention to Alternatives." *Journal of Personality and Social Psychology* 73: 758–766.

12. Maner, J. K., M. T. Gailliot, and S. L. Miller. 2009. "The Implicit Cognition of Relationship Maintenance: Inattention to Attractive Alternatives." *Journal of Experimental Social Psychology* 45: 174–179.

Dig Deeper

Eibl-Eibesfeldt, I. 1989. *Human Ethology*. New York: Aldine de Gruyter.
Fisher, H. 2004. *Why We Love*. New York: Henry Holt and Company.

Q6: Is Love Really Blind?

Lisa A. Neff

Dear Diary: Couldn't be more happy. Am involved with most wonderful person ever. Brilliant, funny, sophisticated, and gorgeous to boot. Am certain new partner will never engage in dysfunctional, annoying behaviors in manner of ex-partners. Cannot imagine a more perfect person.

All of us have probably been there. Granted, maybe you didn't record your incessant gushing in a diary stashed away under your pillow, but you've had these types of feelings before. At the beginning of a relationship, your new love interest can do no wrong. All those quirky things your partner does are endearing and fabulous. Such idealization isn't only true in dating relationships—newlyweds tend to put their partners on a pedestal as well. They don't call it *newlywed bliss* for nothing. At the beginning of a marriage, newlyweds are deeply in love, describe their partners in extremely positive terms, and demonstrate unbridled optimism about the future of the marriage.[1] Talk to any newlywed couple and they will tell you: sure, they know the statistics, they know other couples have problems, but not them—they couldn't be happier. It can even be a bit nauseating to hear. So, in those euphoric early stages of a relationship, many people have a tendency to idealize their partners a bit, suggesting there might actually be some truth to the old adage that *Love is blind*. After all, recognizing that love messes with our perceptions is still the only legitimate explanation for the Jesse James/Sandra Bullock romance, and why anyone finds Flavor Flav, Gary Busey, Courtney Love, or Carrot Top endearing. But the truly important question is whether having this idealized view of your partner is really good for a relationship over time.

Are satisfying and healthy relationships based on a love that is blind?

Shakespeare was on to something: Researchers have found that holding idealized views of your partner not only leads to greater relationship happiness, but also may be critical for maintaining a long-term relationship.[2] Specifically, if you have an idealized view of your partner, this may benefit the relationship in two ways. First, believing all those wonderful things about your partner should make you feel secure in your decision to be with that person—"My partner really is the 'right' one." Second, if you idealize your partner, you most likely will be providing your partner with all kinds of positive feedback—"Honey, you are so brilliant and beautiful." As a result, your partner may develop higher self-esteem and feel more confident and secure about your love.

It turns out that the happiest couples don't always view their relationships in the most accurate manner. Happy couples often exhibit something known as *relationship superiority,* reporting that their relationships have more positive aspects and fewer negative aspects than do the relationships of most others.[3] Other research suggests that the happiest individuals may even hold "positive illusions" about their relationship partners. In fact, some studies have found that in lasting relationships, individuals often view their partners more positively than partners view themselves.[2] In other words, these studies suggest that relationships will be most successful if Katie believes Tom to be an even kinder, sexier, more dependable, and more talented person than Tom considers himself to be. In other words, individuals in happy relationships tend to put a positive spin on their partner's traits, and, as a result, may end up seeing their partners somewhat inaccurately.

Should we deceive ourselves into believing our partner is perfect?

So that's it? If we want to have a happy relationship, we should all idealize our partners and gloss over those less-than-perfect traits our partners may have? Basically, we should lie to ourselves? Not so fast! Not everyone agrees that positive illusions are good for a relationship.[4] You may just be setting yourself up for a fall when you put your partner on a pedestal. It might be better to start off a relationship, particularly a marriage, with a clear and accurate view of who your partner is so that you may be less surprised by and better able to cope with your partner's negative qualities as they inevitably surface in the relationship. And let's face it—at some point you are likely to become painfully aware of your partner's inability to put dirty clothes in the hamper or to show up to events on time. If your love is based on the false premise that your partner is perfect, your love probably won't last very long once you are forced to confront the proverbial skeletons that keep finding a way out of the closet.

Or consider this: If your partner is idealizing you, you might be in the uncomfortable position of having to live up to expectations that you are just unable or unwilling to confirm. And worse, you might question whether your partner really loves you or simply an "ideal" image of you. Imagine your partner praises your cooking abilities, yet every time you attempt to make a romantic meal for the two of you, it turns out to be a disaster of Bridget Jones proportions. You know, the soup that inexplicably came out blue, the charred steak that hardly resembles meat…you get the picture. If your partner is idealizing your abilities under these circumstances, you may begin to wonder if your partner even knows you at all.

Although some people do show positive illusions in relationships, some studies have found that the most satisfied spouses do not idealize their partners, but rather view their partners fairly accurately.[4] These studies indicate that relationship happiness is greater when individuals agree with their partners' own views of their particular traits and abilities. Importantly, couples seem to be happier even when agreeing with the partners' self-views means seeing the partner in a negative light. For instance, if Tom believes himself to be lacking in social skills, this research suggests the relationship will be more successful if Katie also believes that Tom lacks in social skills. This perspective argues, then, that individuals need to have some truthful awareness of who their partners are and what qualities they possess.

What kinds of relationship perceptions make for satisfying relationships?

Which is it? Should we idealize our partners, or should we have a more accurate view of them, even if this means seeing them in a more negative light? Is this one of those annoying "It depends" kinds of answer? Well, sort of, in that the answer is that both perspectives are true—it is just the *when* that depends. The happiest and healthiest relationships are based on an element of accuracy *and* an element of positive illusions or "blindness."[5] It is best to be accurate in your views of your partner's specific traits and abilities, while at the same time idealizing your partner's overall worth as a person. When it comes to things like organizational skills or social skills, having an accurate view of your partner allows you to better predict events in your relationship (e.g., you won't expect your partner to be the life of the party if you recognize that he/she is a little socially awkward) and should make your partner feel more understood in the relationship. When it comes to broad qualities, however, like how kind and wonderful your partner is, a bit of idealization may help both of you feel more secure in the relationship. Newlyweds who both idealize their partner's overall qualities *and* have an accurate view of their partners' specific traits and abilities provide better support to one another and are less likely to divorce in the early years of marriage! After all, isn't that what we all want? A partner who understands that we may not be the most organized person in the world, or that we certainly won't have our cooking skills revered on the *Food Network* anytime soon, but who loves us anyway.

Conclusion

Is love blind? Not exactly. True love may involve recognizing your partner's specific strengths and weakness and loving your partner in spite of (or perhaps because of) those imperfections.

TAKE-HOME POINTS

- ♡ We often idealize our partners at the beginning of a relationship and think our relationship is better than the relationships of most others (relationship superiority).
- ♡ Idealization has some pitfalls, however, as it can lead to disappointment when negativity surfaces in the relationship.
- ♡ The happiest and longest-lasting relationships have partners who idealize general traits of their partners (such as kindness) while having a more accurate view of their specific traits (such as singing ability).

References

1. Veroff, J., E. Douvan, T. L. Orbuch, and L. K. Acitelli. 1998. "Happiness in Stable Marriages: The Early Years." In *The Developmental Course Of Marital Dysfunction*, edited by T. N. Bradbury, 152–179. New York: Cambridge University Press.
2. Murray, S. L., J. G. Holmes, and D. W. Griffin. 1996. "The Benefits of Positive Illusions: Idealization and the Construction of Satisfaction in Close Relationships." *Journal of Personality and Social Psychology* 70: 79–98.
3. Van Lange, P. A. M., and C. E. Rusbult. 1995. "My Relationship Is Better Than—and Not as Bad as—Yours Is: The Perceptions of Superiority in Close Relationships." *Personality and Social Psychology Bulletin* 21: 32–44.
4. Swann, W. B., Jr., C. De La Ronde, and J. G. Hixon. 1994. "Authenticity and Positivity Strivings in Marriage and Courtship." *Journal of Personality and Social Psychology* 66: 857–869.
5. Neff, L. A., and B. R. Karney. 2005. "To Know You Is to Love You: The Implications of Global Adoration and Specific Accuracy for Marital Relationships." *Journal of Personality and Social Psychology* 90: 480–497.

Dig Deeper

Gagné, F. M., and J. E. Lydon. 2004. "Bias and Accuracy in Close Relationships: An Integrative Review." *Personality and Social Psychology Review* 8 (4): 322–338.

Kwang, T., and W. R. Swann. 2010. "Do People Embrace Praise Even When They Feel Unworthy? A Review of Critical Tests of Self-Enhancement versus Self-Verification." *Personality and Social Psychology Review* 14 (3): 263–280.

Miller, P. E., S. Niehuis, and T. L. Huston. 2006. "Positive Illusions in Marital Relationships: A 13-Year Longitudinal Study." *Personality and Social Psychology Bulletin* 32 (12): 1579–1594.

Q7: Does Love Last Forever?

Lorne Campbell

In the movie *Moulin Rouge*, Ewan McGregor's character sang to his beloved that "Love is a many splendid thing; Love lifts us up where we belong; All you need is love!" in his attempt to woo Nicole Kidman's character into forming a loving romantic relationship. The message he was trying to convey is clear: Love is everlasting and will shield couples from the harsh realities of life. Sure, your neighbors are annoying, the gas bill is overdue, the baby won't stop crying, and the mother-in-law is visiting for two months, but *love* is enough to turn that frown upside down!

The hot-and-bothered type of love

When you are first falling in love, the feelings that come with it are extremely intense. They may not always be so intense that you pull a Tom Cruise on Oprah and jump up and down on a couch like a crazy person on national television, but the initial feelings of love are pretty exciting nonetheless. Often in these early stages, seeing or even thinking about your partner can set your heart racing and give you boundless energy. This type of love, known as *passionate love*, also involves a great deal of preoccupation that makes it difficult to focus on anything other than your partner (somehow the fact that you went over your cell phone limit doesn't matter so much when you are deeply in love). At this time, you tend to be infatuated with your partner...not so much in a creepy, building a shrine in your closet type of way, but in a "My partner is the greatest, I can't get enough of her" sort of way.[1] As a result, as we pointed out earlier in this chapter, people who are passionately in love also tend to idealize their partner such that they see only the good sides of their partners and think they are perfect.[2]

Because this type of love is so fun and exciting, it is also addictive, leaving us clamoring for more.[3] Unfortunately, as we noted earlier, although it is easy to be passionately in love early in relationships, it is hard to maintain over long periods of time. Often, the sizzle of the passion starts to fizzle out. Specifically, passionate love has been found to decrease following various life transitions, including moving in together, getting engaged, getting married, and having a child.[4]

When you think about it, this isn't terribly surprising. It can be hard to be infatuated with your "perfect" partner right after you had an argument about the proper position in which to leave the toilet seat or whose turn it is to change a diaper. These types of activities just don't have the inherent excitement and novelty of first dates or first kisses.

The friendly type of love

Luckily, although passionate love may fade over time, another type of love, *companionate love,* tends to grow over time. Companionate love is based on friendship, affection, comfort, and shared interests with a person whose life is intertwined with your own. Whereas passionate love is highly energized, companionate love is more calm and relaxed.[5] In the past, a good time used to be going to a club so that you could spend the night dancing with your partner. However, when companionate love takes over, partners spend more time on more ordinary tasks. As Frank said in the movie *Old School* when describing a married guy's big day, "Well, um, actually a pretty nice little Saturday, we're going to go to Home Depot. Yeah, buy some wallpaper; maybe get some flooring, stuff like that. Maybe Bed, Bath, and Beyond, I don't know, I don't know if we'll have enough time!" You know it's love when you find these types of activities exciting!

This might sound like the type of relationship only older married couples have, but almost 50% of premarital young adults consider their romantic partner to be their best friend.[6] If this still sounds boring, you should know that companionate love is a very good indicator of future relationship success. In fact, when researchers asked couples who have been married for more than 15 years why their marriage lasted, the top two reasons given were that their partner was their best friend, and that they liked their partner.[7] However, perhaps more important, researchers have discovered that beyond the initial infatuation, or *honeymoon phase,* of love, long-term relationships provide people with a "secure-base."[8] We become attached to our partners in both an emotional and a physical sense. The word *partner* is very meaningful in this regard, meaning that we have someone to provide emotional support in bad times, someone to share the good times with, and someone to work with us and help us achieve important life goals. As love matures within relationships, the feelings of emotional dependency that people have for their partners provides them with a sense of comfort and security.

Conclusion

In the end, passionate and companionate love are not completely independent. Those who experience lots of companionate love still experience passion, and vice versa. However, one generalization can be taken from this: passionate love gets us married, companionate love keeps us happily married.

TAKE-HOME POINTS

♡ Passionate love is intense, all-consuming, and tends to fade over time.

♡ Companionate love, a deep love based on liking and intimacy, develops over time.

♡ Love can last forever—typically by moving from intense passionate love to a warm and companionate love.

References

1. Dion, K. L., and K. K. Dion. 1973. "Correlates of Romantic Love." *Journal of Consulting and Clinical Psychology* 41: 51–56.
2. Murray, S. L., and J. G. Holmes. 1997. "A Leap of Faith? Positive Illusions in Romantic Relationships." *Personality and Social Psychology Bulletin* 23 (6): 586–604.
3. Fisher, H. E. 1998. "Lust, Attraction and Attachment in Mammalian Reproduction." *Human Nature* 9: 23–52.
4. Tucker, P., and A. Aron. 1993. "Passionate Love and Marital Satisfaction at Key Transition Points in the Family Life Cycle." *Journal of Social and Clinical Psychology* 12 (2): 135–147.
5. Hatfield, E., and R. L. Rapson. 1993. *Love, Sex, And Intimacy: Their Psychology, Biology, and History.* New York: Harper-Collins.
6. Hendrick, S. S., and C. Hendrick. 1993. "Lovers as Friends." *Journal of Social and Personal Relationships* 10: 459–466.
7. Lauer, R. H., and R. Lauer. 1985. "Marriages Made to Last." *Psychology Today* June: 22–26.
8. Zeifman, D., and C. Hazan. 1997. "Attachment: The Bond in Pair Bonds." In *Evolutionary Social Psychology*, edited by J. A. Simpson and D. T. Kenrick, 237–264. Mahwah NJ: Lawrence Erlbaum.

Dig Deeper

Baumeister, R. F., and E. Bratslavsky. 1999. "Passion, Intimacy, and Time: Passionate Love as a Function of Change in Intimacy." *Personality and Social Psychology Review* 3: 49–67.

Berscheid, E., and H. T. Reis. 1998. "Interpersonal Attraction and Close Relationships." In *Handbook of Social Psychology*, Vol. 2, 193–281, edited by S. Fiske, D. Gilbert, G. Lindzey, and E. Aronson. New York: Random House.

Reis, H. T., and A. Aron. 2008. "Love: What Is It, Why Does It Matter, and How Does It Operate?" *Perspectives on Psychological Science* 3: 80–86.

CHAPTER 3

Intimacy and Attachment

Transitioning from a budding romance to a long-term relationship requires a strong foundation. A sense of emotional attachment or connection with one's partner is a key ingredient that promotes relationship
success. Interestingly enough, our ability to form these connections emanates
from earlier experiences in childhood with our parents. Paging Dr. Freud! Well,
not exactly, but there is some truth to the notion that our heterosexual romantic
relationship partners share qualities with our opposite-sex parents. Relationships
also rely on shared intimacy and closeness; however, too much of a good thing
can be smothering. Finally, people often mistakenly believe that individuals'
sexuality is a key ingredient in relationships. Yet, we'll see that homosexual and
heterosexual relationships are much more similar than they are different.

Q8: ARE SOME PEOPLE MORE READY FOR RELATIONSHIPS THAN OTHERS?

Robin S. Edelstein

Sure, the guy you just met is a Taylor Lautner lookalike and a surefire
candidate for hunk of the year, but will he be a good relationship
partner? And what makes someone a good relationship partner anyway? As you've probably noticed, people think about and approach
relationships differently. Some researchers believe that there are three
main approaches to close relationships called *attachment styles*.[1] There
are certain people who always find themselves involved in relationship drama (*anxious*), whereas others tend to avoid relationships altogether (*avoidant*), and some people always seem to be in happy

and satisfying relationships (*secure*). Researchers believe that these attachment styles start in childhood and are rooted in our relationships with our primary caregivers[2] (that's right, it's all mom and dad's fault—how very Freudian of us). A person's approach to relationships can tell you a lot about what kind of partner they will be.

Anxious attachment

People with an anxious attachment style tend to be obsessed with relationships and their relationship partners. As a result, anxious people tend to be jealous, worry that their partners will cheat or leave them for someone else, and generally lose sleep over the fact that their partners don't care about them.[1] This creates a need for constant reassurance from their partners[3]—"Do you really love me?" "Promise that you'll never leave me" "Am I the only one for you?" "Why don't you say that you love me more?" "You'll never hurt me, right?" A relationship with an anxious person tends to be like living in a soap opera, full of drama—lots of fighting, crying, breaking up, making out, and making up. Even though their lives revolve around relationships, anxious people don't have the most satisfying relationships.[4] This is likely because they are too busy fretting about what their partner is thinking or doing. Quite frankly, they can be a real pain in the ass!

Ironically, this worrying and obsessing can backfire, driving you crazy and ultimately leading you to do the very thing that an anxious person fears most: giving them a one-way ticket to Heartbreak Hotel. Not surprisingly, anxious people do not deal well with breakups.[5] If you've ever been stalked by someone you thought you broke up with, there's a good chance he or she had an anxious attachment style. Take a look outside your window. See that person in the bushes? Not only is he obsessed with you, but he likely has an anxious attachment style as well. (Note: If there REALLY is a person in the window, put the book down and call 911—*then* keep reading).

Avoidant attachment

However, avoidant people probably won't stalk you, won't call all the time, and won't really seem like they want to have a relationship with you in the first place. People with an avoidant attachment style find it difficult to be close and intimate with others, especially relationship partners.[6] This is a partner who has a lot of "walls" and doesn't want to let others in. They also like to feel independent and self-sufficient, preferring not to depend on other people—kind of like a cat's "I'll give you attention when I'm ready for it" approach. For this reason, avoidant individuals have a hard time being supportive of relationship partners, particularly in stressful situations.[7] So if you're looking for emotional support while you're getting a tattoo (you know those things are permanent, right?), needing your hair held back as you worship the porcelain goddess, or support when your grandmother is sick, you may want to avoid an avoidant partner.

Most avoidant individuals do end up in relationships at some point, but they still manage to find ways to keep their distance. For example, they're more likely to be promiscuous, both in and out of relationships.[8] By playing the field and having only short-term relationships (or flings) with people, the amount of closeness with any one partner is limited. It turns out that there really isn't much time for deep meaningful conversation when you are busy trying to get someone naked. Funny how that works.

As a result of having less-meaningful interactions with partners, avoidant people tend to have less-satisfying relationships.[4] And when their relationships end, avoidant individuals don't seem particularly upset.[9] In fact, they treat it more like parole—as if they are being released from relationship jail. They're ready to regain their independence and move on to another partner.

Secure attachment

The good news is that the majority of folks are not particularly anxious or avoidant, but instead have a secure approach to relationships (the bad news is that they're probably already in a relationship[10]). Secure people are comfortable depending on and trusting others, having others depend on them, and tend not to be overly worried about losing their partners.[1] They are comfortable with both physical and emotional intimacy, and can be supportive of relationship partners in times of need. Not surprisingly, secure people (and their partners) tend to be the most satisfied with their relationships.[4] Secure individuals are upset when their relationships end, but not straightjacket-and-padded-room upset like anxious folks may be.[5] And if there is a secure person outside your window, they probably aren't hiding in the bushes. Rather, they're likely holding a boombox above their head in John Cusack–style from *Say Anything*.

Attachment in action

To see the impact attachment styles have on relationships in the "real world," a group of researchers observed people saying goodbye to their romantic partners as they boarded planes at an airport (this was back in the days when you could actually go to the gate with the passenger; around the same time people actually used the word *boombox*).[11] While waiting for their flights, people were asked to take a brief survey that asked about their relationships, including their attachment style and how they were feeling prior to departing. Meanwhile, another researcher spied on them from afar, noting how the couples behaved as they waited for their flights: Did they ignore each other, cry, hug, kiss, make cutesy faces at each other? The researchers discovered that those who were avoidantly attached didn't kiss their partners as much, spent less time looking at their partners, and (not surprisingly) avoided their partners more than those who said they were securely or anxiously attached. Avoidant individuals were probably first in line to board the plane! It was almost like they couldn't wait to get away. Perhaps that extra leg room is just more important than you are. The researchers did not observe links between anxious attachment and people's behaviors, but people with an anxious attachment style did say that they were more upset about the impending separation. So, if you're ever in the mood to "test" your partner (which we don't necessarily recommend) and are wondering what kind of attachment style your partner has but you don't want to make them fill out a questionnaire, you can simply see how he or she acts or feels as you get ready to take a trip!

Can attachment change?

What if you're not secure? What if your partner is clingy or emotionally shut-off? Are you doomed to have bad relationships forever? Not necessarily—attachment styles can change over time.[12] As they get older, people generally get less anxious and less avoidant.[10]

Not interested in waiting it out? Your other option to become more secure is to be in a stable and satisfying relationship with a secure partner.[13] The flipside is also true. If you happen to be a secure person involved with an avoidant or anxious person, you can help your partner become more secure. Be careful, however—some insecure relationships can be quite stable, especially those between anxious women and avoidant men.[14] An example of this is a stereotypical relationship between a woman who can't be loved enough, and a man who can't be left alone enough. Not only will this relationship tend to be unhappy, but it is one way to make sure that your attachment style doesn't change!

Conclusion

As you can see, even though attachment styles can be simplified into three categories, they have important implications for relationships. If you are fortunate enough to be secure, your relationship outlook is positive. If you found yourself saying "Uh-oh" while reading about avoidant or anxious attachment styles, you may now be able to take steps toward becoming more secure.

TAKE-HOME POINTS

- ♡ People with an *anxious* attachment style are overly concerned with abandonment and rejection in relationships; those who are *avoidant* try to maintain physical and emotional distance from relationship partners; people who are *secure* are confident about partners' responsiveness and comfortable getting close to others.
- ♡ Secure people tend to have the most stable and satisfying relationships; those who are anxious tend to have more volatile and dramatic relationships; and avoidant people tend to have somewhat distant and short-lived relationships.
- ♡ Attachment styles are relatively stable over time, but they're not unchangeable. People tend to become less avoidant and anxious with age and when they're in satisfying relationships.

References

1. Hazan, C., and P. Shaver. 1987. "Romantic Love Conceptualized as an Attachment Process." *Journal of Personality and Social Psychology* 52: 511–524.
2. Cassidy, J. 2000. "Adult Romantic Attachments: A Developmental Perspective on Individual Differences." *Review of General Psychology* 4: 111–131.
3. Shaver, P. R., D. A. Schachner, and M. Mikulincer. 2005. "Attachment Style, Excessive Reassurance Seeking, Relationship Processes, and Depression." *Personality and Social Psychology Bulletin* 31: 343.
4. Feeney, J. A. 2008. "Adult Romantic Attachment: Developments in the Study of Couple Relationships." In *Handbook of Attachment: Theory, Research, and Clinical Applications,* 2nd ed., 456–481, edited by J. Cassidy and P. R. Shaver. New York: Guilford Press.
5. Davis, D., P. R. Shaver, and M. L. Vernon. 2003. "Physical, Emotional, and Behavioral Reactions to Breaking Up: The Roles of Gender, Age, Emotional Involvement, and Attachment Style." *Personality and Social Psychology Bulletin* 29: 871–884.
6. Edelstein, R. S., and P. R. Shaver. 2004. "Avoidant Attachment: Exploration of an Oxymoron." In *Handbook of Closeness and Intimacy,* edited by D. J. Mashek and A. P. Aron, 397–412. Mahwah NJ: Lawrence Erlbaum Associates.
7. Edelstein, R. S., K. W. Alexander, P. R. Shaver et al. 2004. "Adult Attachment Style and Parental Responsiveness during a Stressful Event." *Attachment and Human Development* 6: 31–52.
8. Schachner, D. A., and P. R. Shaver. 2002. "Attachment Style and Human Mate Poaching." *New Review of Social Psychology* 1: 122–129.
9. Fraley, R. C., K. E. Davis, and P. R. Shaver. 1998. "Dismissing-Avoidance and the Defensive Organization of Emotion, Cognition, and Behavior." In *Attachment Theory and Close Relationships,* edited by J. A. Simpson and W. S. Rholes, 249–279. New York: Guilford Press.
10. Mickelson, K. D., R. C. Kessler, and P. R. Shaver. 1997. "Adult Attachment in a Nationally Representative Sample." *Journal of Personality and Social Psychology* 73: 1092–1106.
11. Fraley, R. C., and P. R. Shaver. 1998. "Airport Separations: A Naturalistic Study of Adult Attachment Dynamics in Separating Couples." *Journal of Personality and Social Psychology* 75: 1198–1212.
12. Fraley, R. C. 2002. "Attachment Stability from Infancy to Adulthood: Meta-Analysis and Dynamic Modeling of Developmental Mechanisms." *Personality and Social Psychology Review* 6: 123–151.
13. Kirkpatrick, L. A., and C. Hazan. 1994. "Attachment Styles and Close Relationships: A Four-Year Prospective Study." *Personal Relationships* 1: 123–142.
14. Kirkpatrick, L. A., and K. E. Davis. 1994. "Attachment Style, Gender, and Relationship Stability: A Longitudinal Analysis." *Journal of Personality and Social Psychology* 66: 502–512.

Dig Deeper

Campbell, L., J. A. Simpson, J. Boldry, and D. A. Kashy. 2005. "Perceptions of Conflict And Support in Romantic Relationships: The Role of Attachment Anxiety." *Journal of Personality and Social Psychology* 88: 510–531.

Ein-Dor, T., M. Mikulincer, G. Doron, and P. R. Shaver. 2010. "The Attachment Paradox: How Can So Many of Us (the Insecure Ones) Have No Adaptive Advantages?" *Perspectives on Psychological Science* 5: 123–141.

Mikulincer, M., and P. R. Shaver. 2007. *Attachment in Adulthood: Structure, Dynamics, and Change*. New York: Guilford Press.

Q9: Is There Any Truth Behind The Saying That "We Marry Our Father/Mother"?

Robin S. Edelstein

In the Greek tragedy *Oedipus Rex*, the protagonist—Oedipus—has been separated from his biological parents since infancy. As an adult, he returns to his place of birth and, in a tragic and creepy turn of events, unknowingly murders his father and marries his mother. When Oedipus and his mother finally learn the truth, they are (naturally) devastated; she commits suicide and Oedipus blinds himself with his mother's dress pins (again, creepy). In this story, Oedipus and his mother had no way to know that they were mother and son, but Sigmund Freud, the founder of psychoanalytic theory, thought that their experiences held at least some kernel of truth. Freud proposed that young children go through a stage of development in which they unconsciously experience sexual attraction to their opposite-sex parent and, as a result, experience feelings of competition toward their same-sex parent. Drawing on the story of *Oedipus Rex*, in the case of boys, Freud called this situation an *Oedipal conflict* (Freud, ever the misogynist, had even more complicated ideas about what happened with girls); he thought that young children must resolve this conflict before normal gender roles and sexual relationships could be established.[1] Not surprisingly, historians have noted that Freud had a contentious relationship with his father and was the quintessential "mommy's little boy."

Most contemporary psychologists no longer believe that young children actually go through this kind of process, or that children of any age are sexually attracted to either one of their parents. But many psychologists do believe a more benign version of Freud's theory, which is often called the *prototype hypothesis*.[2] According to the prototype hypothesis, early experiences with parents help to shape our preferences for the qualities that we look for in a partner and the kinds of experiences that we ultimately have with those partners—*not* because we are sexually attracted to our parents, but because these important relationships help us create a template that guides us in later relationships.

Is there any evidence that we are attracted to partners who resemble our parents in some way?

You may be thinking, *Eww! I would never date someone like my dad/ mom!* In fact, however, there's more similarity between our parents and our partners than you would expect just by chance. For example, in one study, researchers compared pictures of men's wives with those of the dudes' biological mothers. They found that there was a noticeable degree of similarity between the facial features of the wives and the mothers (at least the similarity was noticeable to the experimenter; we'll safely assume the wives and mothers-in-law turned a blind eye to such overlap).[3] In fact, people who looked at the pictures but did not know whose mother-in-law was whose, were able to match up the mothers-in-law/daughters-in-law pairs surprisingly well. Similar results have been obtained in studies of women's romantic partners and their biological fathers. The next time you have a chance, sneak a glance at your partner and then compare them to your same-gendered parent. Weird, isn't it?

One problem with these studies is that—as much as you may wish it weren't so—we tend to look like our biological parents. So, it's possible that our partners look like our parents because we tend to choose partners who look like *us*.[4] Remember question 3, where we talked about how we are attracted to people who are similar to us? Well, who is more similar to us than our own family? To cleverly get around this problem, researchers studied women who were adopted and compared pictures of women's romantic partners to their adoptive fathers.[5] As it turns out, findings with adopted women are very similar: Their male partners show a noticeable physical similarity to their *adoptive* fathers (who presumably did not closely resemble the women themselves). These findings suggest that the similarity between women's partners and their fathers isn't necessarily because women chose partners who looked like themselves. Instead, women chose partners who looked like the most important male figure in their lives: their (adoptive) father. Even more interestingly, women who said that they had received a lot of emotional support from their adoptive fathers were especially likely to choose partners who looked like their fathers. Similar results have been obtained for men and their choice of romantic partners; this isn't only a "daddy's girl" phenomenon.[3]

Having a closer relationship with our opposite-sex parent may lead us to choose romantic partners who resemble them more. This could be a really good thing, especially if you like your mother. By "marrying your mother," you are at least in a relationship with a woman who has likable qualities. Our preference for partners who resemble our parents also extends to other characteristics, such as a partner's ethnicity, age, and personality (again, similarity and familiarity are pretty powerful). For instance, people who have parents of different ethnicities are more likely to marry someone of the ethnicity of their opposite-sex parent than of their same-sex parent.[6] And women who have fathers who are older than average are more likely to choose partners who are also older than average.[7]

Is there any evidence that we are attracted to partners who have similar personalities to our parents?

There's less research on the topic of personality, but at least one study suggests that our partners and our parents tend to be similar to one another in traits like openness to experience, agreeableness, and emotional stability. Interestingly, people are more satisfied with their romantic relationship when their partners are very similar to their opposite-sex parent in agreeableness, but people are *less* satisfied with their romantic relationships when their partner is very similar to their opposite-sex parent in neuroticism.[8] So, our tendency to choose relationship partners who resemble our parents may not always be a good thing; it depends on the specific characteristics we're talking about.

How do we end up with partners like our parent?

Do you size up that guy at the bar, and think to yourself, "He looks just like my dad...I wonder if he's a good kisser?" Or say to your buddies, "Dude, she's hot like my mom; I'd totally hit that!" (Please say "No.") In reality, how we end up with a partner who reflects the characteristics of our mom or dad likely operates unconsciously. For example, let's say you meet a new person (Jack) who shares some characteristics with an important person in your life (your dad). Just like your dad, Jack is always on time, he's super organized, and he has expensive taste in fine single-malt scotch. Research shows that you are likely to assume that Jack shares other characteristics with your dad (like terrible cooking skills), even though you don't really know whether he does share these characteristics.[9] If you have positive feelings toward your dad, then you're likely to project those feelings onto Jack as well, and you may just end up liking him (despite his terrible cooking skills!). This process, called *transference* (another concept first developed by Freud), can also happen if we encounter people who simply *look* like an important person in our lives.[10] So if that guy at the bar looks a little bit like your dad (but not *too* much; see the answer to the next question), you might find him more attractive, especially if you have a close relationship with your dad.

If someone resembles my parent, will I find them more attractive?

Just making people unconsciously aware of their opposite-sex parent can make them more attracted to new potential partners, even if those new people don't look like the parent at all. In one study, participants were asked to rate how sexually attractive they found pictures of a series of opposite-sex strangers.[4] Half of the participants were subliminally primed with a picture of their opposite-sex parent (meaning that the picture was presented so quickly that they could not consciously perceive it; it affected them on an unconscious level), and half of the participants were primed with a picture of someone else's opposite-sex parent. People who were primed with their own opposite-sex parent rated the pictures they saw as more sexually attractive than people who were primed with someone else's parent. Again, it's important to remember that many of these processes happen unconsciously—or at least out of our immediate awareness. If your best friend reminds you that the guy at the bar looks *just* like your dad, you might actually decide that he's not so attractive after all![4]

As an aside, a less-researched idea in family attraction is a concept called *genetic sexual attraction,* which refers to attraction between biologically related individuals who were unknown to each other until adulthood (typically siblings raised apart due to adoption; think *The Empire Strikes Back* and that awkward kiss between Luke and Leia).[11] This is, not surprisingly, an extremely controversial idea, but organizations such as http://www.adoption.org do counsel individuals looking to meet family members to be aware that this attraction does sometimes happen. Very little research on this potential phenomenon has been conducted, but those who do discuss it suggest that our attraction to people similar to us, coupled with a lack of desensitization and familiarity that normally occurs when we grow up with close biological relatives, could explain genetic sexual attraction. In fact, research on non-genetically related children raised together as siblings suggests that being raised together makes people extremely unlikely to be sexually attracted to each other; cultural taboos and familiarity keep us from being attracted to our actual family members.[4]

Conclusion

So, was Freud right? Are we doomed to unconscious sexual attractions to our opposite-sex parent, and is that why we seek out partners who are similar to them? Not entirely. Evolutionary psychologists propose that we evolved to prefer partners who are similar to us (which could increase cooperation, altruism, and the benefits of shared adaptations) but not *too* similar (so that we have to worry about inbreeding and too much genetic overlap).[12] Thus, the ideal mate may be someone who resembles your parent in some minimal way, but is not exactly like them (whew!).

TAKE-HOME POINTS

- ♡ We tend to be attracted to relationship partners who are similar in personality or physical appearance to our opposite-sex parent.
- ♡ At least some of our attraction to people who resemble our opposite-sex parent happens at an unconscious level.
- ♡ We most likely evolved to prefer partners who are similar to us in some way, but not *too* similar; cultural taboos and socialization processes prevent us from developing attractions to actual family members.

References

1. Freud, S. 1924. "The Passing of the Oedipus Complex." *International Journal of Psycho-Analysis* 5: 419–424.
2. Owens, G., J. A. Crowell, H. S. Pan, D. Treboux, E. O'Connor, and E. Waters. 1995. "The Prototype Hypothesis and the Origins of At-

tachment Working Models: Adult Relationships with Parents and Romantic Partners." *Monographs of the Society for Research in Child Development* 60: 216–233.

3. Bereczkei, T., P. Gyuris, P. Koves, and L. Bernath. 2002. "Homogamy, Genetic Similarity, and Imprinting; Parental Influence on Mate Choice Preferences." *Personality and Individual Differences* 33: 677–690.

4. Fraley, R. C., and M. J. Marks. 2010. "Westermarck, Freud, and the Incest Taboo: Does Familial Resemblance Activate Sexual Attraction?" *Personality and Social Psychology Bulletin* 36: 1202–1212.

5. Bereczkei, T., P. Gyuris, and G. Weisfeld. 2004. "Sexual Imprinting in Human Mate Choice." *Proceedings of the Royal Society B: Biological Sciences* 271: 1129–1134.

6. Jedlicka, D. 1984. "Indirect Parental Influence on Mate Choice: A Test of the Psychoanalytic Theory." *Journal of Marriage and the Family* 46: 65–70.

7. Perrett, D., I. S. Penton-Voak, A. C. Little, et al. 2002. "Facial Attractiveness Judgements Reflect Learning of Parental Age Characteristics." *Proceedings of the Royal Society of London. Series B: Biological Sciences* 269: 873–880.

8. Geher, G. 2000. "Perceived and Actual Characteristics of Parents and Partners: A Test of a Freudian Model of Mate Selection." *Current Psychology* 19: 194–214.

9. Andersen, S., and S. Chen. 2002. "The Relational Self: An Interpersonal Social–Cognitive Theory." *Psychological Review* 109: 619–644.

10. Kraus, M., and S. Chen. 2010. "Facial-Feature Resemblance Elicits the Transference Effect." *Psychological Science* 21: 518–522.

11. Greenberg, M. and R. Littlewood. 1995. "Post-Adoption Incest and Phenotypic Matching: Experience, Personal Meanings and Biosocial Implications." *British Journal of Medical Psychology* 68: 29–44.

12. Bateson, P. 1983. "Optimal Outbreeding." In *Mate Choice*, edited by P. Bateson 257–277. Cambridge UK: Cambridge University Press.

Dig Deeper

Lieberman, D., D. M. T. Fessler, and A. Smith. In Press. "The Relationship between Familial Resemblance and Sexual Attraction: An Update on Westermarck, Freud, and the Incest Taboo." *Personality and Social Psychology Bulletin*. Found online at http://psp.sagepub.com/content/early/2011/04/27/0146167211405997.abstract

Little, A. C., I. S. Penton-Voak, D. M. Burt, and D. I. Perrett. 2003. "Investigating an Imprinting-Like Phenomenon in Humans: Partners and Opposite-Sex Parents Have Similar Hair and Eye Colour." *Evolution and Human Behavior* 24: 43–51.

Q10: Isn't Being Too Close to a Partner a Bad Thing?

Debra Mashek

What is the nature of closeness?

Romantic relationships are, by their very nature, *close*. Partners share things about themselves, do things together, spend a lot of time together, and influence each others' decisions.[1] These are good things for relationships, but is it possible to have too much of a good thing in your relationship? Let's consider this question by thinking about the following image[2]:

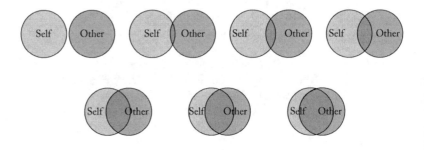

Imagine that the circle on the left (the one labeled "Self") represents you and that the circle on the right (the one labeled "Other") represents your romantic partner. Which pair of circles do you think best represents your relationship? Relationship researchers often use this 1-item measure, called the *Inclusion of Other in Self Scale,* or simply *IOS,* to get a sense of how close an individual perceives her or his relationship with another person. In fact, this measure accurately taps both what researchers refer to as *behavioral closeness* (how much you and your partner do things together) and *cognitive closeness* (how much you and your partner see your selves as intertwined). Admittedly, it may seem odd that this one picture can really assess something as complex as closeness in a romantic relationship. No measure is perfect, but in this case, the saying "Less is more" is true: researchers have shown across countless studies that the IOS provides an effective measure of the complex idea of closeness.

Everyone likes more closeness, right?

Whenever we talk about this scale with our students, the question inevitably arises: "Isn't it a bad thing to select the last pair of circles? Doesn't that mean that the person is totally smothered by the relationship?" The answer, not surprisingly, is that it depends. Just as some people crave the timeless blending of chocolate and peanuts, whereas others prefer to keep the chocolate off their nuts, people have different levels of comfort with closeness. Just because someone indicates a near-perfect overlap between self and other does not mean that the individual, or the relationship, is too close. To illustrate, consider the "Cupplerobe," a quirky little garment that, as the name suggests, is designed to hold two people at once. Some individuals find this idea rather appealing (hence the infomercials), but the mere thought of being physically yoked in such a contraption is enough to make others jump out of their skin. In other words, when it comes to closeness, one robe definitely does not fit all. Thus, it really makes sense to not just ask people how they see their relationship, but to also ask them how they would describe their *ideal* relationship with a partner—that is, what does the person really want? If reality echoes that desire, then all is well. If there's a discrepancy between reality and desire, trouble looms.

Can people want a different amount of closeness than they have?

Now, take a second look at the circles in the IOS. Which pair of circles do you think best represents your ideal relationship with your partner? Here is where things get interesting. Did you select the same pair of circles when thinking about your ideal relationship as you did when thinking about your actual relationship? If you did, then we can assume that, at least at this point in time, you are satisfied with the degree of closeness in the relationship. You're in good company. Approximately 35% to 59% of college students involved in dating relationships report experiencing levels of closeness that match their ideals.[3] Another chunk of daters (between 38% and 46%) indicate wanting *more* closeness; that is, the circles they select for their ideal relationship reveal more overlap than the pair of circles they select for their actual relationship. As you may have guessed, some people (13% to 19%) *do* feel *too close* to their partners; these people describe their ideal relationship as less close than their current relationship.

Keep in mind that these percentages reflect the proportion of people who responded to actual and desired closeness at a given point in time (i.e., right now). But what if you looked more broadly at how you've felt in the relationship over the previous 3 months? Interestingly, a whopping 57% of college students involved in relationships reported that they felt too close to their current partner *at least once* in the preceding 3 months.[3] Clearly, in the world of daters, a majority feel there can be too much of a good thing.

How does feeling too close make you feel?

Researchers asked study participants to write down words that made them feel too close.[4] They then asked another group of participants to evaluate how well each of these words captured the essence of what it means to desire less closeness with an intimate partner. Any guesses about which words floated to the top of the sea of descriptors? Hint: The words definitely fit into the not-so-warm-and-fuzzy camp. They include "feeling trapped," "being smothered," "needing space," and "wanting freedom." One guy who felt too close to his partner summed up the experience as follows: "For seven years, every decision, from what to eat for dinner to where to live, has been made by the two of us together. I want to make some decisions on my own. I don't want my life to be tied to my partner." Another woman proclaimed, "My boyfriend thinks our spirits should be as one—a unified entity. There is just way too much 'we' and 'us' in our relationship, not enough 'me' and 'I.'"

It turns out that people's language use is an important marker of relationship quality as well, and accordingly, the issue of "we-ness" versus "me-ness" is likely at the heart of what it means to feel too close.[5] Generally speaking, using more plural pronouns indicates a greater sense of closeness. So the next time you are alone with a friend and ask how much he likes the latest *American Idol* and he says, "We really aren't fans of the new judges," you can safely assume he is close to his partner because he is by himself but still saying "we."

Should there be a balance between "we" and "me"?

Relationships struggle to balance the intimacy of the relationship with the autonomy of the individuals within that relationship,[6] and just as a relationship cannot exist without some level of intimacy, individuals cannot exist without some level of autonomy. It's not surprising that many of us bristle when our friends treat us as though we are connected at the hip with our partners. When they ask, "Are you free for dinner Saturday night?" often they mean the plural *you* (as in Brad and Angelina, aka "Brangelina") rather than the singular you. It is also true that many people get annoyed when newly coupled friends are suddenly incapable of doing anything without each other. Assumptions such as these, whether made by our friends or ourselves, slowly challenge the distinction between me-the-individual and we-the-couple. Ultimately, you have to strike a comfortable balance for yourself. Being in a relationship where both partners are fully independent may not be ideal, much like a relationship where you lose all individuality isn't ideal.

Are some people more sensitive to being too close?

As you might expect based on answers to other questions in this book, some of us are likely more prone than others to experience this sense of being smothered in relationships. One individual difference dimension related to closeness is what researchers call *attachment avoidance* (see question 8). People with this personality characteristic are especially sensitive to issues of closeness. Avoidant individuals are wary of closeness with others and perceive that their partners want to be closer to them than they are comfortable with. These are the folks that bristle at the thought of their partner's toothbrush making its way into their bathroom or balk at the idea of a shared bank account. Not surprisingly, individuals with attachment avoidance are more likely to report that their partners desire more closeness than they want in their relationships.[7]

Are there certain situations that provoke the desire for less closeness?

Along with being associated with existing individual differences such as attachment avoidance, the desire for less closeness can be caused by specific situations, as illustrated in the lab by *priming*.[4] In one interesting study, researchers exposed some participants who were in dating relationships to those not-so-warm-and-fuzzy words that describe what it means to want less closeness. The key with priming is to expose the word subtly so that participants aren't aware that they are encountering the words. In this study, researchers embedded the "too-close" words in a word search puzzle like those you cherished in *Highlights* magazine as a kid. Other participants were exposed to words not at all relevant to relationships. One fascinating finding from this study is that those people who did the puzzle with the "Oh, you're smothering me" words were more likely than the other group to desire less closeness with their partner after completing the puzzle. Even more interestingly, people with high levels of avoidance were especially sensitive to these subtle word-search exposures. Simply reminding these folks about the possibility of feeling too close seemed to sensitize participants to this possibility and trigger this very perception about their own relationships.[4]

Conclusion

Closeness, in many ways, is like eating Oreos or Gummi Bears. A little is tasty, but eating the whole bag is likely to be a mistake. Taking the analogy further, some people have iron stomachs and can tolerate a whole lot, whereas for others just a little bit makes them sick. The key is to figure out what kind of person you are, what your partner wants in the relationship, and to find a balance that promotes both the development of the relationship as well as one's own comfort and independence.

TAKE-HOME POINTS

♡ Although closeness is an essential ingredient in romantic relationships, it is possible to feel too close to others.
♡ Different people have different degrees of comfort with closeness; when in a relationship, we should balance the closeness needs and desires of both people.

References

1. Berscheid, E., M. Snyder, and A. M. Omoto. 1989. "The Relationship Closeness Inventory: Assessing the Closeness of Interpersonal Relationships." *Journal of Personality and Social Psychology* 57 (5) 792–807.
2. Aron, A., E. N. Aron, and D. Smollan. 1992. "Inclusion of Other in the Self Scale and the Structure of Interpersonal Closeness." *Journal of Personality and Social Psychology* 63 596–612.
3. Mashek, D., and M. Sherman. 2004. "Desiring Less Closeness with Intimate Others." In *Handbook of Closeness and Intimacy*, edited by D. Mashek and A. Aron 343–356. Mahwah NJ: Lawrence Erlbaum Associates, Inc.
4. Mashek, D., B. Le, K. Israel, and A. Aron. In Press. "Wanting Less Closeness in Romantic Relationships: A Prototype Analysis and Experimental Validation." *Basic and Applied Social Psychology*.
5. Agnew, C. R., P. A. M. Van Lange, C. E. Rusbult, and C. A. Langston. 1998. "Cognitive Interdependence: Commitment and the Mental Representation of Close Relationships." *Journal of Personality and Social Psychology* 74: 939–954.
6. Baxter, L. A., and B. M. Montgomery. 1996. *Relating: Dialogues and Dialectics.* New York: The Guilford Press.
7. Mikulincer, M., and P. R. Shaver. 2007. *Attachment in Adulthood: Structure, Dynamics, and Change.* New York: Guilford Press.

Dig Deeper

Mashek, D. and M. Sherman. 2004. "Desiring Less Closeness with Intimate Others." In *Handbook of Closeness and Intimacy*, edited by D. Mashek and A. Aron, 343–356. Mahwah NJ: Lawrence Erlbaum Associates, Inc.

Q11: How Similar or Different Are Homosexual and Heterosexual Relationships?

Jennifer J. Harman

Michael is a 32-year-old accountant and is madly in love. He had a few serious relationships during college, dated a lot of people, but had never met "The One"—until Casey, a 28-year-old retail manager, at a party about a year ago. They hit it off immediately. Casey is smart, charismatic, and makes Michael feel great about himself. They share many mutual interests, such as cooking, watching independent films, and skiing. Over the first 3 months of their relationship, they spent more and more time together. After 6 months, they moved in together, and Michael was amazed that, a year later, he was as in love as he had ever been. He decided that he wanted to propose to Casey and get married. He views this as the next step toward starting a family with Casey.

Michael's relationship with Casey sounds like many other relationships: Two people meet, fall in love, and decide to commit themselves to a long-term partnership. Well, their relationship is like many other *heterosexual* relationships. In this case, Casey and Michael are both men and would not be allowed to marry in many parts of the world. Most Americans agree that certain civil rights (e.g., employment) of people like Michael and Casey should be protected, and that their private, adult, consensual sexual practices should not be restricted.[1] However, there is much more disagreement as to whether a same-sex relationship between couples like Michael and Casey is "bad," and whether their marriage would "undermine" the traditional American family.[2] Much of the debate stems from the belief that intimate and committed relationships between two members of the same sex are inherently immoral, unnatural, or a threat to the institution of marriage and to children. Many of the arguments offered to support these beliefs are religious or philosophical, but often the arguments are based on the idea that heterosexual relationships are both different and better than homosexual relationships. But are there really any differences between homosexual and heterosexual relationships?

Roles

Generally, there are not many differences at all between hetero-sexual and homosexual relationships.[3] They fall in love the same way, have the same concerns about long-term compatibility and doubts, and experience the same desire for long-term commit-ment. Just as heterosexuals hope one day to marry, most gays and lesbians would like to marry someone of the same sex legally one day. Rates of domestic violence are similar across both relation-ship types.[4] Most same-sex couples resemble typical dual-earner heterosexual relationships, in that both partners work and share their financial responsibilities as well as household chores when they live together. The partner who contributes the most resources to the relationship typically performs fewer household tasks, in-dependent of gender or relationship type.[5] There is a stereotype about gay couples that one partner takes on a more masculine role ("butch"), and the other a more feminine role ("femme"), yet this belief is not supported by research. Many also assume that gender roles in relationships such as Michael and Casey's are related to sexual acts or behaviors that partner's may prefer to enact together (i.e., dominant versus receptive sexual role[6]), but there is no data to support this either.

Sex

Sexual satisfaction for both heterosexual and same-sex couples is related to overall relationship satisfaction. In the early stages of a relationship, gay men report higher rates of sexual intercourse than heterosexuals and lesbian women; however, reports of sexual fre-quency decline in relationships across all types.[6] In fact, among couples who have been together 10 or more years, heterosexual re-lationship partners report having sexual relations more frequently than same-sex couples. Both heterosexual and homosexual males are more likely to be non-monogamous than females, and gay men are more likely to report having sex with other partners outside of a partnered relationship than heterosexual and lesbian couples.[6] One reason for this difference is that norms about exclusivity have been found to vary considerably in same-sex relationships, particularly among gay males. Some relationships have clear expectations and agreements about how and what types of sexual behaviors are acceptable outside of the relationship, and others implicitly assume that their relationship is monogamous. Navigating "open" relationships can be challenging, but research shows that as long as both partners agree about their expectations for each other, then there are no significant differences in relationship satisfaction for individuals in monogamous or non-exclusive relationships.[7]

Parenting

Would Michael and Casey make good parents? Stereotypes about gays and lesbians have led to strong beliefs that they would not, such as the belief that homosexuals are mentally ill. In reality, however, homosexuality is not a psychological disorder, and there is no reliable research evidence suggesting that Michael or Casey would be any "crazier" than partners in a heterosexual relationship. There is also no evidence that homosexuals are any more likely than heterosexuals to sexually or physically abuse their children. Another argument that has been proposed is that lesbian mothers are not "motherly enough," yet there is considerable research showing that lesbian and heterosexual women do not differ significantly in their parenting practices,[8] and that same-sex parents are just as effective, if not *more effective* than heterosexual parents.[9]

How would Michael's and Casey's children be affected by being raised by gay parents? Many believe that having a gay parent will make a child have sexual identity issues or have problems with their own gender role. Yet children of gay parents experience no differences in their sexual identity formation relative to children of heterosexual parents,[10] nor do they differ in any other aspect of their personal or social identity development.[11] Interestingly, children of gay and lesbian parents have more flexible views of acceptable gender behaviors,[12] which may be considerably more adaptive than individuals holding firm gender roles. These children also have normal social adjustment with peers and adults.[8] In terms of any possible negative impact that having a gay parent may have, it is generally to the result of prejudice and discrimination from others in society, yet there is not any conclusive evidence that these children are the target of bullying or ostracism any more than any other child would be.[13]

Individual Well-Being

Same-sex relationships are often highly stigmatized in society, and this stigmatization can result in a number of psychological and physiological outcomes, including heightened stress and poorer mental health.[14] Trying to hide their relationships can have negative consequences for homosexuals as well, such as decreased commitment to their relationships, lower self-esteem, and negative physical symptoms.[15] Such findings beg the question, can the legal recognition of same-sex marriage improve or otherwise minimize such outcomes? The evidence overwhelmingly indicates that it would. In a large on-line survey, individuals in legally recognized same-sex relationships have been found to report less internalized homophobia, greater meaning in life, fewer depressive symptoms, and less stress than those who have not been allowed to marry or form a civil union legally.[16]

Marriage Rights

So what is the issue with people like Michael and Casey getting married? Most of the debate relies on religious opinions, with the belief that same-sex marriage is not "real" marriage. Religious groups often define *marriage* as the "union of a man and a woman," a definition presumed to predate formal legal definitions and is therefore used by opponents of same-sex marriage as the valid standard.[17] Another argument proposed by individuals against same-sex marriage is that legalization would undermine "traditional" marriage. There is no reliable data to support this. The Family Research Council provides as support, for example, a Boston *Globe* newspaper article citing that 40% of same-sex marriages in Vermont had been previously married to an opposite-sex person.[17] This belief assumes, erroneously, that sexual orientation is a choice, and that if same-sex marriages were not legal, these particular individuals would have either not divorced or found a different opposite-sex person to marry after divorce. There is no research evidence to substantiate such a claim.

Many in opposition to same-sex marriage also cite research that gay males in relationships are more likely to have non-exclusive relationships than heterosexuals. If Michael and Casey had a consensually agreed-upon, non-exclusive relationship and were married, this arrangement would not necessarily undermine the institution of marriage any more than heterosexuals' behavior in their own marriages would. In fact, infidelity rates are high in heterosexual marriages without open arrangements, ranging from 25% to 50% of married men having sex outside of their marriage.[6] Arguably, if the legal institution of marriage has not been undermined by such high rates of heterosexual infidelity that has been occurring without agreement between partners, allowing stable relationships that have such agreements would not undermine it either.

Finally, some people believe that if people like Michael and Casey were allowed to marry, then we would have to start letting people marry whoever they want: minors, animals, multiple people, tugboats, to carry it to extremes. For example, the Traditional Values Coalition believes that advocates of same-sex marriage want to legalize it "as a way of destroying the concept of marriage altogether—and of introducing polygamy and polyamory (group sex) as 'families.'"[18] There is also a belief that legalizing same-sex marriage will force public schools to "promote" homosexuality. Once again, such notions are scientifically unsubstantiated: Gay marriage is currently legal in more than a dozen countries, and domestic partnerships are currently legal in nearly another 20 additional countries. Across all of these countries, there is no evidence that any of the concerns raised by individuals or groups opposed to same-sex marriage have a legitimate basis in the available scientific data.

Conclusion

As you can see, many of the beliefs surrounding homosexual relationships seem to be misguided at best, or grounded in stereotypical and prejudiced beliefs at worst. Upon examining data from scientific studies, it becomes clear that homosexual and heterosexual relationships are much more similar than they are different. Consider this reason number 1,000,001 to rely on research rather than personal opinion.

TAKE-HOME POINTS

♡ There are very few differences in the quality or content of heterosexual and homosexual relationships; gay and lesbian relationships operate much like heterosexual relationships.

♡ Evidence indicates that gays and lesbians are equally good, if not better, parents compared to heterosexual parents.

References

1. Kaiser Foundation. November 2001. *Inside-out: A Report on the Experiences of Lesbians, Gays, and Bisexuals in America and the Public's View on Issues and Policies Related to Sexual Orientation.* Menlo Park CA: Author.
2. Loftus, J. 2001. "America's Liberalization in Attitudes towards Homosexuality, 1973–1998."*American Sociological Review* 66: 762–782.
3. Brehm, S. S., R. S. Miller, D. Perlman, and S. M. Campbell. 2002. *Intimate Relationship,* 3rd ed. Boston: McGraw Hill.
4. Alexander, C. J. 2002. "Violence in Gay and Lesbian Relationships."*Journal of Gay and Lesbian Social Services* 14: 95–98.
5. Sutphin, S. T. 2010. "Social Exchange Theory and the Division of Household Labor in Same-Sex Couples."*Marriage and Family Review* 46: 191–206: 2010.
6. Blumstein, P., and Schwartz, P. *American Couples.* New York: Simon & Schuster 1983.
7. Blasband, D., and Peplau, L. A. 1985. "Sexual Exclusivity versus Openness in Gay Male Couples."*Archives of Sexual Behavior* 14: 395–412.
8. Patterson, C. J. 2000. "Family Relationships of Lesbians and Gay Men."*Journal of Marriage and Family* 62: 1052–1069.
9. Armesto, J. C. 2002. "Developmental and Contextual Factors That Influence Gay Fathers' Parental Competence: A Review of the Literature." *Psychology of Men and Masculinity* 3: 67–78.
10. Patterson, C. J. 2004. "Lesbian and Gay Parents and Their Children: Summary of Research Findings." In *Lesbian and Gay Parenting: A Resource for Psychologists,* 5-22. Washington DC: American Psychological Association.
11. Stacey, J., and Biblarz, T. J. 2001. "(How) Does Sexual Orientation of Parents Matter?" *American Sociological Review* 65: 159–183.
12. Golombok, S., and Tasker, F. 1996. "Do Parents Influence Sexual Orientation of Their Children? Findings from a Longitudinal Study of Lesbian Families."*Developmental Psychology* 32: 3–11.
13. Tasker, F., and Golombok, S. 1995. "Adults Raised as Children in Lesbian Families."*American Journal of Orthopsychiatry* 65: 203–215.

14. Miller, C. T., and Major, B. 2000. "Coping with Stigma and Prejudice." In *The Social Psychology of Stigma*, edited by T. F. Heatherton, R. E. Kleck, M. R. Hebl, and J. G. Hull, 243–272. New York: The Guilford Press.

15. Lehmiller, J. J. 2009. "Secret Romantic Relationships: Consequences for Personal and Relational Well-Being." *Personality and Social Psychology Bulletin* 35: 1452–1466.

16. Riggle, E. D., Rostosky, S. S., and Horne, S. G. 2010. "Psychological Distress, Well-Being, and Legal Recognition in Same-Sex Couple Relationships." *Journal of Family Psychology* 24: 82–86.

17. Family Research Council. N. D. "InFocus." Retrieved on 11/30/2010 from http://www.frc.org/get.cfm?i=if03h01

18. Traditional Values Coalition 2002–2010. "Do Homosexuals Really Want to Marry?" Retrieved on 11/30/2010 from http://www.traditionalvalues.org/urban/eight.php

Dig Deeper

Kurdek, L. A. 1991. "Sexuality in Homosexual and Heterosexual Couples." In *Sexuality in Close Relationships*, edited by K. McKinney and S. Sprecher, 177–191. Hillsdale NJ: Erlbaum.

Lehmiller, J. J. 2010. "Differences in Relationship Investments between Gay and Heterosexual Men." *Personal Relationships* 17: 81–96.

Peplau, L. A., and Spalding, L. R. 2000. "The Close Relationships of Lesbians, Gay Men, and Bisexuals." In *Close Relationships: A Sourcebook*, edited by C. Hendrick and S. S. Hendrick, 111–123. Thousand Oaks CA: Sage. http://www.apa.org/about/governance/council/policy/parenting.aspx

CHAPTER 4
Long-Term Relationship Processes

Yes, relationships are exciting, but they are also extremely challenging. We regularly face tough decisions within our relationships. From deciding to commit 'til death do us part, choosing whether to cohabitate, sticking with our partners during a long-term separation, or seeking a little assistance when things get rough, the uncertainty surrounding many of the decisions we make during the course of a relationship are enough to bring out the Norman Bates in each of us. In this chapter, we address five common concerns or worries people have about things that often come up in relationships as they progress from initial attraction to (and through) marriage.

Q12: Is Distance Bad for Relationships?

Timothy J. Loving

Tell someone that you are in a long-distance relationship (LDR, or relationships in which the two partners do not live in the same city or are otherwise not in physical proximity of one another), and you may as well put on a pointy hat and grab some cake, because you just started your very own pity party. We tend to believe that people are in relationships because they like their partners, so merely mentioning an LDR immediately creates the impression that you must be miserable. Why? Because you can't be with the person you like (or love). Despite the overwhelming belief that they suck, LDRs are remarkably common. For those of college-age, approximately 25%–50% of college students' romances are long distance,[1–3] and 70% of students become involved in a long-distance romantic relationship at some point while in college.[4] In addition, a growing proportion of people in relationships are choosing to live apart for the sake of career promotion (i.e., dual-career commuter couples), in that they maintain separate residences in different cities so that both partners can focus on careers.[5] Are these geographically separated relationships doomed? Maybe, but not necessarily because of the distance (technically speaking, many relationships are doomed). In reality, geographic distance between partners is both good and bad for romantic relationships. In fact, some would argue that the pros of LDRs significantly outweigh the cons. How can that be?

Maintaining a "Me versus We" Balance

One of the more interesting paradoxes in life is that, at least in Western cultures (i.e., the United States), we feel both a need to be connected to others[6] and to maintain a sense of independence;[7] see also question 10). Involvement in a romantic relationship makes this paradox particularly salient, creating a constant push-and-pull between our independent selves (i.e., the ME part of our identity) and our relationship selves (i.e., the WE part of our identity). One of the great benefits of LDRs is that they facilitate maintenance of this balance. In other words, people in LDRs get to have regular "Me" time to be able to take care of individual needs (e.g., hitting the gym, going tanning, perhaps even doing some laundry), but they also get to have "We" time to fulfill those needs that require the company of another person (e.g., like riding a see-saw).

This often-underappreciated facet of LDRs has some important implications. First, a long-distance relationship is going to be more successful to the extent that the partners get to see each other in person somewhat regularly (a good rule of thumb appears to be at least once every 3 months, but more frequent visits are even better).[8] Otherwise, the couple members run the risk of not experiencing the rewards that attracted them to each other in the first place. Absence may make the heart grow fonder,[9] but absence also makes us forget things (i.e., "Out of sight, out of mind"). There's a fine line between those two possible outcomes. Basically, we like to be with people who we like...at least every now and then.

Rose-Colored Glasses Are Your Friend

LDRs may also help us like our partners *more*. Seriously. One of the key *benefits* of LDRs is that we don't see our partners every day. That's right, I said it. Although being away from someone we care about can be challenging, it turns out that distance allows us to wear the rose-colored glasses of love for longer than we'd get to if we lived with or near our partners. Researchers call this *idealization*, in that we tend to exaggerate our partners' positives and ignore their negatives. In a typical proximal relationship, however, we ultimately become more aware of things that make our partners less than, how shall we say...perfect. To be clear, idealizing a very horrible relationship partner (e.g., an abusive partner) is in no way a good thing. But for the majority of relationships, a little idealization goes a long way[10] (see also question 17). One of the real beauties of LDRs is that individuals tend to idealize their partners for longer because they are less likely to have to be around their partners during all the day-to-day mundane aspects of life. Put another way, it's easy to overlook the annoying things about your partner if you only have to experience them every now and then (and, believe it or not, you can be annoying too, so that distance likely keeps your partner attracted to you as well).

* * *

Given what I've noted, it should come as no surprise that individuals in LDRs actually tend to be more satisfied with their relationships relative to individuals in proximal relationships[10] and are less likely to need their partners to help them feel good.[11] It's true. The idealization experience is partially responsible for this finding; it's a lot easier to be happy with a partner whose faults are less apparent (e.g., you're more attractive if I don't know that you trim your nose hair every day). Some researchers suggest that the reason for the idealization is that people in LDRs engage in *restricted communication*, such that they're less likely to talk about or otherwise display the less than positive aspects of their personalities.[10] It is also possible that people who choose to stay together in the face of geographic separation are just more committed in the first place; otherwise, they would wave goodbye and move on to the next partner. This potential bias in research looking at LDRs does not, however, account for the fact that breakup rates of LDRs increase dramatically once the couple is no longer geographically separated, especially when couples were apart for particularly long periods of time.[12] Given these findings, one could argue that distance, and maintaining that distance, is good for relationships.

Yet there are other forces at play here—relationships thrive on novelty.[13] The rewards or passion we experience for a partner are greater when the time we spend with our partners is both special and novel (e.g., going to the movies is better than watching *Wheel of Fortune* at home). Again, LDR couples are at an enormous advantage when it comes to maintaining novelty in their relationships. Think about it: When couple members do get to see each other, one of the partners is spending time in a novel environment (because they are visiting the other partner in his or her digs). Or, if couple members meet somewhere else (the "meet half-way" approach), the environment is novel for both of them. Sure beats the hour-long conversation that goes something like this (Note: What follows is a dramatization that may or may not reflect the author's actual life):

> Partner A: Where do you want to eat tonight?
>
> Partner B: I don't know, where do you want to eat tonight?
>
> Partner A: I asked you first.
>
> Partner B: You give me three options and I'll choose one.
>
> Partner A: (Provides three options, most likely all of which are "regular" options)
>
> Partner B: How about we just order a pizza.
>
> Partner A: Fine.

Compare that exchange to the following conversation that may occur between couple members in a long-distance relationship:

> Partner A: I missed you so much. I can't wait to show you this new restaurant I found in a really cool part of town.
>
> Partner B: Sounds great. Let's have sex first.
>
> Partner A: Great!.

You get the picture (of this example, that is).

In support of these hypothetical scenarios, individuals in LDRs report taking efforts to make the most of their time with their partners. In other words, they want to make the time special and memorable because they have limited time together.[1,14] If only people in proximal relationships could do the same! (Note: Previous sentence should be read with a tone of heavy sarcasm.) Again, the novelty in a relationship is likely to take a nose-dive when a couple, previously separated, gets back together in the same region. The loss of novelty and independence is just too much for some people to handle.[15]

These greater efforts at making together-time special is similar to the greater maintenance work that LDR couples do. For example, the geographically separated engage in more relationship-focused talk[16] when they communicate. This is partly because LDRs increase relationship uncertainty,[8] so it's likely the couple members look for some reassurances that the relationship is on solid footing more often than proximal couples (barring unhealthy levels of anxiety; see question 8). In addition, individuals in LDRs, not surprisingly, report missing their partners, and missing someone tends to encourage us to do things that are good for our relationships.[17]

Now, this isn't to say that LDRs are all peaches and cream. There's a reason that we tend to doll out sympathies when we learn somebody is in a LDR. As noted earlier, they involve a lot of uncertainty,[3,8] which is mostly centered on anxieties about what's happening "there." Fortunately, getting to see each other on occasion reduces uncertainty. The operative term here is *see;* there is no substitute for face-to-face contact! Otherwise, LDRs are remarkably similar to proximal relationships in general functioning.

Conclusions

Long-distance relationships can be tough for those involved, primarily because we're not able to be with someone we care about. However, that distance also comes with a number of benefits that actually help maintain LDRs, based on relational idealizations and increased novelty that come with decreased physical proximity.

TAKE-HOME POINTS

- ♡ Long-distance relationships help individuals maintain a sense of independence and connectedness.
- ♡ LDRs may increase uncertainty about the future, but that uncertainty can make people work harder at their relationships.
- ♡ LDRs keep things novel and arousing.

References

1. Sahlstein, E. M. 2004. "Relating at a Distance: Negotiating Being Together and Being Apart in Long-Distance Relationships." *Journal of Social and Personal Relationships*, 21(5): 689–710.
2. Stafford, L. 2005. *Maintaining Long-Distance and Cross-Residential Relationships*. Mahwah NJ: Lawrence Erlbaum Associates.
3. Van Horn, K. R., A. Arnone, K. Nesbitt, et al. 1997. "Physical Distance and Interpersonal Characteristics in College Students' Romantic Relationships." *Personal Relationships* 4(1): 25–34.
4. Guldner, G. T., and C. H. Swensen. 1995. "Time Spent Together and Relationship Quality: Long-Distance Relationships as a Test Case." *Journal of Social and Personal Relationships* 12 (2): 313–320.
5. Rhodes, A. R. 2002. Long-Distance Relationships in Dual-Career Commuter Couples: A Review of Counseling Issues. *The Family Journal* 10 (4): 398–404.
6. Baumeister, R. F., and M. R. Leary. 1995. "The Need to Belong: Desire for Interpersonal Attachments as a Fundamental Human Motivation." *Psychological Bulletin* 117 (3): 497–529.
7. Gabriel, S., and W. L. Gardner 1999. "Are There 'His' and 'Hers' Types of Interdependence? The Implications of Gender Differences in Collective versus Relational Interdependence for Affect, Behavior, and Cognition." *Journal of Personality and Social Psychology* 77 (3): 642–655.
8. Dainton, M., and B. Aylor. 2002. "Patterns of Communication Channel Use in the Maintenance of Long-Distance Relationships." *Communication Research Reports* 19 (2): 118–129.
9. Le, B., T. J. Loving, G. W. Lewandowski, Jr., et al. "Missing a Romantic Partner: A Prototype Analysis." *Personal Relationships* 15 (4): 511–532.
10. Stafford, L., and J. R. Reske. 1990. "Idealization and Communication in Long-Distance Premarital Relationships." *Family Relations: Journal of Applied Family & Child Studies* 39 (3): 274–279.
11. Le, B., and C. R. Agnew. 2004. "Need Fulfillment and Emotional Experience in Interdependent Romantic Relationships." *Journal of Social and Personal Relationships* 18 (3): 423–440.
12. Stafford, L., and A. J. Merolla. 2007. "Idealization, Reunions, and Stability in Long-Distance Dating Relationships." *Journal of Social and Personal Relationships* 24 (1): 37–54.
13. Aron, A., C. C. Norman, E. N. Aron, C. McKenna, and R. E. Heyman. 2000. "Couples' Shared Participation in Novel and Arousing Activities and Experienced Relationship Quality." *Journal of Personality and Social Psychology* 78 (2): 273–284.
14. Rhodes, A. R. 2002. "Long-Distance Relationships in Dual-Career Commuter Couples: A Review of Counseling Issues." *Family Journal: Counseling and Therapy for Couples and Families* 10 (4): 398–404.

15. Stafford, L., A. J. Merolla, and J. D. Castle. 2006. "When Long-Distance Dating Partners Become Geographically Close." *Journal of Social and Personal Relationships* 23 (6): 901–920.
16. Dellmann-Jenkins, M., T. S. Bernard-Paolucci, and B. Rushing. 1994. "Does Distance Make the Heart Grow Fonder? A Comparison of College Students in Long-Distance and Geographically Close Dating Relationships." *College Student Journal* 28 (2): 212–219.
17. Le, B., M. S. Korn, E. E. Crockett, and T. J. Loving. In Press. "Missing You Maintains Us: Missing a Romantic Partner, Commitment, Relationship Maintenance, and Infidelity." *Journal of Social and Personal Relationships.*

Dig Deeper

Helgeson, V. S. 1994. "Long-Distance Romantic Relationships: Sex Differences in Adjustment and Breakup." *Personality and Social Psychology Bulletin* 20 (3): 254–265.
Lydon, J. E., T. Pierce, and S. O'Regan. 1997. "Coping with Moral Commitment to Long-Distance Dating Relationships." *Journal of Personality and Social Psychology* 73 (1): 104–113.
van Anders, S. M., and N. V. Watson. 2007. "Testosterone Levels in Women And Men Who Are Single, in Long-Distance Relationships, or Same-City Relationships." *Hormones and Behavior* 51 (2): 286–291.

Q13: How Do I Know If I've Found Ms./Mr. Right?

Jody L. Davis

You may have had the experience of believing that you've found "The One" for you, but later discovered that you were mistaken—as the saying goes, "Hindsight is 20/20." If you can't trust your intuitions, then how can you determine whether a partner is Ms. or Mr. Right? Let's start by laying to rest the myth that there is a single person out there who is the perfect match for you (see question 19). (This should relieve a lot of pressure; what if The One didn't like you or happened to live in Nepal? It'd be you and your 18 cats for eternity.) Complicating matters is the fact that people generally are bad at knowing what qualities they want in a partner.[1] Therefore, we do not recommend simply comparing a partner to your "What I want in an ideal partner" wish-list. Nevertheless, a broad review of the research literature reveals some universal criteria that Ms. or Mr. Right ideally would meet. More important, the criteria change depending on whether you're looking for The One or the "One-Time Thing." Assuming that you are interested in a long-term match, we address this topic by highlighting pertinent characteristics about you, about your partner, and—most importantly—about your relationship.

What role do you play?

Let's start with you. To be clear, this topic isn't about whether you are the *other person's* Ms. or Mr. Right (we'll give you the benefit of the doubt—clearly, as a reader of this book, you're pretty outstanding). Rather, it might be informative for you to examine *how* you love your partner. Would you say that your feelings for your partner are characterized primarily by intense emotion and sexual excitement? If you are preoccupied with thoughts about your partner, and your relationship is based on great chemistry, then it's possible that you are experiencing passionate love (also see question 10). Great, right? Well, not if you are in the relationship for the long haul. After only two years of marriage, behaviors such as saying "I love you" and having sex occur about half as often.[2] In fact, it's pretty clear that passion for your partner does not guarantee a successful long-term relationship.

In other words, Ms. or Mr. Right may not be the person who has given you the most butterflies in your stomach. We guarantee that there are other fish in the sea who can make you weak at the knees.

What role does your partner play?

Now let's consider your partner. Does she or he have personal qualities consistent with being a caring and skillful relationship partner? You better hope so; over the long haul, these are the types of qualities that make for a lasting romance. For example, one desirable personal quality that affects a wide range of relationship processes—as well as the likelihood of breaking up—is having a secure attachment style. Attachment "security" is characterized by low levels of attachment-related anxiety (translation: the clingy and needy type) and avoidance (translation: the "I can't be bothered to care" type; see question 4 for more).[3,4] What are some indications of attachment security? It's a good sign if your partner trusts you. Imagine that you attend a social gathering without your partner. Would your partner obsess about whom you talked to and express jealousy without justification? If so, then your partner may be a bit anxious. Similarly, it's a good sign if your partner is supportive when you are stressed out. Imagine that a family member is diagnosed with cancer, and you cry periodically about it. Would your partner be uncomfortable with your distress and discourage you from expressing your fears by saying something like, "That's life...deal with it"? A partner who responds to your increasing anxiety by withdrawing rather than providing support may be avoidant—not the type of person that you want to have around during the hard times in life (it's "For better or worse," not "For better and best").

There are a few other core personality traits that you should avoid because of their toxic effect on relationships—part of finding Ms. or Mr. Right is avoiding Ms. or Mr. Wrong! Does your partner have a portrait of himself over his bed? Does she post pictures of herself in a bikini on Facebook? More seriously, does your partner feel entitled to special treatment and like to show off material possessions and social connections? Can you imagine your partner saying any of the following: "Check out my new phone and all the contacts I have! You're cooler just by knowing me." If so, you may be in a relationship with a narcissist. Narcissists can be exciting to be around (think Barney Stinson on "How I Met Your Mother").

However, the short-term narcissism-fueled fun typically turns into long-term suffering because narcissists use relationships to enhance themselves. It won't be long before Mr. Abdominal Muscles insists that you play the role of trophy girlfriend by wearing a certain color that looks best with his skin tone! Wait, what's that? *You* wanted something from the relationship as well? Forget about it; narcissists don't care about the needs of their partners, nor do they make attempts to cultivate their relationships.[5] That's for losers.

Another undesirable trait to watch out for is *neuroticism,* or the tendency to focus on the negatives in life ("The glass isn't just half-empty; it's cracked and full of rotten milk, and I'm going to talk to you about it all night long"). Imagine that your partner wants you to go out to a movie, but you decide to stay in to study for an exam. Would your partner freak out and think that you're no longer interested in the relationship? Or would your partner really drive you crazy by sometimes getting mad when you prioritize school, but other times making you feel guilty if you do poorly in school? It is very unpleasant to have a relationship partner who is moody and tends to see the worst in everything, and such relationships are more likely to break up or end in divorce.[2,3] For example, neuroticism is associated with a particularly destructive process called the *demand-withdraw pattern*: Couples whose interactions are characterized by a pattern in which one partner "demands" while the other withdraws are more likely to divorce (see question 28 for more).[2,6]

What role does your relationship play?

Finally, to predict long-term success, it is most important that you assess how your relationship has been going thus far. Features of relationships are more powerful predictors of relationship fate compared to partners' individual characteristics.[3] Individually, you and your partner could be the most amazing people in the world, but that does not mean that the combination of the two of you will lead to relationship bliss. You can give your relationship a "check-up" by observing patterns of behavior between the two of you. For example, you could look for behaviors that indicate whether your partner feels committed to your relationship. People illustrate commitment to their relationships by engaging in what we call *relationship maintenance behaviors.*

For example, your partner (assuming that he or she isn't a narcissist!) may demonstrate a willingness to sacrifice by sometimes prioritizing your needs above his or her own. It would be a good sign if your partner graciously goes along with your preferences at times (e.g., attends your favorite music concert with you even if he or she dislikes the performer). In addition, your partner may tend to forgive your hurtful behaviors, or accommodate when you behave badly. For example, imagine that you're very hungry after a long day, and you snap at your partner when he's unable to quickly pick something from a restaurant menu. Does he respond in a constructive manner, such as saying, "You're right, I'm taking a long time," or does he order a water and say that he's no longer hungry? All couples inevitably have conflicts and disagreements, but healthy couples are able to avoid a negative spiral of hostile interactions by responding constructively (e.g., forgiving the partner) instead of reciprocating a partner's destructive behavior (e.g., showing contempt for the partner).[6,7] If you're seeing some signs of negative behavior now, what's going to happen when the house is a mess, the dog just ate your favorite pair of shoes, the cable company keeps double-billing you, and—well, you get the point. Basically, life gets complicated. Is this the person that you want in your corner when things get tough?

You also should ask yourself whether your partner promotes your self-development. For example, you could assess the extent to which your partner helps you approach your ideal version of yourself. Does your partner encourage goals that you have for yourself by helping clarify those goals or praising you for movement toward them? Relationships (and partners) are better for you when they help you achieve characteristics of *your* ideal self, not your partner's view of your ideal self.[8] That's right, we said it: You are allowed to be somewhat selfish. Does your partner provide opportunities for you to develop new interests? Successful relationships require that you mix things up every now and then; a partner who contributes to you having novel and interesting experiences helps stave off boredom, leading to greater satisfaction as the years go by in a long-term relationship.[9]

Conclusion

Overall, to the extent that your love has a strong foundation, your partner has personal characteristics well-suited for close-relationships, and your relationship is characterized by healthy, commit-ment-promoting behaviors, then you can consider yourself on the right track! The real challenge lies in making these assessments ac-curately, without overly positive interpretations of your partner. To increase objectivity, it might be a good idea to seek opinions from friends and family members (see question 18). Of course, no person or relationship is perfect; even in healthy, long-term relationships there is a mixture of gratifying and frustrating experiences. Like-wise, any partner has a mixture of positive and negative aspects; therefore, it is critical that you determine whether you can accept your partner's less-desirable qualities, because they are likely to only seem worse later in the relationship![2] The good news is that once you commit to a relationship, your commitment sets into motion a set of perceptions and behaviors—such as derogation of alterna-tive partners and positive illusions (see question 5)—that help you maintain the relationship.[6]

TAKE-HOME POINTS

♡ Passion tends to decline over time, so it is not the best criterion for long-term partner selection.

♡ Individuals who are low in attachment anxiety and avoidance, narcissism, and neuroticism make better relationship partners.

♡ Individuals who demonstrate their relationship commitment through a willingness to sacrifice and forgiveness, and who contribute to the partner's self-development, have better rela-tionships.

References

1. Eastwick, P. W., and E. J. Finkel. 2008. "Sex Differences in Mate Preferences Revisited: Do People Know What They Initially Desire in a Romantic Partner?" *Journal of Personality and Social Psychology* 94: 245–264.

2. Huston, T. L. 2009. "What's Love Got to Do With It? Why Some Marriages Succeed and Others Fail." *Personal Relationships* 16: 301–327.

3. Le, B., Dove, N. L., Agnew, C. R., Korn, M. S., and A. A. Mutso. 2010. "Predicting Nonmarital Romantic Relationship Dissolution: A Meta-Analytic Synthesis." *Personal Relationships* 17: 377–390.

4. Shaver, P. R, and M. Mikulincer. 2007. "Attachment Theory and Research: Core Concepts, Basic Principles, Conceptual Bridges." In *Social Psychology: Handbook of Basic Principles,* edited by A. W. Kruglanksi and E. T. Higgins, 650–677. New York: Guilford Press.
5. Campbell, W. K. 2005. When You Love a Man Who Loves Himself: How to Deal with a One-Way Relationship. Chicago: Sourcebooks Casablanca.
6. Gottman, J. M., and R. W. Levenson. 2000. "The Timing of Divorce: Predicting When a Couple Will Divorce Over a 14-Year Period." *Journal of Marriage and the Family* 62: 737–745.
7. Rusbult, C. E., N. Olsen, J. L. Davis, and P. A. Hannon. (2001). "Commitment and Relationship Maintenance Mechanisms." In *Close Romantic Relationships: Maintenance and Enhancement,* edited by J. H. Harvey and A. E. Wenzel, 87–113. Mahwah, NJ: Lawrence Erlbaum Associates.
8. Rusbult, C. E., E. J. Finkel, and M. Kumashiro. 2009. "The Michelangelo Phenomenon." *Current Directions in Psychological Science* 18: 305–309.
9. Tsapelas, I., A. Aron, and T. Orbuch. 2009. "Marital Boredom Now Predicts Less Satisfaction 9 Years Later." *Psychological Science* 20: 543–545.

Dig Deeper

Amato, P. R. 2010. "Research on Divorce: Continuing Trends and New Developments." *Journal of Marriage and the Family* 72: 650-666.
Arriaga, X. B. 2001. "The Ups and Downs of Dating: Fluctuations in Satisfaction in Newly Formed Romantic Relationships." *Journal of Personality and Social Psychology* 80: 754–765.
Berscheid, E. 2006. "Searching for the Meaning of 'Love.'" In *The New Psychology of Love,* edited by R. Sternberg and K. Weis, 171–183. New Haven, CT: Yale University Press.

Q14: Should I Live with My Partner before We Get Married?

Timothy J. Loving

Cohabitation. To many, it's a dirty 12-letter word (your grandma might even call it "Living in sin") that prompts unsolicited advice from all those junior relationship experts in your life. "Don't do it; it will ruin your marriage!" "Don't do it, everyone knows that you don't buy the cow when you get the milk for free!" Such statements, which essentially refer to what is known as the *cohabitation effect*, promote the idea that cohabitation causes later marriages to fail at a greater rate than marriages naturally fail. Of course, you may have another set of armchair relationship experts who suggest using cohabitation as a test drive that helps promote future marital happiness. So who is right? Does cohabitation deserve the bad rap it's garnered over the last couple of decades?

Answering such a question is admittedly a bit challenging for a very simple methodological reason: We cannot conduct an experiment that establishes cause and effect by randomly assigning couples to cohabitation versus no-cohabitation experimental conditions. In other words, in an ideal world, we would take a group of couples who share similar relationship characteristics (e.g., relationship length). Next, we would randomly assign half the couples to live together for a set amount of time (e.g., 2 years) while the other half would maintain separate residences for the same amount of time. We'd then have all the couples get married and follow their marriages over time to see how they turn out. Clearly, such a design isn't possible (both practically or ethically), because individuals have freedom of choice and self-select to cohabitate or not. Thus, any conclusions we draw about the effect cohabitation may or may not have on relationship outcomes must rely on studies that compare cohabiters (i.e., "Sinners") to non-cohabiters (i.e., "Saints") using fancy statistical techniques (i.e., math) in hopes of determining whether there is any truth behind the so-called *cohabitation effect*. Addressing such a question is critical, as it is now estimated that a minimum of 50% of couples will cohabit prior to marriage (and that doesn't include all those who cohabit and never marry).[1] So, should you live with your partner before getting married? The astute reader of this book has probably already guessed the correct answer: It depends.

Cohabitation: One Size Does Not Fit All

The notion that cohabitation before marriage negatively affects later marital outcomes is driven by early studies that demonstrated just such a negative association. For example, cohabiting couples report more conflict and less relationship satisfaction than their married counterparts[2,3] and are more likely to break up with their partners if they are unhappy with the amount of sex they are getting in their relationships.[4] Admittedly, a lot of this early work was based on analysis of individuals that cohabited back before cohabitation was a more widely accepted part of relationship development.[5] So before you go and break that lease you and your partner just signed or resign yourself to living with your parents until you get married, there are some important qualifiers to these general patterns. More recent work indicates that any effect cohabitation has on later marital outcomes depends largely on couples' future plans for marriage. If a couple plans to get hitched someday, but chooses to cohabit in the meantime for their own reasons (e.g., it's simply more cost-effective), then the outcomes of premarital cohabiters look very similar to the outcomes of non-premarital cohabiting married couples,[6,7] leading researchers to conclude that a *pre-engagement cohabitation effect* is far more likely than a *pre-marital cohabitation effect*.[7] In other words, the real issue at hand is what types of future plans or commitment the couple has made before they decide to move in together. If there are no future plans (marriage or other explicit long-term commitment), then living together before marriage may pose a risk to the relationship.

Why is this? Many individuals choose to cohabit with their partners as a way of "testing the waters," so to speak. The basic idea is that because living with someone is more like marriage than not living together, then perhaps cohabitation will give you a feel for what it's like to be married. Here's the rub: People who feel confident about their future with their partners have no need to take the relationship on a marriage test-drive (not to mention the fact that marriage is different than simply living together—but that's an entirely different issue). Put another way: People who want to ease into things may have already seen the proverbial writing on the wall (and the writing isn't a romantic love poem where everything works out in the end).[8] Thus, these relationships were pretty much doomed anyway, regardless of whether cohabitation was involved.

The Slippery Slope

Interestingly, people who choose to cohabit without plans for getting married or a clear exit strategy from the relationship may often find themselves getting married even if the test-drive doesn't go so smoothly. In short, living with someone is a big investment, and investments promote commitment. As a result, that test-drive may very well result in a purchase nobody was prepared for, such that the experience of cohabitation creates *momentum*, or a slippery slope, that propels a couple to marriage.[9] This same logic applies to folks who just move in together for practical reasons. You know how it goes—You're staying over at each other's house every night and realize it may just be cheaper and more convenient to get a place together. Next thing you know, you've invested in some fine Ikea kitchen supplies, maybe adopted a plant or pet together, and even "accidentally" used each other's toothbrushes. The horror! Guess what? You may have just purchased a one-way ticket to marriage (sorry, refunds are very expensive and involve lawyers). As you can see, the slippery slope idea can have unintended and potentially serious consequences. In this case, individuals who may have never married in the first place may find themselves exchanging vows just because they thought it would be fun to play house. This is clearly not the foundation needed for a successful marriage.

Conclusion

So, should you live with your partner before marriage? Everybody together now....IT DEPENDS! If you're thinking of living together because you want to know if you can adapt to your partner's annoying habits (like the way she slurps her cereal when she eats, or the way he cuts his toenails in the living room), or otherwise have some concerns about your long-term compatibility, then, no, you shouldn't live together. The writing is already on the wall. Read it; it says, "This relationship is not working." But if you and your partner plan to be together forever (how very sweet), and it makes practical sense to shack up, then, by all means, have fun playing house.

TAKE-HOME POINTS

♡ Cohabitation is very common.

♡ "Why buy the cow when you can have the milk for free?" Maybe you like the cow.

♡ Cohabitation before engagement is a larger risk factor for poor marital outcomes than is cohabitation before marriage.

♡ Cohabitation is a big investment that can propel couples to marry, regardless of their initial intentions.

References

1. Bumpass, L. L., and H. H. Lu. 2000. "Trends in Cohabitation and Implications for Children's Family Contexts in the United States." *Population Studies* 54: 29–41.

2. Chen, H., P. Cohen, S. Kasen, J. G. Johnson, M. Ehrensaft, and K. Gordon, K. (2006). "Predicting Conflict within Romantic Relationships during the Transition to Adulthood." *Personal Relationships* 13(4): 411–427.

3. Brown, S. L., and Kawamura, S. (2010). Relationship quality among cohabitors and marrieds in older adulthood. *Social Science Research*, 39(5), 777-786.

4. Yabiku, S. T., and C. T. Gager. 2009. "Sexual Frequency and the Stability of Marital and Cohabiting Unions." *Journal of Marriage and Family* 71: 983–1000.

5. Manning, W. D., and P. J. Smock. 2005. "Measuring and Modeling Cohabitation: New Perspectives from Qualitative Data." *Journal of Marriage and Family* 67(4): 989–1002.

6. Stanley, S. M., G. K. Rhoades, P. R. Amato, H. J. Markman, and C. A. Johnson. 2010. "The Timing of Cohabitation and Engagement: Impact on First and Second Marriages." *Journal of Marriage and Family* 72(4): 906–918.

7. Rhoades, G. K., S. M. Stanley, and H. J. Markman. 2009. "The Pre-Engagement Cohabitation Effect: A Replication and Extension of Previous Findings." *Journal of Family Psychology*, 23 (1): 107–111.

8. Rhoades, G. K., S. M. Stanley, and H. J. Markman. 2009. "Couples' Reasons for Cohabitation: Associations with Individual Well-Being and Relationship Quality." *Journal of Family Issues*, 30 (2): 233–258

9. Stanley, S. M., G. K. Rhoades, and H. J. Markman. 2006. "Sliding versus Deciding: Inertia and the Premarital Cohabitation Effect." *Family Relations*, 55 (4): 499–509.

Dig Deeper

Brown, S. I. 2005. "How Cohabitation Is Reshaping American Families." *Contexts* 4 (3): 33–37.

Manning, W. D., J. A. Cohen, and P. J. Smock. 2011. "The Role of Romantic Partners, Family, and Peer Networks in Dating Couples' Views about Cohabitation." *Journal of Adolescent Research* 26(1): 115–149.

Wiik, K. A., E. Bernhardt, and T. Noack. 2009. "A Study of Commitment and Relationship Quality in Sweden and Norway." *Journal of Marriage and the Family* 71 (3): 465–477.

Rhoades, G. K., S. M. Stanley, and H. J. Markman. 2006. "Pre-Engagement Cohabitation and Gender Asymmetry in Marital Commitment." *Journal of Family Psychology* 20 (4): 553–560.

Q15: ARE PEOPLE LESS HAPPY AFTER THEY GET MARRIED?

Nancy E. Frye

Imagine your grandparents' 50th anniversary party: They are a cute couple; Grandpa looks a bit like Walter Matthau, whereas Grandma looks like Betty White. Just as they are about to cut the cake, your grandfather launches into a speech about how much he loves your grandmother, and how his love for her has only gotten stronger and stronger over time. The thing is, he clearly seems to mean it, and Grandma appears genuinely touched. As you imagine them gazing lovingly into each other's eyes, your mind wanders and you recall how, just last week, they were bickering over what kind of cake they should have for the party, and the best, most direct route for driving to the party. You start to wonder: Do they really love each other more than they did when they got married? It sure didn't seem like it last week. What *has* happened to their feelings for each other over time?

How do people think *their relationships have changed?*

It turns out that your grandparents aren't alone in thinking that, like a fine wine or cheese, their relationship has gotten better with time. If you were to ask most people to draw a graph representing how their feelings about their marriages have changed over time, they'll likely draw a U-shape curve. In other words, they remember being extraordinarily happy early on, but recognize there were some early declines in satisfaction, followed by recent improvements. People perceive just this U-pattern whether you ask them after they've been married for more than 30 years[1] or for only 4 years.[2] In fact, when you ask people to tell you how their feelings for their spouse have changed over time, they tend to pretty consistently report that they've gotten better, especially over the recent past.[3] What's going on here? Well, it turns out that people feel pretty good when they see things as getting better with time; in other words, we're motivated to perceive improvements![4] This general motivation applies to relationships as well as lots of other areas of life as well. If you're just starting an exercise program and are struggling to run a mile, it's not quite so frustrating if you at least see yourself struggling a little bit less each time you go for the mile-that-feels-like-20-miles run. We perceive our relationships similarly: If you're not perfectly blissful with your partner, it's nice to at least think of your relationship as improving with time.

How do people's relationships actually *change over time?*

If there was an overly intrusive relationships researcher stalking your relationship over time and plotting your marriage over the years, what would the researcher see? It turns out that the actual graph of relationship bliss is a little different when it doesn't rely on people's memories. One way researchers avoid using people's sometimes overly optimistic or rosy outlooks on their relationships is by asking people how happy they are in their marriage and how long they've been married rather than having them project how things have changed over time. Specifically, participants report only their current information: married 5 years 3 months and about a 7 out of 10 in terms of happiness. This way, people don't have to try to remember how things have changed; they just say how they feel "right now." When the data are collected this way, people who have been married longer tend to be less happy.[5] But this method of comparing the newly married with the long-time married with the super-long-time married isn't perfect either. First, it doesn't take into account things like the state of the world, which might affect couples who have been married different lengths of time differently. For instance, if the economy is awful and it's becoming increasingly harder to retire, it might not be any surprise that people who have been married the longest (and who are just about ready to retire) might be least happy, because they're experiencing the stress of not being able to retire. Second, this method isn't able to look at things like whether the unhappier people just end up divorcing. If this happens, the people who were unhappy to begin with won't end up being studied—unless, of course, the researchers can catch them quickly before they divorce.

Another way to avoid relying too much on people's sometimes-flawed recollections is to measure relationship satisfaction repeatedly over many years in the form of a longitudinal study (with the operative term being *long*). Obviously, this method is time and labor intensive, but you'd think it would yield the most accurate picture of how satisfaction changes over the course of marriage. Interestingly, despite the drawbacks mentioned previously, research that follows the same couples over time tends to find the same pattern as the cross-sectional designs, with relationship satisfaction going down with time.[1,2,6] It turns out that the rate of this decline is about the same for people who lived together before they got married, had a child before they got married, or who took the more traditional marry-live together-have a child route.[7] Why is reality less blissful than people's recollection? Are people lying? Are they delusional? Well, it's possible they're delusional, but more likely it is something much less nefarious. It's likely just a simple matter of how our memory works (or, more accurately, how it doesn't work). It turns out we aren't very good at remembering details from the past. (What did you eat for dinner last Tuesday? What about two weeks ago?) Instead, we rely on shortcuts or our best guess about how things used to be. (Tuesdays I work late so I probably just ate a quick salad) So, when you ask people about how their relationships have changed over time, you may just be asking them more than they can reasonably know.

What do these declines in satisfaction mean for you and your relationships?

Should marriage vows be, "I promise to be with you until you make me so miserable I can't help but leave you"? Is all hope lost for the Disney-promised happily ever after? Don't worry—and don't be so quick to cancel your wedding plans. There is hope; these declines over time just capture what happens for couples *on average*. In other words, there are exceptions to the rule. Some couples' satisfaction plummets, some couples' satisfaction declines a bit, and some couples' satisfaction stays about the same. That's right—some couples actually get to keep those giddy, blissful happy feelings they felt on their wedding day. What is the key to keeping those blissful feelings over time? Well, these couples are those who don't have much stress in their lives, aren't too neurotic, and express more positive than negative emotions as they talk with each other about their relationship.[8] Sounds easy, huh?

As you think about all this research, and you think about your grandfather's lovely speech to your grandmother, you start to wonder if your grandparents are one of those lucky few couples who manage to defy the odds and remain blissfully happy over time. Then you think about how neurotic both of your grandparents are—all the stress they've gone through, and how sarcastic they tend to be when they argue with each other. You start to think they're probably not one of those lucky few. So, what's up with your grandfather's speech? Is he just delusional? Well, people's memories of their relationships are somewhat related to what actually happened such that people who tend to be especially blissfully happy remember higher average levels of satisfaction than people who tend to be less blissfully happy.[2] But that doesn't mean that their memories don't give them a little wiggle room. Maybe your grandfather's memories of his happiness with your grandmother are rooted in reality. At the same time, however, he's probably looking back on things with some rose-colored glasses, and he's probably remembering a little more improvement than an objective outsider stalking their marriage over time might have seen. All these things likely make your grandfather feel even happier in the present, and have more hope for the future. And remember, it's not the type of delusion that could cause him to run around without any pants on or talk to squirrels, so it's probably best to smile and nod as your grandfather talks glowingly about his increasing happiness over time. No harm, no foul. After all, who's to say that your grandfather's memories aren't more important than a more objective observation? In fact, recalling things this way just might make the years they have left together that much more meaningful.

TAKE-HOME POINTS

- ♡ People tend to remember that their relationships have gotten better with time, especially recently. The more people remember such improvements, the better they feel about their relationships.
- ♡ People's satisfaction, when measured in a way that doesn't rely on their memories, tends to decline on average over time. This varies across couples, however, with some couples experiencing steep declines and other couples experiencing no decline.

References

1. Vaillant, C. O., and G. E. Vaillant. 1993. "Is the U-Curve of Marital Satisfaction an Illusion? A 40-Year Study of Marriage."*Journal of Marriage and the Family* 55 (1): 230–239.
2. Karney, B. R., and N. E. Frye. 2002. "'But We've Been Getting Better Lately': Comparing Prospective and Retrospective Views of Relationship Development." *Journal of Personality and Social Psychology* 82: 222–238.
3. Frye, N. E., and B. R. Karney. 2004. "Revision in Memories of Relationship Development: Do Biases Persist Over Time?" *Personal Relationships* 11: 79–97.
4. Albert, S. 1977. "Temporal Comparison Theory."*Psychological Review* 84: 485–503.
5. VanLaningham, J., D. R. Johnson, and P. Amato. 2001. "Marital Happiness, Marital Duration, and the U-Shaped Curve: Evidence from a Five-Wave Panel Study." *Social Forces* 78: 1313–1341.
6. Halford, W. K., A. Lizzio, K. L. Wilson, and S. Occhipinti. 2007. "Does Working at Your Marriage Help? Couple Relationship Self-Regulation and Satisfaction in the First Four Years of Marriage."*Journal of Family Psychology* 21: 185–194.
7. Tach, L., and S. Halpern-Meekin. 2009. "How Does Premarital Cohabitation Affect Trajectories of Marital Quality?" *Journal of Marriage and the Family* 71: 298–317.
8. Lavner, J. A., and T. N. Bradbury. 2010. "Patterns of Change in Marital Satisfaction Over the Newlywed Years." *Journal of Marriage and the Family* 72: 1171–1187.

Dig Deeper

Anderson, J. R., M. I. VanRyzin, and W. J. Doherty. 2010. "Developmental Trajectories of Marital Happiness in Continuously Married Individuals: A Group-Based Modeling Approach." *Journal of Family Psychology* 24: 587–596.

Sullivan, K. T., L. A. Pasch, M. D. Johnson, and T. N. Bradbury. 2010. "Social Support, Problem Solving, and the Longitudinal Course of Newlywed Marriage." *Journal of Personality and Social Psychology* 98: 631–644.

Q16: Is Relationship Counseling Useful?

Eshkol Rafaeli

People consider calling up a relationship counselor for a variety of reasons, ranging from, "Things are good, and we want them to be even better," to "I worry about these patterns we get ourselves into," all the way to "We're at each other's throats and I fear one of us will not live to see tomorrow." Let's put aside the last reason—serious concerns about physical safety, or other forms of abusiveness in relationship—for a minute (although see question 23 on why people stay in bad relationships) and focus on the first two reasons. Many couples find themselves thinking these types of things, but often wonder whether therapy is the right route for addressing their concerns.

Is Therapy Effective?

Imagine that your relationship is showing some signs of wear and tear, unhappiness, or maybe even infidelity. Should you spend the time and effort to go to couples therapy? Will it help? The short answer is *it could*, especially if it uses one of several tried and tested approaches.[1-3] There are now several such approaches with names like *behavioral couples therapy* (BCT), *cognitive behavioral couples therapy* (CBCT), *emotion-focused couples therapy* (EFCT), and *insight-oriented couples therapy* (IOCT). Clearly, just as C3PO loved R2D2, therapists love to use acronyms.

All of these therapeutic traditions work better, *on average,* than no therapy at all.[2] Admittedly, there have been very few neck-and-neck direct comparisons of these treatments, so right now there's little reason to think that one works better than another. One exception to this is a relatively new approach, called *integrative couples therapy* (ICT), which does seem to work better than its precursor (BCT), particularly for couples who are in a lot of distress. Although BCT was quite effective, the creators were struck by the fact that at least one third of couples didn't benefit from it at all, and even among those who did, many "relapsed" into renewed relationship problems. Thus, the same people who first developed BCT made improvements and developed ICT[3] (more on it later).

There are some similarities among these approaches. For one, all of them rely primarily on what's called *conjoint therapy*—bringing the couple in, together, and conducting most therapy sessions with both partners in the room (think of the therapy sessions in the movie *Couples Retreat*). But the focus of each one is somewhat different. For example, BCT focuses on changing behaviors and activities, CBCT works by changing both the behaviors and the thoughts of both partners, and EFCT works on changing the way emotional vulnerability (e.g., "I don't feel like my partner supports me for who I am") is expressed and reacted to. Notice that the word *change* keeps appearing in the last sentence? Well, ICT, the newer approach, is a bit different: It emphasizes both *change* and *acceptance* strategies—learning to change those things that can be changed and to accept those that can't (much like the serenity prayer posted on many an assistant's wall that states, "God grant me the serenity to accept the things I cannot change; courage to change the things I can; and wisdom to know the difference").

Good therapy, like any good medicine, must rely on sound science, use tried-and-tested methods, and be implemented by skilled professionals who know what they are doing. All the approaches listed previously have been tried and tested, and there are ways of finding professionals who are well versed in them (a few links are suggested in the "Dig Deeper" section). But unlike, say, an antidepressant pill, the personality of the counselor carrying out the therapy is quite important. Finding a counselor who is agreeable to both partners can be tricky, but is really important nonetheless. Without mutual agreement, couples therapy is not likely to move forward very well. Therapists, for their part, usually try to maintain a sense of neutrality; they are there to help the relationship, not to side with one or the other of the partners. But it is not always the case that both partners believe the therapist is neutral. In such cases, it may take time before a couple finds a counselor with whom both couple members are comfortable. The key is to take the time to find that counselor.

Let's be realistic for a second, however; even with mutual agreement and a wise and caring therapist, couples counseling may prove to be too little, too late. There are few guarantees with any kind of therapy, and the rate of divorce *following* couples therapy is considerable (but remember, this could be because those who go in for counseling do so when things are already quite bad). In other words, waiting for problems to get out of control may not be the best strategy; catching problems early and fixing them is more likely to get a relationship back on track. Counseling has its best chance of working when both partners are still invested in the relationship.

Therapy in Good Relationships

Now, what about good relationships? (The ones that haven't had this kind of wear and tear—yet.) Isn't it strange for a happy couple to seek counseling? As they say, "If it ain't broke, don't fix it." If your fiancée suggests you go to *pre*marital counseling, should you start worrying about the *post*marital years? Not really. Couples counselors developed several forms of relationship enhancement or prevention intervention programs. Again, so that they sound *very* important, they have acronyms for them: RE (Relationship Enhancement), PREP (Prevention and Relationship Enhancement Program), and CC (Couples Communication). These are often brief (a weekend workshop, or a short series of evening meetings), sometimes done in groups, and often led by non-therapists. For example, PREP is currently being run in many faith-based organizations, and has been adopted by entire dioceses as a program offered as part of premarital counseling.

These programs stand out in a sea of others because they have been researched and validated most extensively; they all seem to do some good, especially in the short run.[3] One (PREP) has also been shown to have some longer-lasting positive effects. All three programs emphasize some combination of useful themes, varying from problem solving, to communication skills, to ideas for enhancing fun and pleasure in the relationship. That can't hurt—can it?

Therapy in Really Troubled Relationships

At the beginning of this answer, we put aside the question of counseling when serious concerns about physical safety, or abuse, exist. We did this because relationships that get to this sad—or frankly, scary—state, should definitely give us pause. If basic safety can't be guaranteed, counseling is only going to be part of the solution, at best. With counseling (and possibly even before starting it), we'd want to consider what can be done to get both partners out of harm's way—and by *harm*, we mean being the victim, being the perpetrator of any violence—or, as is sometimes the case—being a bit of both. If harm (which, in its extreme form, is often referred to as *Intimate Partner Violence*) occurs, it really must be the first target of change, but it isn't an easy one.[4] With harm (or the threat of it) out of the way, counseling might have a fighting chance of salvaging or improving the relationship.

TAKE-HOME POINTS

♡ Marital or couples therapy can be effective, and some forms of therapy have the records (empirical data) to show this.

♡ Relationship enhancement programs (again, some forms of these) really can enhance relationships—even already happy relationships.

♡ Timing is really important. Nipping problems in the bud (with well-timed therapy) or anticipating them in the first place (with preventive enhancement programs) sure beats trying to fix things after they go wrong.

References

1. Baucom, D. H., V. Shoham, K. T. Meuser, A. D. Daiuto, and T. R. Stickle. 1998. "Empirically Supported Couple and Family Interventions for Marital Distress and Adult Mental Health Problems." *Journal of Consulting and Clinical Psychology* 66: 53–88.

2. Christensen, A., D. H. Baucom, C. T. Vu, and S. Stanton. 2005. "Methodologically Sound, Cost-Effective Research on the Outcome of Couple Therapy." *Journal of Family Psychology* 19: 6–17.

3. Christensen, A., and C. L. Heavey. 1999. "Interventions for Couples." In *Annual Review of Psychology*, edited by J. T. Spence, J. M. Darley, and D. J. Foss, 165–190. Palo Alto, CA: Annual Reviews.

4. Babcock, J. C., C. E. Green, and C. Robie. 2004. "Does Batterers' Treatment Work? A Meta-Analytic Review of Domestic Violence Treatment." *Clinical Psychology Review* 23: 1023–1053.

Dig Deeper

The following websites have more information about these programs:
- ♡ Association for Behavioral and Cognitive Therapies: http://www.aabt.org
- ♡ The American Association for Marriage and Family Therapy: http://www.aamft.org
- ♡ A centralized website for many enhancement programs: http://www.smartmarriages.com
- ♡ Prevention and Relationship Enhancement Program: http://www.prepinc.com

CHAPTER 5

Relationship Cognitions

Illiam Shakespeare wrote in *Hamlet*, "for there is nothing either good or bad, but thinking makes it so." Although Hamlet wasn't referring to relationships, this statement appropriately captures the power that our thoughts have on our perceptions about relationships, especially our own. What do you expect from relationships? If your expectations are too high, you may be perpetually disappointed. However, if they are too low, you may end up settling for a loser. In either case, calibrating your thoughts could help, even though the actual relationship may not change. Perhaps you could gather opinions from others who are close to you in order to get a more accurate and unbiased opinion. But, is it wise to listen to your friends and family? How can someone else help *you* find *your* soul mate? Well, that depends on whether you believe in soul mates to begin with.

Q17: I HAVE HIGH EXPECTATIONS FOR MY RELATIONSHIP. IS THAT BAD?

Lisa A. Neff

"I'm looking for love. Real love. Ridiculous, inconvenient, consuming, can't-live-without-each-other love."

—Carrie Bradshaw, *Sex and the City*

"There's that one perfect person out there to complete you."

—Charlotte York, *Sex and the City*

"From my experience, honey, if he seems too good to be true—
he probably is."

—Samantha Jones, *Sex and the City*

"Soulmates only exist in the Hallmark aisle."

—Miranda Hobbs, *Sex and the City*

When it comes to love and relationships, should you expect
the best, like the eternal optimists Carrie and Charlotte from *Sex
and the City*? After all, most people agree that having a satisfying
relationship is one of the most important things in life (and the
research supports this idea), so why should you settle for anything
less than perfect? If you expect only the best, you might be more
likely to actually achieve a happy and fulfilling relationship. Isn't
that what the power of positive thinking is all about? Then again,
holding such high expectations sets you up for bitter disappointment if the frogs you kiss fail to transform into that magical and
elusive Prince (or Princess) Charming. And think about it: How
many times have you heard politicians and grandparents complain that the reason divorce rates are so high these days is that
couples just don't have realistic expectations of marriage? Some
researchers argue that young couples have expectations that are
overly romanticized, and when the relationship gets hard, they
get frustrated and bail on the relationship. Perhaps it is better to
lower your expectations a bit, like the more practical Samantha
and Miranda?

Positive Expectations May Influence How You Perceive Your Relationship

Relationship science and pop culture (at least *Sex and the City*) actually agree on this one—both have a hard time coming to a definitive
answer. Some scholars argue that highly positive expectations are
critical for maintaining happy and healthy relationships. For instance, several studies show that couples who hold higher relationship expectations also report having higher-quality relationships.[1,2]
So, maybe stubbornly holding on to your mental list of "must haves"
in a relationship is not such a bad thing after all. If you expect the
best in your relationship, you may end up thinking and behaving
in ways that create the relationship you were hoping for. For ex-

ample, when individuals hold higher expectations for their relationships, they are more likely to interpret their partner's behaviors in a positive light.[3,4] Imagine you come home from a long day of work, and although you are noticeably stressed, your partner fails to even ask, "How was your day today?" If you have positive expectations and generally see your partner as supportive and nurturing, you are more likely to interpret his or her silence as, "It's nice that my partner sees that I'm stressed and is giving me some time and space to relax." In other words, our expectations color our views of the world around us, a process known as *perceptual confirmation*. If we expect good things from the relationship, we are more likely to see good things in the relationship. To rephrase an old adage, "Believing is seeing."

Positive Expectations May Influence How You Act

Highly positive expectations can also encourage partners to behave more positively in their relationships. This type of self-fulfilling prophecy is known to researchers as *behavioral confirmation*. If you believe that you and your partner will have a passionate relationship, you might be more likely to engage in behaviors that help fuel those passionate desires, like sneaking away from work to have impromptu lunch dates, sprinkling rose petals on the bed, or making a mix tape (careful, that may have stopped being romantic somewhere in the late 1990s), thereby creating a more passionate relationship. Passion in, passion out. In addition, when couples expect the best, they may be more willing and motivated to work at their relationships during difficult times. It stands to reason that if you think your relationship is great, you'll do things to preserve it. Studies have found that when partners hold more positive expectations, they tend to engage in more constructive behaviors like not avoiding a fight when conflict arises.[4] As a result, these couples feel more satisfied with the resolutions of their conflicts and have relationships that are more likely to last.

Before you decide to adopt "I will only expect the best" as your new relationship mantra, however, consider this: Other scholars have questioned whether holding such high expectations really is beneficial for relationships. It is possible that expectations may become too unrealistic. If you think your relationship will be free of disagreements and will provide complete romantic bliss day after day, you may be watching too many sappy movies or reading too many Nicholas Sparks books. When the relationship fails to meet those high standards (trust us, it will happen), you may experience disappointment.[2] Let's face it, the "Believing is seeing" idea can only go so far. You may expect that you and your partner will never fight or will always have a satisfying sexual relationship, but those beliefs are awfully hard to live up to, especially if kids, work, and in-laws enter the equation. When relationship experiences continually fall short of expectations, partners often become unhappy and stop trying as hard to maintain the relationship: Highly positive expectations can be good for relationships, but only if those expectations are reasonably likely to be confirmed (see also question 29).

Do Expectations Influence Everyone Similarly?

Recent research suggests that the impact of expectations on a relationship may depend on the couple's relationship skills.[5] In a study of newlywed couples, researchers measured spouses' relationship expectations and communication skills soon after the wedding (what an exciting honeymoon!). Researchers then tracked these couples over a four-year period to examine how their marital satisfaction changed during the early years of marriage. Couples with high expectations reported being happier in the marriage four years later, but only if they had good communication skills. If a couple had high expectations, yet were terrible at communicating with one another, they became progressively less happy as time went on. In other words, it isn't enough to expect high-quality relationships. Those expectations produce better relationships only when partners also have good relationship skills that are able to facilitate the achievement of their lofty relationship ideals.

George W. Bush once said, "I'm the master of low expectations." What does that mean for his relationships with Laura? As with high expectations, the effect of low expectations on the marriage depends on couples' relationship skills. Believe it or not, this study found that if couples had lower expectations and poor communication skills, they actually were doing fine four years later. Wait. These people seem to have two strikes against them. Why are they okay? Because of their poorer communication skills, they were more likely to experience problems in the relationship, but the important thing is they were expecting these problems, and that expectation may have buffered them from disappointment in the marriage. It's strange, but true. It may be a case where the common sentiment, "If you want to avoid disappointment, lower your expectations" rings true. In other words, if you anticipate encountering bumps in the matrimonial road, you may be less upset when those rough times roll around. Unfortunately, this also means that if you expect a miserable relationship, you may be more likely to have a miserable relationship, and you are more likely to stay in that relationship (which suggests that relationship longevity isn't always the best way to measure relationship success).

Most surprisingly, however, was the finding that couples with low expectations, but good communication skills, were the least happy of all four years later! This seems counter-intuitive, because these couples are supposed to be good communicators, which should help their relationships. However, it may be the case that partners who believe the relationship is going to be less than stellar end up communicating this belief in a way that makes it more likely to happen. Just imagine a partner who frequently mentions how "all relationships are doomed to fail; being single is the only way to be truly happy." Perhaps, it's just a matter of time before this becomes true. Much like the story of Goldilocks, the lesson of this study is that expectations should not be too high or too low, but rather should match the skill level of the couple in order to ensure that those expectations are likely to be met.

Conclusions

What does all this mean? In a nutshell, high expectations can be a good thing—as long as they don't reach a level that is unattainable. Of course, what is realistic for one couple may be unrealistic for another couple. It is best to consider what skills you and your partner bring to the relational table and then set your sights to a level that may be difficult, but not impossible to reach. If *Sex and the City* is our guide, then being a Miranda may be best, but with a little Carrie and Charlotte thrown in for good measure.

TAKE-HOME POINTS

♡ Some research suggests that if we expect good things from our relationship, we may create a more satisfying relationship.

♡ Other research suggests that high expectations lead to disappointment and poor relationship outcomes.

♡ Ultimately, it seems that whether highly positive relationship expectations are good or bad for a relationship depends on whether those expectations are likely to be confirmed.

References

1. Baucom, D. H., N. Epstein, L. A. Rankin, and C. K. Burnett. 1996. "Assessing Relationship Standards: The Inventory of Specific Relationship Standards." *Journal of Family Psychology* 10: 72–88.

2. Fletcher, G. J. O., J. A. Simpson, and G. Thomas. 2000. "Ideals, Perceptions, and Evaluations in Early Relationship Development." *Journal of Personality and Social Psychology* 79: 933–940.

3. Srivastava, S., K. M. McGonigal, J. M. Richards, E. A. Butler, and J. J. Gross. 2006. "Optimism in Close Relationships: How Seeing Things in a Positive Light Makes Them So." *Journal of Personality and Social Psychology* 91: 143–153.

4. McNulty, J. K., and B. R. Karney. 2002. "Expectancy Confirmation in Appraisals of Marital Interactions." *Personality and Social Psychology Bulletin* 28 (6): 764–775.

5. McNulty, J. K., and B. R. Karney. 2004. "Positive Expectations in the Early Years of Marriage: Should Couples Expect the Best or Brace for the Worst?" *Journal of Personality and Social Psychology* 86: 729–743.

Dig Deeper

Assad, K. K., B. M. Donnelan, and R. D. Conger. 2007. "Optimism: An Enduring Resource for Romantic Relationships." *Journal of Personality and Social Psychology* 93: 285–297.

Huston, T. L., J. P. Caughlin, R. M. Houts, S. E. Smith, and L. George. 2001. "The Connubial Crucible: Newlywed Years as Predictors of Marital Delight, Distress, and Divorce." *Journal of Personality and Social Psychology* 80: 237–252.

Q18: My Family and Friends Don't Like My Partner. Should I Listen to Them?

Jody L. Davis

In an ideal world, relationships with everyone in your social network—friends, family members, romantic partners, and others—would be harmonious, with everyone enjoying one another's company. As the saying goes, "Any friend of yours is a friend of mine!" But oftentimes, whether we want it or not, our friends and family members give us advice or extol opinions about our partners that may not be what we want to hear. Imagine the following scenario: Your friend is in a committed romantic relationship with a guy whom she absolutely adores, but you and her other friends all despise him. Perhaps you are trying to convince her that his tendency to flirt with every girl he meets is just not acceptable, and others are attempting to persuade her that he cannot be trusted. You all may even be trying to convince her that he is, in fact, cheating on her. Who should your friend believe—her social network, whose view of her boyfriend is so different than her own? Or should she trust her own belief that he is perfect?

Who has the most accurate view of your romantic partner?

As you've probably figured out by now, the answer isn't entirely straightforward. On the one hand, you are likely to have greater breadth (i.e., you know a greater variety of things) and depth (i.e., you know much more about those areas) of information about your partner than do your friends and family. That should come as no surprise: It's *your* partner and those long conversations weren't for nothing. On the other hand, your thoughts about your partner can be affected by a host of cognitive biases that may lead you to overlook negative features about your relationship or partner (and they can be unconscious or deliberate biases).[1] These biases explain in part why individuals' perceptions can diverge from one another and suggest that people may not be the best judge of their romantic partners. At the same time, to the degree that you are in a committed or satisfying relationship, your thoughts about your romantic partner may be positive illusions that increase the likelihood of pro-relationship behaviors such as forgiveness. Now, that's not such a bad thing, eh? (See question 17.)

If researchers were looking at positive illusions in your relationship, they would compare your perception of your partner to your partner's actual behaviors, your partner's own perceptions, or to perceptions of social network members (e.g., your roommates, friends). When researchers examine the social network, they find that people describe their own relationships as more committed and more satisfying than their friends perceive them to be.[2] You may report that you and your partner are always happy together, but your friend may report that you're only sometimes happy together (perhaps they hear, and remember, your complaints about your partner). Viewing the partner and the relationship in an overly positive manner can render inaccurate judgments. For example, friends (especially female friends) are more accurate than relationship partners themselves at predicting whether a dating relationship will end.[3] It could be that your best friend is right to be skeptical when you say that you're sure that you'll be with your partner forever!

Maintaining positive illusions and other benevolent cognitions about romantic partners may lead people to make pro-relationship choices. When your partner betrays you (e.g., makes fun of you in public), are your friends more or less likely than you to forgive your partner? In a situation referred to as the *third-party forgiveness effect,* individuals' friends (third parties) are less forgiving of a partner who betrays an individual than the person who was actually betrayed![4] If someone cheats on your friend; you may still be angry with the person even though your friend has long since forgiven the jerk. One reason social network members are less forgiving is that they are less committed to your partner than you are (they may even be hoping that you'll break up and that you'll date someone else); therefore, they tend to interpret your partner's behavior in a less benevolent manner and are less likely to give the benefit of the doubt. For example, if your partner belittles you to impress someone else, you may attribute your partner's behavior to being nervous or to being drunk; however, your friend is more likely to attribute such behavior to your partner being a selfish prick. In general, an outside perspective from social network members can be a useful "reality check."

When friends' views and your views collide

Importantly, disagreement with social network members is likely to yield tension or discomfort, which must be resolved. Otherwise, you walk around "out of balance," so to speak, such that you have to manage two separate close relationships that mix like Pop Rocks and Coke, or oil and water (in research terms, this is known as *a lack of cognitive consistency*). But, what if you insist on maintaining your positive view of your partner in the face of persistent disagreement from social network members? The repercussions could be ugly. It's possible that the quality of your relationship with your friend or family member could suffer due to tension experienced over disagreeing. How many times have you heard of people being accused of putting their relationship ahead of friends and family?

Research also suggests that if a romantic relationship is less stable, receiving general approval of the relationship from friends or family members strengthens relationships. If you're on the fence, knowing your family and friends like your partner may encourage you to try to make it work. In fact, social network members' approval of a dating relationship predicts people's commitment to the relationship, which in turn predicts relationship persistence.[5] In particular, people's *perception* that their friends approve of a relationship (vs. the friends' actual approval) is an important predictor of relationship success; so, simply believing that social network members like your partner increases the odds that your relationship will last. Put simply: It's hard to maintain a relationship with someone whom your friends don't like. Just ask those star-crossed lovers, Mr. Montague and Ms. Capulet.

Conclusion

To summarize, whether you want to admit it or not, your thoughts about your romantic partner are biased. This can be a good thing: keep in mind that people like their own romantic partners more than others do, and that liking partners despite their annoying behaviors is a feature of committed relationships. But, your other close relationships can become strained when your rose-colored glasses are at odds with your friends' and family's doom-and-gloom colored glasses (for the record, the official color of doom and gloom is deep purple). Keep in mind that they may see something very important that you are overlooking. Acknowledge that your perceptions about your partner may be positively skewed. If you think that your partner's habit of quoting movie lines in every conversation is endearing ("May the force be with you"), but your family members think it's obnoxious ("Toga! Toga!"), that could be okay ("Frankly my dear, I don't give a damn"), and even helpful to your relationship's success ("I think this is the beginning of a beautiful friendship"). However, if you think that your partner is a strong, independent person, but your friends think that your partner is selfish and controlling, then there could be a problem. Can you remember a situation when you felt like a friend was being overly positive about a partner? That "friend" could very well be you!

TAKE-HOME POINTS

♡ Social networks notice problems in relationships that the individuals in those relationships often miss themselves.
♡ Individuals' friends (third parties) tend to be less forgiving than the individuals who are betrayed by their partners.
♡ Relationships that have the support of the individuals' social networks are more likely to succeed.

References

1. Loving, T. J., and C. R. Agnew. 2001. "Socially Desirable Responding in Close Relationships: A Dual-Component Approach and Measure." *Journal of Social and Personal Relationships* 18 (4): 551–573.
2. Agnew, C. R., T. J. Loving, and S. M. Drigotas. 2001. "Substituting the Forest for the Trees: Social Networks and the Prediction of Romantic Relationship State and Fate." *Journal of Personality and Social Psychology* 81: 1042–1057.
3. Loving, T. J. 2006. "Predicting Dating Relationship Fate with Insiders' and Outsiders' Perspectives: Who and What Is Asked Matters." *Personal Relationships* 13: 349–362.
4. Green, J. D., J. Burnette, and J. L. Davis. 2008. "Third-Party Forgiveness: (Not) Forgiving Your Close Other's Betrayer." *Personality and Social Psychology Bulletin* 34: 407–418.
5. Etcheverry, P. E., B. Le, and M. R. Charania. 2008. "Perceived versus Reported Social Referent Approval and Romantic Relationship Commitment and Persistence." *Personal Relationships* 15: 281–295.

Dig Deeper

Heider, F. 1958. *The Psychology of Interpersonal Relations.* New York: John Wiley.

MacDonald, T. K., and M. Ross. 1999. "Assessing the Accuracy of Predictions about Dating Relationships: How and Why Do Lovers' Predictions Differ from Those Made by Observers?" *Personality and Social Psychology Bulletin* 25: 1417–1429.

Sprecher, S., D. Felmlee, T. L. Orbuch, and M. C. Willetts. 2001. "Social Networks and Change in Personal Relationships." In *Stability and Change in Relationships: Advances in Personal Relationships,* edited by A. L. Vangelisti, H. T. Reis, and M. A. Fitzpatrick, 257–284. New York: Cambridge University Press.

Sprecher, S., and D. Felmlee. 1992. "The Influence of Parents and Friends on the Quality and Stability of Romantic Relationships: A Three-Wave Longitudinal Investigation." *Journal of Marriage and the Family* 54: 888–900.

Q19: I Believe for a Relationship to Work, Partners Must Be "Soul Mates." Am I Right?

Benjamin Le

Many people claim to be looking for their "soul mate." What exactly is a soul mate? One common perspective is that soul mates represent the other half of one's being (think "You complete me" from *Jerry Maguire*, but in a more cosmic sense). Another perspective is that a soul mate is someone who is your perfect partner—the only one out there with whom you will have a perfect relationship that is naturally easy to maintain. Obviously, investigating the cosmic sense of the word *soul mate* is impossible because there's no way to objectively measure if two people really do *complete* each other (and, if you can think of a way, the research community would love to hear about it!). Researchers, however, can examine individuals' beliefs about the "perfect partner" idea of a soul mate. Thus, we focus on that interpretation of *soul mate* in this response. But first, a bit of background.

Is belief in soul mates related to how a person looks at the world more generally?

As it turns out, someone's belief that there's a perfect partner out there is conceptually similar to individuals' beliefs regarding whether things in life are stable versus malleable. These beliefs, known as *implicit* or *lay theories*, have been applied to many different aspects of people's lives, including intelligence and personality. Do you believe your intelligence level is pretty much set as is? If someone isn't the brightest star in the sky now, do you believe that there's not much they can do to get brighter in the future? Or do you think that intelligence can be changed if someone pays attention in school, works really hard, and studies a lot? You can probably imagine that people differ in these beliefs and that they have an impact on how much effort people put into tasks related to those beliefs. For example, if you believe that your intelligence is malleable, then you will probably study harder because you believe your efforts will pay dividends in terms of exam grades. However, if you believe that your intelligence is fixed, then there's not much you can do to do better (including studying), so you might as well blow off studying and go out with your friends. Why bother studying at all if you can't change things?

Do the ideas of stability versus change apply to romantic relationships?

This basic idea applies to romantic relationship as well.[1] Some people may believe that they and their partners can change (He *will* learn not to leave the toilet seat up), and thus their relationships can change for the better (or worse). Others might believe that their relationships are pretty much fixed and they're not likely to get much better or worse. Just as your implicit theories have an impact on how much you might study for an exam, they also help determine how much effort you'll put into working through problems in your relationships. If you believe your relationship can change, then you would put the effort into making things in your relationship better. But if your partner's personality and the state of your relationship are static, why bother to make an effort?

So what do these beliefs have to do with being soul mates?

In addition to these general beliefs about personality and relationships, researchers have identified a more specific set of beliefs regarding how people think relationships will progress (see also question 13).[2] These beliefs influence how romantic partners think about their relationships and make efforts to keep them going (or not). In particular, two different sets of beliefs have been studied in much depth, and they can be illustrated simply by the following brief survey (take a moment to determine which of the following statements you identify with the most):

___(1) Potential relationship partners are either compatible or they are not.

___(2) The ideal relationship develops gradually over time.

The first question, which reflects a dimension that researchers have labeled *Destiny*, is essentially the degree to which one believes in a soul mate. For example, people high on the Destiny dimension believe that there is only one romantic match for each person, and that when these two people meet, love will strike at first sight, the two are destined to be together. They believe that they should follow their hearts in their relationships, and that "Love conquers all."

The second question taps a set of beliefs that researchers have termed *Growth*. Growth theorists think of relationships as gardens; they must be tended to and nurtured, and they develop slowly over time. To these folks, successful relationships are able to overcome conflict, and they believe that working through challenges makes them stronger as a couple.

How do relationship beliefs influence relationships?

Although it is interesting to be able to identify differences in the way Destiny and Growth theorists think about relationships, what's more important is that these dimensions have important implications for relationship development, satisfaction, and coping with the negative events that couples face. People who endorse the soul mate-oriented Destiny beliefs are actually more *likely* to see their relationships break-up.[3] Why? Well, it turns out that virtually all relationships are faced with challenges, and conflict is a guarantee at some point in the life of a relationship. This really rocks the foundation of those with Destiny beliefs. Whoa, wait a minute! If you don't agree with my choice of curtains and unconditionally love all 13 of my cats, you must not be my soul mate. If we aren't perfectly happy and conflict-free, I must have made an error in judgment about your soul mate credentials—I'm not supposed to fight with my *soul mate*! Thus, when things get rocky, these folks are more likely to cut the cord and move on to the next relationship. Not surprisingly, Destiny theorists are more likely to take responsibility for breaking-up and less likely to maintain a relationship with an ex-partner; if they aren't your soul mate, what's the point in hanging out with them?[2]

In contrast, Growth theorists tend to put effort into resolving conflicts and may even put a positive spin on negative relationship events ("My partner might have cheated on me, but getting through that will only make us stronger!").[2] For them, working through conflict is expected, to some degree, and is part of what brings couples together; it isn't necessarily an indication that the relationship is going badly.[4-6] People who endorse Growth beliefs also tend to be more committed to their partners and are more inclined to date one person longer than those low in Growth beliefs. They also have fewer one-night stands.[2] These results are consistent with the idea that relationships take time to develop; Growth theorists take time to see how relationships play out and are less likely to jump in bed with someone they have just met.

Conclusion

Does all this mean that your relationship will work out better if you are *not* with your soul mate? Not necessarily. Clearly, Growth theorists put more effort in maintaining their relationships and experience less negative effects from downturns in their relationships. Usually this is a good thing; there's a good reason people say "Relationships take work to succeed." However, if a relationship is in trouble or a partner is a particularly bad match, Growth theorists may continue to try to salvage things, needlessly putting energy into a dead-end relationship. They just don't know when to quit! In contrast, people high in Destiny may give up too soon and not give relationships an opportunity to develop or live up to their potential because they bolt at the first sign of trouble. However, Destiny theorists are not destined to a world of serial monogamy; they just need to be honest with themselves about what they are looking for in their relationships and understand their particular belief system. Ultimately, having a sense of your expectations for relationships and knowing how those match up to partners' expectations is likely to be key. If you're a Growth theorist who is with a Destiny theorist, you might be frustrated with your partner's lack of effort to work through problems. Likewise, if you are a Destiny theorist but your partner holds Growth beliefs, he or she is likely to be surprised when you want to kick them to the curb.

TAKE-HOME POINTS

♡ Implicit theories of relationships refer to people's beliefs about the stability versus changeability of aspects of their romantic relationships. Are things likely to remain the same? Or could they get better or worse over time?

♡ Destiny theorists believe in soul mates; that you are meant to be with a particular partner. Any problems in the relationship are a sign that the partner isn't your soul mate, so they are more likely to take responsibility for breaking-up with a partner.

♡ Growth theorists believe that relationships get stronger as they overcome challenges. Therefore, they are more likely to put effort into their relationships when they encounter trouble.

References

1. Kammrath, L., and C. S. Dweck. 2006. "Voicing Conflict: Preferred Conflict Strategies among Incremental and Entity Theorists." *Personality and Social Psychology Bulletin* 32: 1497–1508.
2. Knee, C. R. 1998. "Implicit Theories of Relationships: Assessment and Prediction of Romantic Relationship Initiation, Coping, and Longevity." *Journal of Personality and Social Psychology* 74: 360–370.
3. Le, B., N. L. Dove, C. R. Agnew, M. S. Korn, and A. A. Mutso. 2010. "Predicting Non-Marital Romantic Relationship Dissolution: A Meta-Analytic Synthesis." *Personal Relationships* 17: 377–390.
4. Knee, C. R., A. Nanayakkara, N. A. Vietor, and C. Neighbors, and H. Patrick, H. 2001. "Implicit Theories of Relationships: Who Cares if Romantic Partners Are Less Than Ideal?" *Personality and Social Psychology Bulletin* 27: 808–819.
5. Franiuk, R., D. Cohen, and E. M. Pomerantz. 2002. "Implicit Theories of Relationships: Implications for Relationship Satisfaction and Longevity." *Personal Relationships* 9: 345–367.
6. Knee, C. R., H. Patrick, N. A. Vietor, and C. Neighbors. 2004. "Implicit Theories of Relationships: Moderators of the Link Between Conflict and Commitment." *Personality and Social Psychology Bulletin* 30: 617–628.

Dig Deeper

Knee, C. R., H. Patrick, and C. Lonsbary. 2003. "Implicit Theories of Relationships: Orientations toward Evaluation and Cultivation." *Personality and Social Psychology Review* 7: 41–55.
Knee, C. R., and A. Canevello. 2006. "Implicit Theories of Relationships and Coping in Romantic Relationships." In *Self and Relationships: Connecting Intrapersonal and Interpersonal Processes*, edited by K. Vohs and E. Finkel, 160–192. New York: Guilford.

CHAPTER 6

The Dark Side of Relationships

Unfortunately, relationships aren't all puppy dogs and ice cream. That is, relationships aren't always perfect; they can include some pretty nasty experiences. For example, your partner could betray your trust by cheating. There are many reasons why people cheat, and a few ways to help detect whether your partner is cheating. However, worry about this too much, and you're likely to become overly jealous and drive your partner away. Unfortunately, even when relationships are unhealthy, people may stick with them for a variety of reasons. In other cases, relationships break-up; some for worse, but some for better. Hopefully, this chapter doesn't become a checklist of things your relationship has or should have, but rather serves as a cautionary tale of things to avoid. Just think, however; without these relationship experiences in the world, housewives wouldn't be so desperate and reality television may lose a lot of appeal.

Q20: What Is Cheating, and What Are Its Consequences?

Gary W. Lewandowski Jr.

"True love is hard to find. Sometimes you think you have true love and then you catch the early flight home from San Diego and a couple of nude people jump out of your bathroom blindfolded like a goddamn magic show."

—Mitch Martin, *Old School* (2003)

How much does this type of thing happen in relationships? Okay, not so much the blindfolds and magic show part, but what percentage of people engage in "extra-relationship" sexual activity? The best answer to this question is that we don't really know for sure. Generally speaking, roughly 1 in 3 men and 1 in 5 women have committed sexual infidelity,[1] although these estimates vary from study to study. Yet, although the differences are shrinking, men's self-reported cheating is higher than women's. How can men be cheating so much more than women? It may be the case that men are socialized such that they're more likely to inflate their amount of cheating, or they're more honest about it than are women (who are socialized to protect their "pure" image).

What is considered cheating? Are there different types?

This is a trick question—cheating is cheating, right? It's one of those things that you just know it when you see it (or hear about it from a friend that saw your partner doing it). Well, let's see just how absolute cheating is. Is having sexual intercourse with someone other than your partner cheating? YES! (Assuming you're not in to swinging.) Maybe this game is easy. What if your partner has conversations with someone at work, but doesn't tell you? Hmm. What if you have a crush where you fantasize about someone else when you're with your partner? Is flirting cheating? What about going to a strip club? What about Hooters? What about accepting a friend invitation from an ex-partner on Facebook? What about sexting? The line may be a bit fuzzy after all. If you think about it, within your own relationship, your partner is the one who ultimately decides what is cheating. You might think flirting is okay, but your boyfriend or girlfriend may not. Kissing someone else may not be allowed—unless, of course, your partner is the one encouraging you to do it. So, in essence, the reality of the situation is that cheating is any type of activity with a non-partner that your own partner would find upsetting or a breach of trust in your relationship.

When relationship scientists set out to study infidelity, what do they consider cheating? Generally, they break it down into two main types: sexual versus emotional.[2] *Sexual infidelity* is the type of cheating most people think of when someone engages in physical sexual activity with someone who isn't one's romantic partner. Cheating behaviors in this case can range from kissing—to heavy petting (yes, this is an official science term that basically equates to rounding second base and heading to third)—to, of course, sexual intercourse. *Emotional infidelity* is a bit more ambiguous, but generally involves forming an emotional connection with a non-partner and includes things like a secret texting relationship, engaging in intimate self-disclosure, all the way up to falling in love.

How can I tell if my partner is cheating?

Determining if your partner is cheating may not always be as cut and dried as simply waiting for naked people to jump out of your bedroom closet. However, if you suspect that your partner may be cheating, researchers have identified several things that you can look for to confirm (or refute) your suspicions.[3] There are two types of infidelity: emotional and sexual. If your partner is talking a lot about spending time with someone else (with whom you think they would consider having a relationship) or acting apathetic toward you, these behaviors may indicate either type of infidelity. Clues that your partner may be engaging in emotional infidelity include indications that your partner is unsatisfied with your relationship; reluctance to discuss a specific person; emotional disengagement; increased anger, guilt, anxiety, or hostility; and not wanting to spend time with you (of course, many of these may just mean he or she is just not that into you as well). Indicators that your partner may be engaging in sexual infidelity include changes in the partner's normal routine, changes in sexual interest (either lack of interest or exaggerated interest), and physical clues like lack of arousal. Women tend to be more sensitive to these cues, suggesting that they are more adept at monitoring for and identifying infidelity. Again, however, a very large and important caveat here is that these behaviors only suggest—and do not *guarantee*—that cheating is occurring.

If I cheat, should I tell my partner?

What do you do if you're the one who slips up? Before you decide on whether to come clean, you should know that how a partner discovers your cheating has a great impact on your relationship in different ways.[4] Specifically, researchers examined four different scenarios regarding how a person could discover cheating: They find out from another person, they catch you "red-handed" (with your pants down, so to speak), he or she confronts you and you admit it, and you tell your partner on your own (i.e., "the blindside"). As you may expect, if they catch you in the act or if someone rats you out, partners are the least forgiving and the relationship suffers the most. If you want to minimize the impact of your cheating ways, you should tell your partner about it before they find out another way. Granted, they may still not be happy and they may not forgive you, but taking an open and honest approach gives you the best chance of working things out (if that is indeed what you want). Perhaps the worst possible way is that taken by so many politicians and celebrities—having the cable news channels let your partner know.

What are the consequences of cheating?

Evolutionary theory predicts and research has shown that men are less likely to forgive sexual infidelity and more likely to break-up over sexual infidelity, whereas women are less likely to forgive and more likely to break-up over emotional infidelity.[5] However, these summaries require some qualifiers; partners' responses may depend on why they think cheating occurred.[6] For example, if your partner believes that you cheated because you are a terrible person, he or she is less likely to forgive you and more likely to avoid you or seek revenge. But, if your partner believes you cheated because of extenuating circumstances (e.g., you were at a party, had too much to drink, and succumbed to someone's promiscuous advances), he or she is more likely to forgive you and more likely to try to work things out. (Note: "more likely" doesn't necessarily mean "likely.")

Although the revelation of a partner's infidelity is a common cause for ending a relationship, it does not guarantee that the relationship will end. There is evidence that people stay with partners who cheat because they fear losing the partner or they are not willing to separate because of a strong emotional connection.[7] When somebody stays with a cheater because of fear, he or she is more likely to seek revenge, avoid conflict, and become generally more disrespectful and aggressive towards the partner. For example, in an investigation of how infidelity influences marriage, researchers examined 62 practicing therapists' cases that involved infidelity.[8] In almost 50% of cases, the marriage was preserved following infidelity, but was characterized as negative, empty in quality, or having a doubtful future. The next most frequent outcome, in 34% of the sample, was that the marriage ended in divorce. Finally, couples stayed together 15% of the time and were characterized by therapists as having improving and growing relationships.

Conclusion

People typically become romantically involved with partners whom they love, respect, care about, and trust. Nevertheless, people are often unfaithful. Cheating can take many forms and can reveal itself in relationships in many ways. Regardless, it is safe to say that cheating damages relationships and undermines many of the positive reasons why a person likely entered the relationship in the first place.

TAKE-HOME POINTS

♡ The definition of what makes a behavior *cheating* varies depending on the beliefs of the partners in the relationship.
♡ Researchers generally distinguish between emotional and sexual forms of infidelity.
♡ There are several behaviors that suggest one's partner may be cheating.
♡ Cheating is clearly bad for relationships and produces many negative consequences.

References

1. Tsapelas, I., H. E. Fisher, A. and Aron. 2011. "Infidelity: When, Where, Why." In *The Dark Side of Close Relationships II*, edited by W. R. Cupach, B. H. Spitzberg, W. R. Cupach, and B. H. Spitzberg, 175–195. New York: Routledge/Taylor & Francis Group.
2. Miller, S. L., and J. K. Maner. 2009. "Sex Differences in Response to Sexual versus Emotional Infidelity: The Moderating Role of Individual Differences." *Personality and Individual Differences* 46 (3): 287–291.
3. Shackelford, T. K., and D. M. Buss. 1997. "Cues to Infidelity." *Personality and Social Psychology Bulletin* 23 (10): 1034–1045.
4. Afifi, W. S., W. L. Falato, and J. L. Weiner. 2001. "Identity Concerns Following a Severe Relational Transgression: The Role of Discovery Method for the Relational Outcomes of Infidelity." *Journal of Social and Personal Relationships* 18 (2): 291–308.

5. Shackelford, T. K., D. M. Buss, K. and Bennett. 2002. "Forgiveness or Breakup: Sex Differences in Responses to a Partner's Infidelity." *Cognition and Emotion* 16 (2): 299–307.
6. Hall, J. H., and F. D. Fincham. 2006. "Relationship Dissolution Following Infidelity: The Roles of Attributions and Forgiveness." *Journal of Social and Clinical Psychology* 25 (5): 508-522.
7. Roloff, M. E., K. P. Soule, and C. M. Carey. 2001. "Reasons for Remaining in a Relationship and Responses to Relational Transgressions." *Journal of Social and Personal Relationships* 18 (3): 362–385.
8. Charny, I. W., and S. Parnass. 1995. "The Impact of Extramarital Relationships on the Continuation of Marriages." *Journal of Sex and Marital Therapy* 21 (2): 100-115.

Dig Deeper

Cupach, W., and B. Spitzberg, Eds. 2011. *The Dark Side of Close Relationships II.* New York: Routledge/Taylor & Francis Group.

Hall, J. H., and F. D. Fincham. 2006. "Relationship Dissolution Following Infidelity." In *Handbook of Divorce and Relationship Dissolution,* edited by M. A. Fine and J. H. Harvey, 153–168. Mahwah NJ: Lawrence Erlbaum Associates.

Q21: WHY DO PEOPLE CHEAT IN RELATIONSHIPS?

Gary W. Lewandowski Jr.

In the movie *Unfaithful*, Diane Lane's character seems to have it all: a nice house, kids, and a hunky husband to boot (played by Richard Gere). Yet, following a chance encounter with an attractive younger man, she finds herself being, well, unfaithful. Why would she risk all of the nice things in her life in order to cheat? There are several reasons why people might be unfaithful to their partners, including individual factors (i.e., their personalities), aspects of their relationships, or something particular about the situation.

Why do celebrities seem to cheat so much?

Quick, think of as many celebrities as you can who have allegedly been caught cheating. Go! Tiger Woods, Arnold Schwarzenegger, Jude Law, Bill Clinton, David Letterman, Kobe Bryant, Eliot Spitzer, LeAnn Rimes, Hugh Grant, Bill Clinton some more, Jon Edwards, that guy Sandra Bullock was married to, and Brett Favre. That took just about 30 seconds. Why is it so easy to come up with celebrity cheaters? It's just that common of a phenomenon (at least among male celebrities and politicians). So why do they do it? The simple answer is, because they can.

In the case of celebrities, they have high mate value because potential interlopers (i.e., home wreckers) find them desirable because of their physical attractiveness, money, power, notoriety, or combination thereof (mostly power). As a result, their pool of potential partners is large, and because of their celebrity status, some of these potential partners are happy to be willing accomplices in the affair. In the context of the investment model (see question 23), celebrities have a high quality of alternatives, which in turn undermines commitment. There really are a lot of other fish in their proverbial seas. Unfortunately, this means that even if they are satisfied and highly invested in their relationships, commitment isn't a sure bet. When people feel less of a sense of commitment, they are more likely to cheat. Researchers from Southern Methodist University in Texas found that students who reported lower levels of commitment at the beginning of the semester were more likely to cheat, either physically or emotionally, later in the semester.[1] In a follow-up study, a different set of students recorded all of their interactions during Spring Break. Even over that short week, those with lower commitment reported more physical and emotional intimacy with alternative partners. Thus, it may not be the case that the rest of the world is more virtuous and more faithful than celebrities. Instead, it may just be that they don't have the same temptations or ability to capitalize on them. Of course, when those who are less rich and famous cheat, their affairs don't end up on TMZ, so it may be that we are just more aware of celebrities who cheat.

Are some people more likely to cheat than others?

Other than celebrities, are there people who will be faithful to the end, whereas others are just cheating cheaters? One individual difference that seems to predict cheating is *sociosexuality,* which refers to the extent to which a person considers sexual behavior and emotional feelings to be intertwined (see question 31).[2] When people have an unrestricted sociosexual orientation, they are more capable of having sex without "catching feelings." Practically every person from the cast of MTV's *Jersey Shore* exhibits this pattern. A large-scale research study of 500 participants found that unrestricted sociosexuality relates to a higher sex drive, more sex partners, and a greater likelihood of cheating on one's primary partner.[3] Men are more likely to be unrestricted, which may partially explain their higher reported rates of cheating.

A person's attachment style (see question 8) may also influence cheating behavior. When 800 participants were asked about their attachment and cheating behavior, those who had more of an anxious attachment (e.g., dependency and a great deal of worry about how much the partner cares for them) were more likely to cheat.[4] A similar study of more than 500 undergraduate and more than 250 members of the community found that those who were highly anxious tended to cheat because they weren't receiving enough attention in their primary relationship.[5] In contrast, those with dismissive attachment styles (i.e., those who feel less need for relationships) tended to cheat in order to gain space and freedom in the primary relationship.

Some people may be more likely to cheat because of underlying biological and hormonal influences. For example, women with higher estrogen levels are more likely to cheat.[6] Similarly, men with higher testosterone levels have more interest in sex outside of their relationships.[7] Even though we don't carry around testosterone and estrogen testing kits to use on our partners (although that would be cool, wouldn't it?), people can determine levels of these hormones without realizing it by listening to their partners' voices.[8] Men with greater testosterone have deeper voices (e.g., Barry White), whereas women with more estrogen have higher voices (e.g., Mariah Carey). It seems we may have some inherent knowledge of this hormonal link to both infidelity and voice pitch. In one study, participants listened to audio clips of male and female voices that had been digitally altered to be higher or lower and indicated how likely that person would be to cheat. Men with masculine deep voices and females with feminine high voices were perceived to be at a higher risk for infidelity.

A woman's ovulatory cycle may also influence her likelihood of cheating.[9] Specifically, women are more likely to cheat when they are most likely to get pregnant (when she is ovulating). Whoa— why is this? Evolutionarily speaking, women should desire to obtain the best genes possible (think Jon Hamm) for their offspring. But the super-sexy mate may not stick around to raise the child, so she needs to have a more stable partner who will provide security (think Phil, the dad with three kids, from the TV series *Modern Family*). As a result, if a woman finds herself in a relationship with a lesser-quality partner (think Napoleon Dynamite), she'll cheat when she is most fertile so that her offspring have the benefit of better genes. These hormonal effects might make it sound like a person can't help cheating because he or she is at the mercy of their hormones, but that's not what the research shows. Hormones may make resisting harder, but people have the ability to be self-aware and self-reflective, and should be held accountable for their own choices.

Once a cheater, always a cheater?

You and your partner have been a happy couple for some time. One day the conversation turns to past relationships (potentially dangerous territory—proceed with caution!) and your partner reveals that he was less than faithful in a previous relationship. Of course, your partner assures you that he would never cheat on you and that he was a different person back then; the past is in the past. But should you believe him? Although we aren't aware of any research that addresses this question directly, you should know that there is a common aphorism in psychology that says, "The best predictor of future behavior is past behavior."[10] Basically, if you have ever gone over the speed limit, cheated on a test, or cheated on your taxes, you're likely to do it again. This happens because the first time you do something (like cheat on your partner), you have to weigh several options ("Will I get caught?" "Am I the type of person who cheats?") and then make the decision ("This is worth the risk"). The next time around requires less thinking and processing because you've weighed your options once before (and presumably gotten away with it), which allows the behavior to occur automatically. In essence, past cheating behavior greases the skids, making it easier to slide into bed with someone who isn't your primary partner. As Ann Landers said, "If you marry a man who cheats on his wife, you'll be married to a man who cheats on his wife." So, there isn't direct evidence that someone will always be a cheater, but the research on a variety of other behaviors certainly suggests it is more likely.

What about the relationship leads someone to cheat?

Frankly, it could be a lot of things and researchers have approached this question in a variety of ways. In a nationally representative sample of more than 2,800 participants, researchers looked at infidelity in married as well as cohabitating couples.[11] At a general level, attending fewer religious services, cohabitating, and having less overlap between partners' social networks (i.e., having fewer common or "joint" friends) were risk factors for infidelity. In addition, those with lower relationship satisfaction were more likely to have engaged in recent infidelity. This raises the proverbial "chicken versus the egg" debate. Does lack of satisfaction lead to cheating, or does cheating lead to less satisfaction in the relationship? To answer this question, researchers examined couples in the context of a longitudinal study covering 17 years.[12] Their data suggests that dissatisfaction by itself is not a risk factor for cheating, but that when people believed that a divorce was on the horizon, they were more likely to cheat. Once people cheated, their satisfaction in their marriage decreased, and they perceived divorce as more likely. Looks like it's neither the chicken nor the egg.

With this in mind, you'd probably want to identify potential deficiencies in the relationship. One potential contributing factor is that one's partner doesn't provide enough new and exciting experiences within the relationship.[13] When one's partner provides insufficient opportunities for self-growth within the relationship, then people report a greater inclination for cheating in order to fulfill their needs. To find an alternative partner who can meet those needs, you'd likely need to do a bit of window-shopping. To test this, people in a current relationship rated the relationship's ability to provide self-expansion (i.e., new and exciting experiences), then had the chance to interact with someone that could have been an alternative partner.[14] In reality, they interacted with a computer that provided preplanned answers that suggested a great deal of self-expansion. For example, if participants asked, "Do you like to hear different perspectives on topics?" the program responded, "Yes, it keeps life interesting." Not surprisingly, those who had relationships with less self-expansion enjoyed the interaction more, and picked more questions that assessed the potential partner's ability to provide self-expansion.

In a follow-up study, nearly 150 participants rated their own self-expansion and then were given a chance to participate in a "get acquainted" activity with highly attractive single partners. Participants knew they could select as many or as few people to interact with as they wanted. How many should they pick? Assuming they were happy and committed…ZERO! If you are in a happy and self-expanding relationship, it is probably a terrible idea to pick anyone, because you might be tempted to do more than just chat. As with the previous study, those in less self-expanding relationships selected more potential interaction partners. These studies are important, because people are less likely to consciously make the decision, "Today I'm going to cheat on my partner!" even if their relationship isn't very expanding. Instead, they likely engage in a series of behaviors that increase the chances of it happening, starting with paying more attention to alternate partners.

Are there situational factors that make people more likely to cheat?

We can't overlook a major determinant of whether you check out alternatives—quite simply, there must be alternate partners to check out in the first place. This highlights the role of situational factors on cheating. As any good social scientist will tell you, a person's surroundings and environment have powerful influences on behavior. To assume that there are only cheaters and non-cheaters in the world is an oversimplification. Sometimes we find ourselves in situations full of potential partners, and other times it's a sausage-fest. (Is there an equivalent term for women?)

Case in point: When you aren't at home with your partner, the next most likely place you'd be is at work. As you might expect, when you work at a place where there are greater opportunities for sexual partnerships, infidelity is more likely to occur.[11] So if your husband wants to work at Victoria's Secret or your wife wants to work at Home Depot…just say no. Okay, so you've solved this issue by making sure your partner works in a setting that is devoid of human contact. However, it is also possible that stress from work could influence cheating. Stress, whether from excessive demands, making difficult decisions, or preventing yourself from strangling your boss, requires effort that leads to ego-depletion, or a state where the person feels worn down.[15] When you feel worn down from one activity, it makes it harder to control yourself in other situations.

To see if ego-depletion, or psychological fatigue, affects the likelihood of cheating, researchers created a sense of stress in participants (all of whom were currently in committed romantic relationships) by bringing them into a room smelling of freshly baked cookies.[16] In the room, participants saw two plates, one with the cookies and the other with radishes. Those in the depletion condition had to ignore the cookies and eat the radishes. The other group (who got the far better deal) got to eat the cookies while ignoring the radishes. Next, participants were given the opportunity to interact with an attractive stranger in order to help out a local dating service. In reality, the stranger was part of the experiment (a confederate) and asked standard questions and provided standard answers. During the conversation, the confederate asked two key questions: (1)"Do you have a number I could text you at? You seem like definitely the kind of person I would really like to get to know more," and (2)"Do you think you would want to meet up for a coffee date with me sometime soon?" Granted, participants weren't given the chance to physically hook-up with another person, but would you really be happy if your partner indulged either of these requests? Probably not. It turns out that participants who ate radishes (those in the depletion condition) were three times more likely to give out their phone number and to accept a coffee date. Forgoing temptation (like fresh-baked cookies) while doing something unpleasant (eating radishes) is stressful and ego-depleting in a way that can lead to a lack of restraint around other kinds of temptations. Experiencing a long, stressful, and ego-depleting day at work is likely to make cheating more tempting.

Conclusion

Overall, your best bet is form a relationship based on trust with someone you care about and respect. Then, spend time making sure that the relationship is satisfying, fulfilling, and provides sufficient excitement so that that neither partner will be inclined to stray. Also, you should obviously never eat radishes or let your partner within the same zip code as a celebrity.

TAKE-HOME POINTS

♡ Celebrities seem to cheat a lot, and it may be due to more opportunities or to their higher mate value.
♡ Some individuals are more likely to cheat than others.
♡ Individuals who have cheated in the past are more likely to cheat in the future.
♡ Factors within the relationship, such as impending divorce or lack of growth, can lead to greater infidelity.
♡ A person's surroundings or experiences can lead to more cheating.

References

1. Drigotas, S. M., C. Safstrom, and T. Gentilia. 1999. "An Investment Model Prediction of Dating Infidelity." *Journal of Personality and Social Psychology* 77 (3): 509–524.

2. Simpson, J. A., and S. W. Gangestad. 1991. "Individual Differences in Sociosexuality: Evidence for Convergent and Discriminant Validity." *Journal of Personality and Social Psychology* 60 (6): 870–883.

3. Ostovich, J. M., and J. Sabini, J. 2004. "How Are Sociosexuality, Sex Drive, and Lifetime Number of Sexual Partners Related?" *Personality and Social Psychology Bulletin* 30 (10): 1255–1266.

4. Bogaert, A. F., and S. Sadava. 2002. "Adult Attachment and Sexual Behavior." *Personal Relationships* 9 (2): 191–204.

5. Allen, E. S., and D. H. Baucom. 2004. "Adult Attachment and Patterns of Extradyadic Involvement." *Family Process* 43 (4): 467–488.

6. Durante, K. M., and N. P. Li. 2009. "Oestradiol Level and Opportunistic Mating in Women." *Biology Letters* 5: 179–182.

7. McIntyre, M., S. W. Gangestad, P. B. Gray, J. Chapman, T. C. Burnham, M. T. O'Rourke, and R. Thornhill. 2006. "Romantic Involvement Often Reduces Men's Testosterone Levels—But Not Always: The Moderating Role of Extrapair Sexual Interest." *Journal of Personality and Social Psychology* 91 (4): 642–651.

8. O'Connor, J., D. Re, and D. Feinberg. 2011. "Voice Pitch Influences Perceptions of Sexual Infidelity." *Evolutionary Psychology* 9: 64–78.

9. Pillsworth, E. G., and M. G. Haselton. 2006. "Male Sexual Attractiveness Predicts Differential Ovulatory Shifts in Female Extra-Pair Attraction and Male Mate Retention." *Evolution and Human Behavior* 27 (4): 247–258.

10. Ouellette, J. A., and W. Wood. 1998. "Habit and Intention in Everyday Life: The Multiple Processes by Which Past Behavior Predicts Future Behavior." *Psychological Bulletin* 124 (1): 54–74.

11. Treas, J., and D. Giesen. 2000. "Sexual Infidelity among Married and Cohabiting Americans." *Journal of Marriage and the Family* 62 (1): 48–60.

12. Previti, D., and P. R. Amato. 2004. "Is Infidelity a Cause or a Consequence of Poor Marital Quality?" *Journal of Social and Personal Relationships* 21 (2): 217–230.

13. Lewandowski, G. W., Jr., and R. A. Ackerman. 2006. "Something's Missing: Need Fulfillment and Self-Expansion as Predictors of Susceptibility to Infidelity." *The Journal of Social Psychology* 146 (4): 389–403.

14. VanderDrift, L. E., G. W. Lewandowski, Jr., and C. R. Agnew. 2011. "Reduced Self-Expansion in Current Romance and Interest in Relationship Alternatives." *Journal of Social and Personal Relationships* 28: 356–373.

15. Baumeister, R. F., K. D. Vohs, and D. Tice. 2007. "The Strength Model of Self-Control." *Current Directions in Psychological Science* 16: 351–355.

16. Ciarocco, N., J. Echevarria, and G. W. Lewandowski, Jr. In Press. "Hungry for Love: The Influence of Self-Regulation on Infidelity." *Journal of Social Psychology.*

Dig Deeper

Levine, S. B. 2010. "Infidelity." In *Handbook of Clinical Sexuality for Mental Health Professionals,* 2nd ed., edited by S. B. Levine, C. B. Risen, and S. E. Althof, 87–102. New York: Routledge/Taylor & Francis Group.

Vangelisti, A. L., and M. Gerstenberger. 2004. "Communication and Marital Infidelity." In *The State of Affairs: Explorations in Infidelity and Commitment,* edited by J. Duncombe, K. Harrison, G. Allan, and D. Marsden, 59–78. Mahwah NJ: Lawrence Erlbaum Associates.

Q22: Isn't a Little Jealousy a Good Thing?

Robin S. Edelstein

While killing time during your lunch hour, you (Brenda) see that your boyfriend Dylan is now Facebook friends with Kelly. Whoa—stop the bus! What in the name of Facebook friends is going on here? Didn't Dylan have a thing for some girl named Kelly before you got together? Dylan is definitely up to something, and that *something* certainly involves this Kelly chick. It may be time to look through all of Dylan's "friends" and see what he's up to. Better yet, you could steal his password and *really* see what he's been up to. But before you begin the termination process, you might want to step back a bit so that you can avoid unleashing the wrath of the "green-eyed monster." Jealousy can strike when you least expect it: on Facebook…or when you see your girlfriend talking to a guy at a party and you wonder about her motives (and his)…or when you find somebody else's underwear in your girlfriend's laundry basket (okay, maybe this last one is worth a little jealousy). What does it say about your relationship if you're always obsessing about what your partner is up to, or who else might have their sights on him? And who wants to be with someone who doesn't trust them? Too much jealousy can obviously be a problem. But what if your partner is *never* jealous? Could a *little* jealousy actually be a good thing in a relationship?

What is jealousy?

Jealousy occurs when we feel that an important relationship might be threatened.[1] It is important to note that all jealousy is not created equally. For example, *reactive jealousy* results from a specific event with a realistic threat such as when you actually see someone clearly flirting with your girlfriend. A threat may also be imaginary…like when you wonder what your boyfriend is doing on that "business trip" in Las Vegas (what happens in Vegas stays in Vegas, right?). You may be worried about the Vegas trip because of *suspicious jealousy,* when an individual is constantly vigilant about the partner's behavior and may even resort to snooping. Regardless of the type, jealousy, especially when it results from insecurity or lack of trust in the relationship, undermines relationship quality.

Not surprisingly, however, although jealousy is generally a pretty negative emotion, it can actually have some positive effects in relationships—at least in small doses. By being cognizant of our partner's wandering eye, or aware of others who are trying to catch our partner's eye, we help avoid losing an important relationship.[2] Believe it or not, people often deliberately engage in *mate-poaching*—meaning they pursue partners who are already in a relationship, and those pursuits are surprisingly successful![3] At the same time, if you fail to monitor your partner's behaviors to some degree, you could end up staying with someone who's being unfaithful to you. So, in order to protect your relationship, it's important to pay at least some attention to what your partner is doing and who your competition might be. And if your relationship isn't really worth protecting because your partner is being unfaithful, that's important to know, too.

Can jealousy be a good thing?

We're most likely to experience jealousy in relationships when we feel more serious, committed, and interdependent.[1] Jealousy can also show your partner that you're invested in the relationship (and vice versa). After all, if you weren't invested in the relationship, would you really care that much about what your partner was doing (and with whom)? (Of course, there's a danger that this kind of thinking can lead people to justify a partner's excessive jealousy with thoughts like, "She only hacked into my email account and deleted all my high-school female friends because she loves me so much"—more on that later.) Feelings of jealousy may sometimes even lead to positive behaviors that can make a relationship stronger. For example, if you start feeling jealous, you might stop to reexamine your relationship; if you think that your relationship is worth fighting for, you might be more attentive to your partner, or be less likely to take your partner for granted.[4] These kinds of behaviors might even make your partner less likely to stray in the first place, and there's some evidence that people who have a (somewhat) jealous partner are more satisfied and committed to their relationships, especially if their partners also make *them* feel less jealous.[5]

Is purposefully making your partner jealous a good idea?

It's probably not surprising, then, that most people have deliberately tried to make their partners jealous at some point during the relationship, often in hopes of getting more attention or as a way of "testing" their relationship.[6] This strategy can sometimes be effective at keeping a romantic partner interested, especially for people who are more secure in their relationships. Paradoxically, secure individuals (see question 8) have less to be jealous about in the first place, which may be why purposefully eliciting jealousy doesn't undermine relationship quality.[6] Women may be more likely than men to try to make their partners jealous,[7] and they're also more likely to focus on maintaining the relationship when they feel jealous themselves.[8] Men, however, may be more likely to retaliate by finding new partners when they feel jealous. As a result, if you're a heterosexual female, or a gay male, trying to elicit jealousy might not be the most effective strategy to use with your boyfriend, and it may just encourage him to stray.

The dark side of jealousy

Of course, we all know that jealousy has another side, one that is potentially very dangerous. The dark side of sexual jealousy is highlighted in the popular media, from movies like *Fatal Attraction* and *Mean Girls* to television shows like *The Bachelor*. As you may have noticed, these sorts of love triangles never seem to end very well for those involved (and, sometimes, innocent bystanders even get caught up in the wreckage). In the real world, sexual jealousy is a commonly cited cause of relationship breakups, and excessive jealousy during a relationship has been associated with violent stalking behavior after the relationship ends.[9] In fact, jealousy is one of the most common motives for violence and homicide between romantic partners.[2] Even under less extreme circumstances, excessive and unwarranted jealousy can destroy an otherwise healthy relationship.

Conclusion

Although jealousy can have some positive effects in relationships, it's important for both partners to keep jealous feelings in check and not to let them get too out of control. Although an extremely jealous partner might also be an extremely invested partner, too much jealousy is definitely not a good thing, and you shouldn't let that investment become an excuse (or a justification) for excessive jealousy. If you really feel like you can't trust your partner, maybe your suspicions are correct. And if you feel like you need to do a lot of work to keep your partner interested, maybe this isn't the right relationship for you. So, is a little jealousy a good thing in a relationship? A *little*, yes—but just remember that a little bit of jealousy can go a long way!

TAKE-HOME POINTS

- ♡ A little bit of jealousy can be a good thing in a relationship; it's a sign of investment and can keep partners from taking each other for granted.
- ♡ Although people often try to make their partners jealous, this strategy doesn't tend to be very effective.
- ♡ Too much jealousy can definitely be a problem in a relationship; it's a sign of lack of trust as well as a common cause of relationship breakups (and worse).

References

1. White, G. L., and P. E. Mullen. 1989. *Jealousy: Theory, Research, and Clinical Strategies*. New York: Guilford Press.
2. Buss, D. 2000. *The Dangerous Passion: Why Jealousy Is as Necessary as Love and Sex*. New York: Free Press.
3. Schmitt, D. P., and D. M. Buss. 2001. "Human Mate Poaching: Tactics and Temptations for Infiltrating Existing Mateships." *Journal of Personality and Social Psychology* 80: 894–917.
4. Pines, A., and E. Aronson. 1983. "Antecedents, Correlates, and Consequences of Sexual Jealousy." *Journal of Personality* 51: 108–136.
5. Sheets, V. L., L. L. Fredendall, and H. M. Claypool. 1997. "Jealousy Evocation, Partner Reassurance, and Relationship Stability: An Exploration of the Potential Benefits of Jealousy." *Evolution and Human Behavior* 18: 387–402.
6. Guerrero, L. 1998. "Attachment-Style Differences in the Experience and Expression of Romantic Jealousy." *Personal Relationships* 5: 273–291.
7. White, G. L. 1980. "Inducing Jealousy: A Power Perspective." *Personality and Social Psychology Bulletin* 6: 222–227.
8. Shettel-Neuber, J., J. B. Bryson, and L. E. Young. 1978. "Physical Attractiveness of the 'Other Person' and Jealousy." *Personality and Social Psychology Bulletin* 4: 612–615.

9. Roberts, K. A. 2005. "Women's Experience of Violence during Stalking by Former Romantic Partners." *Violence Against Women* 11: 89–114.

Dig Deeper

Dijkstra, P., D. P. H. Barelds, and H. A. K. Groothof. 2010. "An Inventory and Update of Jealousy Evoking Partner Behaviours in Modern Society." *Clinical Psychology and Psychotherapy* 17: 329–345.

Guerrero, L. K., and P. A. Andersen. 1998. "The Dark Side of Jealously and Envy: Desire, Delusion, Desperation, and Destructive Communication." In *The Dark Side Of Close Relationships,* edited by B. H. Spitzberg and W. R. Cupach, 33–70. Mahwah NJ: Lawrence Erlbaum Associates.

Muise, A., E. Christofides, and S. Desmarais. 2009. "More Information Than You Ever Wanted: Does Facebook Bring Out the Green-Eyed Monster of Jealousy?" *Cyber Psychology and Behavior* 12: 441–444.

Q23: WHY DO PEOPLE STAY IN BAD OR ABUSIVE RELATIONSHIPS?

Nancy E. Frye

In an ideal world, once people find a relationship, they would live out the Hollywood version of life (that is, the "riding off into the sunset" version of things, not the version of things where their significant other turns out to be a double-agent working for the CIA). Granted, this usually doesn't happen; you probably don't ride off into the sunset and the CIA thing is unlikely to pan out. Sometimes, things go in pretty much the exact opposite direction of the stereotypical Hollywood ending. It may be on a small scale, where you and your partner are constantly bickering and finding that your relationship just isn't that nice to be in anymore. Or it may be more serious, where your partner is constantly monitoring your Facebook account and asks you to justify every friend you have.

To be sure, these are the signs of a bad relationship, but unfortunately, it can get much worse. *Abusive relationships* involve physical abuse such as punching, hitting, kicking, and slapping; or verbal abuse such as insulting or otherwise emotionally tormenting a partner. For example, one person could start belittling the other (in a way that goes way past the scope of "You really thought that shirt and those pants matched?!"), or things could get physical, with objects or punches being thrown. In short, men and women behave badly at times and it can spell disaster for any relationship and can be dangerous for the victim's well-being. But, even if such behavior is enough to make you want to end a relationship, thoughts of ending the relationship don't always lead to actually doing so; people stay even when everyone else is yelling "Get out!" Which leads to the question: Why do people stay in bad relationships?

The economics of relationships

Part of the answer comes down to economics. Don't worry – the words *macro* and *micro* do not appear henceforth. But, part of economics involves comparing alternatives. Deciding whether to stay in a relationship or leave it is a little like deciding between an iPad and a new LCD TV. If you buy the latest iPad, you may not be able to buy a new LCD TV as well—at least not without racking up a monstrous credit card bill. So, you need to compare the iPad and a new LCD TV, and decide which adds more to your life. Similarly, people weigh what they think would happen if they left their partners against what they think would happen if they stayed, and they tend to go with the better (or at least less horrible) of the two projected outcomes. For instance, people who have little or no income on their own might feel like they have to stay in their relationship, no matter how bad it gets, because the alternatives (like eviction or starvation) are even worse. This can be seen in research that asked people directly to think about the alternatives to their relationship, by asking them to rate how much they agreed with statements like, "My alternatives to our relationship are close to ideal (dating another, spending time with friends or on my own, etc.)." The less undergraduates in relationships agreed with statements like that, the less likely they were to have broken up with their partner a few months later.[1] The economics of relationships are so powerful that they can even predict whether people return to abusive relationships. Women who had left their partner and gone to a shelter and who had little education and no income of their own were more likely to later return to their partner than those women who had more education and an income of their own.[2] So, the fewer options people have—in terms of other relationships, how happy they'd be on their own, and how much money they have—the more likely they are to stay in a bad relationship.

Another part of the economics involved comes down to investments. The more time and effort that people put into something, the harder time they have just giving up on it. Despite the saying "You shouldn't throw good money after bad," people do this sort of thing all the time. Once people have defended their significant others to their friends and family, celebrated anniversaries, and possibly had kids, ending the relationship can feel like throwing away all that time, effort, and energy. This link between investments and staying in a relationship was found in that study of those college students mentioned previously; the college students were less likely to leave their partner if they agreed more with statements like, "I have told my partner many private things about myself (I disclose secrets to him/her)."[1] The importance of investments can also be seen in the study mentioned concerning women in the shelter, who were more likely to return to their husband if they had been with him longer and had more children with him.[2]

"Ours is not to reason why"—or is it?

The stability of relationships where partners have few alternatives and have invested quite a lot seems like it should look pretty similar to the stability of relationships where partners are blissfully in love—partners in both types of relationship seem likely to end up having to figure out what to do for their fifth (or fiftieth) anniversary. We'll get to whether this is *really* likely to be the case in a second. First, however, what about the day-to-day life of these relationships? If people stay because of those economics, does their relationship look any different than if they stay because they're so blissfully happy they can't imagine life without their partner?

It turns out the answer is yes—all relationships are not created equally. If people stay, despite the relationship being not so great, because they just don't see any alternative to their partner, they actually behave differently toward their partner. This can be seen in looking at how people respond when their partner has messed up (or *transgressed*, in fancy researcher speak). In one study, people were asked to think of a time when their relationship partner had transgressed. This could have been any kind of transgression, from forgetting a birthday to kissing someone else. Then, the researchers looked to see how the reactions to transgressions might be related to why people were staying in their relationship. Those people who were staying because of the economics (i.e., staying because they were worried they just didn't have any alternatives to their partner) weren't quite so forgiving as the people who were staying because they wanted to stay. Those people who didn't see alternatives tended, down the road, to act a bit cold to their partner, deny affection to their partner, and not help their partner out as much after their partner had transgressed. So, the next time you forget your partner's birthday (or accidentally kiss someone else), think about why your partner is staying with you; if it's because you're on a desert island and no one else is around, you should prepare yourself for a cold shoulder.[3]

Now, what about that stability question? If people feel they have few alternatives and that they've made a lot of investments in their relationship, are they doomed to stay in a bad relationship for-ever? To find out, researchers asked people why they stayed married (a question that is a bit rude and impertinent, but researchers can get away with such things). Then, they followed people over time to see whether the reasons why they stayed married were related to whether they actually did stay married. It turns out that people who said they only stayed married because marriage was the lesser of the two evils (e.g., because they were on the equivalent of a desert island with no one else around, because they couldn't afford to live on their own) actually tended to figure out a way to leave, if they were given enough time. Over the 17 years of the study, people who reported they stayed married only because they had barriers to leaving were more than one and a half times more likely to divorce their partner than people who reported they stayed married because their partner was the "bee's knees" and they were head over heels in love.[4]

"It's not that bad now and will get better in the future"

The economics of relationships give some idea why people may stay in not so great relationships, and looking at divorce over time gives some hope that people may actually figure out a way, with enough time, to leave a bad relationship. But staying in a bad relationship day in and day out, over decades, can't just be about alternatives and investments, can it? It turns out there's a bit more to the story.

In addition to economics, classic concepts from Shakespeare also play a role. Think about the line from *Hamlet*: "There's nothing either good or bad, but thinking makes it so." This sentiment applies not only to trying to decide whether you should kill your uncle (if you're Hamlet), but it also applies to relationships. Even the worst of the worst in bad relationships tend not to be completely bad. People tend to put more emphasis on the better parts of their rela-tionships ("Sure, my partner belittles me in front of his friends and calls me names, but he did take me to the Bahamas last summer").[5] This view of things can help make it easier to stay in a relationship that the rest of the world may view as pretty horrendous.

In addition, like Little Orphan Annie, people may think that "The Sun'll Come Out Tomorrow"—telling themselves that things in the relationship are going to get better if they just wait (and "stick up their chin and grin…"). People are actually pretty good at seeing improvement in all sorts of areas, regardless of whether that improvement is really there. For instance, a bunch of people who had taken a study skills training program vehemently believed that their study skills had gotten better over the course of the program. The thing is, however, when researchers compared measures of their study skills before the program to measures of their study skills after the program, there were no differences.[6] How can this be? How can people remember improvement where there's none at all? It turns out that when people looked back on their initial level of study skills, they were underestimating them—by a lot. As a result of their inaccurate thoughts about where they started, they saw things as having gotten better over time. Which makes them a winner. And who doesn't like to be a winner?

Such findings provide interesting insight into why people may stay in objectively poor relationships. It turns out that people seem to do something very similar when thinking about their relationships. Basically, they tend to look at how things are changing over time in a way that lets them see improvement. To test this hypothesis, researchers asked people at different points in time how happy they were in their relationships. They later asked them about how their relationships were changing over time. People tended to say that their relationships were getting better over time, even if the measures taken at each time point showed no improvement at all (or even, in some cases, the measures showed declines in the relationship). If people are this bad at *remembering* how their relationships have changed over time, think about how terrible they must be at *predicting* how their relationships will change in the future. People, after all, are not psychic. And it can be really easy to think about all the ways the future will be better than the present (think along the lines of "I'll lose five pounds as soon as I'm less stressed"; how often does that ever really happen?). Just like with studying and weight loss, peoples' expectations about how their relationships are going to change in the future have pretty much nothing to do with how their relationships actually do change.[7] As a result, people may wait it out, thinking that the abuse will stop. It seldom, if ever, does.

Conclusions

Why is it that people stay in bad relationships? In short, the answer comes down to economics, Shakespeare, and Little Orphan Annie:

because they have to, they're just not focusing on the right stuff, or they make themselves feel good by thinking things are better today than yesterday. Seldom do they stay because they want to.

TAKE-HOME POINTS

♡ People may feel they simply don't have any alternatives to a bad relationship or they'd lose too many investments if they left a relationship, and so will stay in the relationship even if it's a bad one.

♡ People expect things to get better, so they may stay in a bad relationship, thinking that, over time, it'll become a good relationship.

♡ Just because a relationship lasts a long time does not mean the people in it are happy.

References

1. Rusbult, C. E., J. M. Martz, and C. R. Agnew. 1998. "The Investment Model Scale: Measuring Commitment Level, Satisfaction Level, Quality of Alternatives, And Investment Size." *Personal Relationships* 5: 357–391.
2. Rusbult, C. E., and J. M. Martz. 1995. "Remaining in an Abusive Relationship: An Investment Model Analysis of Nonvoluntary Dependence." *Personality and Social Psychology Bulletin* 21: 558–571.
3. Roloff, M. E., K. P. Soule, and C. M. Carey. 2001. "Reasons for Remaining in a Relationships and Responses to Relational Transgressions." *Journal of Social and Personal Relationships* 18: 362–385.
4. Previti, D., and P. R. Amato. 2003. "Why Stay Married? Rewards, Barriers, and Marital Stability." *Journal of Marriage and the Family* 65: 561–573.
5. Neff, L. A., and B. R. Karney. 2003. "The Dynamic Structure of Relationship Perceptions: Differential Importance as a Strategy of Relationship Maintenance." *Personality and Social Psychology Bulletin* 29: 1433–1446.
6. Conway, M., and M. Ross. 1984. "Getting What You Want by Revising What You Had." *Journal of Personality and Social Psychology* 47: 738–748.
7. Sprecher, S. 1999. "'I Love You More Today than Yesterday': Romantic Partners' Perceptions of Changes in Love and Related Affect over Time." *Journal of Personality and Social Psychology* 76: 46–53.

Dig Deeper

Langer, A., E. Lawrence, and B. A. Barry. 2008. "Using a Vulnerability-Stress-Adaptation Framework to Predict Physical Aggression." *Journal of Consulting and Clinical Psychology* 76: 756–768.

Lawrence, E., and T. N. Bradbury. 2001. "Physical Aggression and Marital Dysfunction: A Longitudinal Analysis." *Journal of Family Psychology* 15: 135–154.

Rhoades, G. K., S. M. Stanley, G. Kelmer, and H. J. Markman. 2010. "Physical Aggression in Unmarried Relationships: The Roles of Commitment and Constraints." *Journal of Family Psychology* 24: 678–687.

Q24: How Will My Breakup Affect Me?

Gary W. Lewandowski Jr.

"We need to talk" may be the four most dreaded words one can hear from a partner. After a few hours of intense "discussion," the only thing left to do is to update your relationship status on Facebook. You're going to be okay. After all, your partner took responsibility and clearly stated, "It's not you; it's me." How very nice. Besides, it isn't totally over; your partner said, "We may be better off as friends," which indicates you'll stay in touch. Wait, on second thought, maybe that stuff didn't help at all. That's right, you got dumped. It might seem like it's the end of the world and that you'll never get over it, but chances are if you did a casual survey of your family or friends, you would find out that most of them, if not all, got dumped or experienced a breakup at some point in their lives. And guess what? They've all made it through the experience alive, perhaps much to their own surprise.

How good are people's predictions about how bad their breakups will be?

Although your friends may have emerged from their breakups in one piece, they may not have thought such an outcome was remotely possible back when the relationship was going strong. In fact, research on the topic suggests we're not very good at forecasting our emotional reactions to a breakup.

For example, researchers at Northwestern University and Carnegie–Mellon University had a group of college freshman, who tend to be prone to breaking-up, answer questions about their relationships over a nine-month period. When their relationships were still intact, participants predicted how distressed they would be if the relationships ended.[1] Later, when their relationships ended, participants answered a parallel question about how distressed they actually were about their breakups. The results showed that participants anticipated experiencing more distress than they actually endured. In other words, when we're involved with someone, we think we'd be devastated if we lost them (which makes sense); but, it turns out, life does indeed go on.

What is the negative side of a breakup?

Just because the breakup's aftermath may not be as bad as you think, it may still be a tough experience. Again, research with college students highlights the emotional aftermath of breakup. In one study, approximately 200 college students who experienced a breakup in the previous three months were asked to provide information about their current well-being.[2] Breaking-up was associated with experiencing depression, anxiety, betrayal, rejection, intrusive thoughts, and sleep disturbance. Distress was also more pronounced when the breakup occurred more recently, when the participant was the one broken up with (i.e., the *Dumpee*), and when a new relationship had not been started. It is important to note that breakups aren't just depressing; they may also have consequences for the individual's sense of self.[3] Anything that you would provide as an answer to the question "Who am I?" is your *self-concept*, and positive relationships can help add to your self-concept by making you more knowledgeable, less anxious, or even more patient. However, once that relationship is lost, those new aspects of the self-concept may be lost as well, leading to a loss of self. To determine how a breakup influences the self, researchers asked, "How were you affected by the breakup of your relationship?" Researchers then analyzed the responses to look for important themes or types of comments, and paid careful attention to whether participants demonstrated a loss of self through statements such as "I'm confused about who I am," and "I lost part of myself." These types of statements were especially likely to be provided when the former relationship was fulfilling and provided sufficient opportunities for self-growth (i.e., the participants had more to lose). So, The Script may have had it right when they sang in the song "Breakeven" "…when a heart breaks, no it don't break even, even, no. What am I supposed to do when the best part of me was always you…"

Can breakup be a positive thing?

On the flip side, there is also the possibility that your breakup not only won't kill you, but could actually make you stronger. (Thanks, Nietzsche!) For example, nearly 100 college students were asked an open-ended question about how much they had grown as a person following their breakup.[4] On average, they listed five positive changes—for example, feeling more self-confident, gaining communication skills, and learning what type of partner is better for them in the future—for every negative change. It also turns out that if you end a relationship with a partner who is dull, boring, or doesn't help you become a better person, you increase your chances of experiencing positive outcomes.[5] Reported positive outcomes include a range of positive emotions (e.g., competent, empowered, optimistic, thrilled, wise) as well as a sense of personal growth. The really great news is that only one third characterized their breakup as negative, with more than 66% of participants describing it as positive or equally good and bad, with 41% of those saying that the breakup was a positive experience overall. So, when Brittney Spears decided to make Kevin Federline "FedEx," it may have been the best thing she could have done for her self-concept. (She may not be the most stable individual, but she's far more interesting than Federline.)

How can I get better?

So, if some people have these positive breakups, is there a way to help the rest of us who are wandering around Dumpsville (population: YOU) feeling rejected? One simple strategy you could use is to write about your breakup experience. There is a body of literature that shows writing about an emotional or upsetting experience can lead to improvements in mental and physical health.[6] Specifically, when participants in these studies write about experiences such as death, tragic events, and physical or sexual abuse for a little bit each day, there are benefits in terms of fewer doctor's visits, less absenteeism from work, and decreases in distress or depression. If this can work for these types of events, it should certainly work for breakup—and the good news is, it does. In a study of people who were single after experiencing a recent breakup, participants were randomly assigned to write either about the negative or positive aspects of their breakups.[7] Compared to a group who wrote about a neutral topic, both the positive and negative writing groups felt better about the breakup. Perhaps most important, the group who focused on the positive aspects did the best and reported the fewest negative emotions (e.g., empty, rejected, traumatized) and the greatest number of positive emotions (e.g., relief, confidence, strength). "Dear Diary, I'm getting a divorce from Ryan Reynolds. On the upside, I'll be able to date pretty much anyone in the world that I want because I'm rich, attractive, and well, basically I'm still Scarlett Johansson. Wow, I do feel better. Thanks Diary!"

The "Dear Diary" approach of writing about breakup highlights the more general strategy of spending time thinking about the past relationship.[8] Here, you'll want to be careful to avoid thinking about things in a way that can actually make you feel worse. Specifically, you should avoid obsessing about the things that bother you, dwelling on the small details, and focusing on how others don't have it as hard as you. Instead, reflect on what you can learn from the experience, try to derive benefits from the positive, and focus on moving on with your life.

Conclusion

Sure, breaking-up is hard to do, but it's a natural part of life. Although it may hurt and it may feel like you'll never have a relationship again, it isn't the end of the world. In fact, people think it will be worse than it actually is, and in many cases, people experience breakups as positive. And really, why not? In many ways, breakups are the natural outcome when two people aren't able to make a relationship work. Or more simply, high-quality fantastic relationships between ideally matched partners don't generally break-up. So rather than view a breakup as a major loss, perhaps it's really just an opportunity to go out and find the type of partner who will provide you with a lifetime's worth of relationship happiness.

TAKE-HOME POINTS

♡ People are bad at predicting their breakup's negative impact and tend to overestimate how bad it will be.

♡ Breakups result in many negative experiences, such as loneliness, distress, and loss of self.

♡ Breakups also often result in positive outcomes, like positive emotions and personal growth.

♡ Writing about your breakup experience, especially focusing on the positive aspects, promotes better adjustment after a breakup.

References

1. Eastwick, P. W., E. J. Finkel, T. Krishnamurti, and G. Loewenstein. 2008. "Mispredicting Distress Following Romantic Breakup: Revealing the Time Course of the Affective Forecasting Error." *Journal of Experimental Social Psychology* 44 (3): 800–807.
2. Field, T., M. Diego, M. Pelaez, O. Deeds, and J. Delgado. 2009. "Breakup Distress in University Students." *Adolescence* 44 (176): 705–727.
3. Lewandowski, G. W., A. P. Aron, S. Bassis, and J. Kunak. 2006. "Losing a Self-Expanding Relationship: Implications for the Self-Concept." *Personal Relationships* 13: 317–331.
4. Tashiro, T., and P. Frazier. 2003. "'I'll Never Be in a Relationship Like That Again': Personal Growth Following Romantic Relationship Breakups." *Personal Relationships* 10: 113–128.
5. Lewandowski, G. W., Jr., and N. Bizzoco. 2007. "Addition through Subtraction: Growth Following the Dissolution of a Low Quality Relationship." *Journal of Positive Psychology* 2 (1): 40–54.
6. Pennebaker, J. W. 1997. "Writing about Emotional Experiences as a Therapeutic Process." *Psychological Science* 8: 162–166.
7. Lewandowski, G. W., Jr. 2009. "Promoting Positive Emotions Following Relationship Dissolution through Writing." *The Journal of Positive Psychology* 4 (1): 21–31.
8. Saffrey, C., and M. Ehrenberg. 2007. "When Thinking Hurts: Attachment, Rumination, and Postrelationship Adjustment." *Personal Relationships* 14 (3): 351–368.

Dig Deeper

Fine, M. and J. Harvey, Editors. 2006. *Handbook of Divorce and Relationship Dissolution*. Mahwah NJ: Lawrence Erlbaum Associates.
Tashiro, T., P. Frazier, and M. Berman. 2006. "Stress-Related Growth Following Divorce and Relationship Dissolution." In *Handbook of Divorce and Relationship Dissolution*, edited by M. Fine and J. Harvey, 361–384. Mahwah NJ: Lawrence Erlbaum Associates.

CHAPTER 7

Resources, Power, and Conflict

All couples argue at some point or another, and money is often the topic of choice. Thus, who makes more money and decisions regarding whether to combine income may hold long-lasting implications for couples. At the most basic level, arguments occur when two people prefer different things in their relationships. Interestingly, although they say, "Money is power," determining who gets their way in a relationship is far more complicated than counting dollars and cents. Furthermore, the tactics someone uses to get his or her way in a relationship matter more than the mere presence of conflict. Sticks and stones may break your bones, but contrary to what your momma told you, words *will* hurt you as well. How you react to those words (or other misdeeds by your partner) is quite informative, and that information can be used for better *or* worse by your partner.

Q25: SHOULD WE COMBINE OUR MONEY?

Marci E. J. Gleason

One of the most famous lines in literature is the opening to *Pride and Prejudice* by Jane Austen; "It is a truth universally acknowledged, that a single man in possession of a good fortune, must be in want of a wife." It is famous because (1) *Pride and Prejudice* is the best book ever (Note: This is a personal opinion of this author); (2) it succinctly and with sly humor summarizes the theme of the book; and (3) it accurately points out that marriage and money were inexorably linked in the late 1700s in England. This latter point is, although less so today, still true in many cultures.

Marriage for Money and Power

Let's take a step back for a bit: For hundreds of years, marriage was largely a financial or political arrangement made by people other than the two individuals getting married.[1] It was a way to consolidate resources and reinforce connections between different groups of people—think the arranged marriages between European royal families. In the past, women had no property rights, and so upon marriage, if her family (her father) wanted to give her resources, they had to pass directly from her father to her husband. These resources were commonly referred to as *dowries* and could consist of money or other goods (e.g., a flock of sheep, plot of land). Not surprisingly, women with large dowries were more likely to be sought after by suitors (aka "Gold Diggers") because the money and material goods would belong to the former suitor—now husband—upon marriage. By law, women had little to no rights over their finances (this was true until the mid to late 1800s in the United States[1]), so the question of whether to combine money at marriage was moot.

Thankfully, the times they were a-changing, and in the United States and other modern Western cultures, marriage is no longer commonly determined by financial and political concerns, but people are expected and encouraged to marry for love.[1] (In fact, most of Jane Austen's book describes the turmoil that arose when society started believing that marriage should be based on love rather than property—Jane Austen was clearly on the side of love.) A recent example of the turnover to a love-based model of marriage is evident in the fact that Prince William of England married Kate "the commoner" Middleton presumably motivated by love, when only 30 years before his father was encouraged very forcefully to enter into an arranged marriage with a woman he did not appear to love.

Marrying for love, but the bills must get paid

Today we marry for love, often referred to as *companionate marriage,* and both partners have equal rights to their property upon entering marriage. Couples largely decide what happens to resources after marriage, but each state has its own laws governing who has rights to assets in a marriage. The different laws about the allocation of assets come into play when a couple divorces and when one member or both members of the couple go into debt, inherit property, are given a large gift, and on and on. For instance, in some states, if your partner goes on a spending spree and runs up huge credit card bills, you will be also be held responsible for that debt. (Time to freeze the credit card in a block of ice and block QVC from your TV.) The legal distinctions go on and on, but what becomes clear from them is that couples, married couples in particular, are tied together not only emotionally but also financially.

This leads to difficult decisions that partners must make about how finances should be handled within their relationship. Choosing a system of money management is a task that couples should not take lightly, because fighting over money is one of the most common conflicts couples' report.[2] Unfortunately, we may not be that good at choosing partners who have similar money management styles and priorities to our own. Recent research surveyed individuals about their tendencies to be conservative (a group they labeled *tightwads*) or liberal (the *spendthrifts*) with money, and found that people are more likely to be married to someone whose orientation is the opposite of their own, and that the less matched people were on this spending dimension, the less satisfied they were in their marriage.[3] Furthermore, it seemed that the tendency to choose partners who had a different fiscal orientation may be driven by the fact that people disapprove of their own tightwad or spendthrift tendencies. So if money is a big source of conflict and we have a tendency to choose people who are likely to disagree with us on how money is spent, can choices in how to manage money alleviate conflict?

What are the choices in money management?

You can think of money organization as occurring along a continuum. On one side, you have couples who keep their money entirely separate from each other; on the other side are the couples who combine all of their money. Of course, in between, are the couples who do a little bit of both. By far, the most common approach is that of couple's pooling all of their money and spending out of that common pot. This accounts for how more than 75% of married couples approach their finances and more than 50% of couples who are cohabiting.[4] This is the most traditional approach to couple finances—the whole "What's mine is yours and what's yours is mine" idea. Advantages of combining money include the ability for both members of the couple to have equal access to assets and for both partners to potentially have equal say in spending choices. Couples also view pooling money as a way to signal commitment.[5]

Increasingly, couples are choosing not to completely pool their assets, but to instead keep some assets separate. When couples don't have a completely pooled approach, they have many shared assets including things like houses, cars, and at least one joint back account, but also have assets that are not jointly held. The most typical manifestation of this is a couple in which each partner has an individual bank account while also maintaining a joint bank account.[6] In this situation, the joint account is often used for expenses that are considered shared (e.g., the mortgage or rent, the utility bill, groceries) and the individual accounts are used for things that are considered separate (e.g., clothing, gifts, hobbies, trips to the spa or strip club, other splurge purchases). This allows for different spending habits between the spouses while still maintaining a large degree of common pooling.

Maintenance of completely separate assets with partners having no shared account or shared assets is the least common approach, but is increasing as more partners take an individualized approach to marriage (e.g., an approach to marriage that promotes maintaining independence from one's partner).[6] Keeping their assets separate is one way to maintain independence. People who have previously been divorced or are marrying later in life are more likely to adopt this model, perhaps because they have learned that interdependence can be messy or are just accustomed to a certain level of independence.

To pool or not to pool

Back to the original question: Should you combine your money? There is no definitive answer to how these different styles affect relationship satisfaction and longevity. However, if you remember question 23, the more *investments* (such as shared assets) a couple has in their relationship, the stronger their level of commitment tends to be. Not only is sharing money symbolic of commitment, it may also increase commitment. People who keep their assets separate report they do so in order to retain their independence and are more likely to endorse the idea that one should leave a relationship when it is no longer satisfying (not a sign of deep commitment).[6]

Conversely, for individuals who have very different spending habits, having independent accounts (entirely or in part) might help alleviate tension over spending choices. If your partner has a penchant for buying Star Wars memorabilia or Beanie Babies, you might prefer that they do that on their own dime (and that means you can indulge your love of fine wine or microbrews guilt-free).

The most typical advice given to couples is that they discuss how money will be handled and agree to a method of handling it. Open communication is key. Regardless of the approach you choose in the beginning, there is a strong tendency for couples to pool their assets as they are together for a longer period of time and this tendency is even more pronounced when couples do things like buy a house together or have children—perhaps because both of these activities tend to make money a bit more scarce, leaving little left to discuss or use to buy that fine wine.

TAKE-HOME POINTS

♡ Historically, marriage was a primarily financial arrangement with the husband making all financial decisions. Today, marriage is typically entered into because of a desire for companionship and love.

♡ Most married couples, and many cohabitating couples, pool all of their assets, but an increasing number of couples are keeping at least some money separate.

♡ It is unclear how decisions over pooling money affect marriages in terms of satisfaction and longevity, but there is evidence that joint assets increase commitment.

References

1. Coontz, S. 2005. *Marriage, a History: From Obedience to Intimacy, or How Love Conquered Marriage.* New York: Viking.
2. Kline, G. H., N. D. Pleasant, S. W. Whitton, and H. J. Markman. 2006. "Understanding couple conflict." In *The Cambridge Handbook of Personal Relationships,* edited by A. L. Vangelisti and D. Perlman, 445–462. New York: Cambridge University Press.
3. Rick, S. I., D. A. Small, and E. J. Finkel. In Press. "Fatal (Fiscal) Attraction: Spendthrifts and Tightwads in Marriage." *Journal of Marketing Research.*

4. Smock, P. J., and E. Jennings. 2009. "Money and Couple Relationships." In *The Encyclopedia of Human Relationships,* edited by H. T. Reis and S. Sprecher, 1111–1115. Thousand Oaks, CA: Sage.

5. Burgoyne, C. B., V. Clarke, J. Reibstein, and A. Edmunds. 2006. "'All My Worldly Goods I Share with You'? Managing Money at the Transition to Heterosexual Marriage." *The Sociological Review* 54: 619–637.

6. Lauer, S. R., and C. Yodanis. 2011. "Individualized Marriage and the Integration of Resources." *Journal of Marriage and Family* 73: 669–683.

Dig Deeper

Coontz, S. 1997. *The Way We Really Are.* New York: Basic Books.

Pahl, J. 1995. "His Money, Her Money: Recent Research on Financial Organization in Marriage." *Journal of Economic Psychology* 1: 361–376.

Q26: WILL MY HUSBAND RESENT ME IF I MAKE MORE MONEY THAN HE DOES?

Jennifer J. Harman

"Oh, please let him earn more money than I do. You may not understand that now, but believe me, you will one day. Otherwise, that's a recipe for disaster."

—Alex Goran (Vera Farmiga), *Up in the Air*, 2007

This was relationship advice given to the character Natalie Keegan by an older female colleague in the 2009 movie *Up in the Air* when they were discussing important characteristics for a marital partner. Although some historians think this sentiment may be outdated as attitudes toward gender and marriage have changed, others think that the increased status of women can result in backlash against them. So, what happens to relationships when wives start earning more money than their husbands? Do husbands resent their wives?

Income, power, and equity in marriages

Although women on average still earn significantly less money than men (approximately 75.5 cents for every dollar in the United States[1]), women have made some strides. In 1970, only 4% of wives earned more money than their husbands; 22% of wives did in 2007. Married women today, compared to 1970, are also more likely to have a higher education level than their spouses.[2] Basically, over the past few decades, men have had access to a larger and larger number of financially secure and educated spouses; women have seen decreases.

Can differences in income lead to power imbalance in a relationship? Some psychological theories predict that any valuable resource, such as money, can be exchanged for other benefits, like power. The data, however, are not as clean cut. Some surveys show that married women's increased income allows them to make more household decisions,[3] and whoever makes less money in the relationship tends to take on a greater burden of housework, regardless of gender.[4] Other studies, however, show that a man's power and status in the home remains about the same—even when their wife makes more money![5] In other words, not only does he get to have a "sugar-momma," but he doesn't have to do extra housework as well.

Role expectations may partially account for these differing results. Traditionally, husbands have been the "breadwinners" and wives have been the "homemakers." Today, however, modern gender roles have both partners sharing these roles.[6] If a husband and wife are traditional, the wife usually defers to her husband ("Yes, honey, you can have the remote"). But if partners are more modern-minded, they may coordinate their power and influence across situations ("You pick the TV show, but I pick the vacation destination"). In one study of marriages in which the wife earned more money than the husband, money provided little power advantage for the women in their relationships; couples used their role expectations for each other to drive how they interacted and made decisions.[5] These couples worked together to establish and maintain roles in their relationship based on their expectations for what each partner should be doing, with traditional gender roles informing those expectations.

Expectations and relationships

Now, to the original question: How might these expectations influence perceptions of one's partner? In a survey of married adults, husbands who were perceived as providing more to the family reported feeling appreciated and their wives reported feeling grateful.[7] Who doesn't enjoy a nice paycheck? It's a win–win situation. If the wife was perceived as the "provider," the husband was not any more grateful than other husbands, and women did not feel particularly appreciated. Here, husbands get the benefit of someone else being the provider, but aren't exactly thankful for it. On the bright side, other than not feeling *more* appreciated, there didn't seem to be any negative consequences when women earned more money in these relationships, from either the male or female's perspective. In another large survey, relationship problems were not associated with a wife making more money than her husband.[8] Clearly, we've come a long way since the 1950s TV show "Father Knows Best," but we still have a way to go.

So when might a husband resent his wife for earning more?

Husbands experience more resentment when gender role expectations in the relationship do not match their actual relationship experience. If the man is more modern and the woman is more traditional, there are typically fewer problems, because the woman usually does what the man wants in terms of taking on the heavier load of cooking, cleaning, and child rearing.[9] However, there can be problems when the woman is more modern and the man is more traditional. In these relationships, the wife may resist her husband's wishes (e.g,, she isn't super keen on being barefoot, pregnant, and cooking Sunday dinners while he watches football all day). As a result, the traditional man may be annoyed that his expectations are not being met.[6] Women in these relationships are typically unhappy, and their husbands are more withdrawn and less trusting.[10] These expectations even play a role in decisions to marry. When men have modern gender role views and expect to share the provider role with a spouse, they are likely to marry earlier, whereas men who expect to play the provider role delay marriage longer, until they are more financially stable (given that age and income are positively correlated). Lower-income individuals tend to hold more traditional gender-role expectations than do higher-income individuals, and this has been used as one explanation as to why some lower-income men are less likely to marry.[11]

How do women's earnings affect parenting?

Children and parenting expectations might also create problems in marriages when the wife makes more money. Parental roles oftentimes force modern women into less powerful caretaking positions and modern men into more powerful positions (i.e., after a child is born, household task division adheres more closely to traditional divisions, resulting in substantially more work for women). Indeed, for women who make more money than their spouses, role strains associated with parenting and inequity in household chore assignment were found to be stronger predictors of marital problems.[8] Basically, a woman earning more money is helpful for the marriage only if she also isn't doing the lion's share of the housework. Conversely, stay-at-home fathers who take on the homemaker role entirely (aka "Mr. Mom") often face considerable stigma from society for violating traditional gender roles.[12] (We'd have to ask Gaylord

Focker if the stigma is more or less pronounced for male nurses.) The long-term ramifications of this role reversal are yet unknown, but strains and stressors from within and outside the family structure can ultimately cause problems in relationships.

* * *

How can you best navigate these potential problems? First, select a mate who shares your expectations for how to balance decision making and other roles in the relationship. This is one way to ensure fewer problems. If both partners work outside the home, communication and conflict management skills can help them address role strain more effectively, which can also increase marital satisfaction and marital quality.[13] The actual way that household decisions and responsibilities are divided (assuming all decisions are not based on heated matches of rock-paper-scissors) matters less than how fair each partner believes their division to be.[14] So, communication about what both partners think is fair in terms of household responsibilities, role expectations, and decision-making authority can help a lot too.

Conclusion

Overall, it seems that wives earning more money than their husbands isn't necessarily going to doom a relationship. However, the one clear downfall is that women don't necessarily get a fair deal in terms of division of household labor. Marital satisfaction seems to be based more on shared expectations regarding gender roles and clear and open communication and less on who has the bigger paycheck.

TAKE-HOME POINTS

♡ Women still earn less, on average, than men, but this gap is closing.
♡ Conflict arises when gender role expectations do not match, such as when a husband holds traditional gender roles and his wife has a more egalitarian viewpoint.
♡ Selecting a mate with similar expectations about decision making and household responsibilities can help lessen relationship problems.

References

1. Longley, R. 2004. "Gender Wage Gap Widening, Census Data Shows: First Decline in Women's Real Earnings since 1995." About.com US Government Info. Retrieved on December 2, 2010, from http://usgovinfo.about.com/od/censusandstatistics/a/paygapgrows.htm

2. Fry, R., and D. Cohn. 2010, January 19. "New Economics of Marriage: The Rise of Wives." Pew Research Center. Retrieved on May 4, 2011, from http://pewresearch.org/pubs/1466/economics-marriage-rise-of-wives

3. Pew Social Trends Staff. 2008, September 25. "Women Call the Shots at Home; Public Mixed on Gender Roles in Jobs." Pew Research Center. Retrieved on December 1, 2010, from http://pewsocialtrends.org/2008/09/25/women-call-the-shots-at-home-public-mixed-on-gender-roles-in-jobs

4. Bittman, M., P. England, N. Folbre, L. Sayer, and G. Matheson. 2003. "When Does Gender Trump Money? Bargaining and Time in Household Work." *American Journal of Sociology* 109: 186–214.

5. Tichenor, V. 2005. "Maintaining Men's Dominance: Negotiating Identity and Power When She Earns More." *Sex Roles* 53: 191–205.

6. Amato, P. R., and A. Booth. 1995. "Changes in Gender Role Attitudes and Perceived Marital Quality." *American Sociological Review* 60: 58–66.

7. Deutsch, F. M., J. Roska, and C. Meeske. 2003. "How Gender Counts When Couples Count Their Money." *Sex Roles* 48: 291–303.

8. Rogers, S. J., and P. R. Amato. 2000. "Have Changes in Marriage Relations Affected Marriage Quality?" *Social Forces* 79: 731–753.

9. Scanzoni, J., and M. Szinovacz. 1980. *Family Decision-Making: A Developmental Sex Role Model.* Beverly Hills: Sage.

10. Haber, L. C., and J. K. Austin. 1992. "How Married Couples Make Decisions." *Western Journal of Nursing Research* 14: 322–342.

11. Koball, H. L. 2004. "Crossing the Threshold: Men's Incomes, Attitudes toward the Provider Role, and Marriage Timing." *Sex Roles* 51: 387–395.

12. Rochlen, A. B., R. A. McKelley, and T. A. Whittaker. 2010. "Stay-at-Home Fathers' Reasons for Entering the Role and Stigma Experiences: A Preliminary Report." *Psychology of Men and Masculinity* 11: 279–285.

13. Perrone, K. M., and E. L. Worthington, Jr. 2001. "Factors Influencing Ratings of Marital Quality by Individuals within Dual-Career Marriages: A Conceptual Model." *Journal of Counseling Psychology* 48: 3–9.

14. Lavee, Y., and R. Katz. 2002. "Division of Labor, Perceived Fairness, and Marital Quality: The Effect of Gender Ideology." *Journal of Marriage and the Family* 64: 27–39.

Dig Deeper

Baker, R., G. Kiger, and P. J. Riley. 1996. "Time, Dirt, and Money: The Effects of Gender, Gender Ideology, and Type of Earner Marriage on Time, Household-Task, and Economic Satisfaction among Couples with Children." *Journal of Social Behavior and Personality* 11: 161–177.

Gray-Little, B. and M. Burks. 1983. "Power and Satisfaction in Marriage: A Review and Critique." *Psychological Bulletin* 93: 513–538.

O'Reilly, S., D. Knox, and M. Zusman. 2009. "What College Women Want in a Marriage Partner." *College Student Journal* 43: 503–506.

Q27: Why Does One Person in a Relationship Tend to Always Get His or Her Way?

M. Minda Oriña

Why does one person in a relationship always get his or her way? Because the other person lets them. Okay, well, it's actually not quite that simple. Probably the best way to think about this topic is to consider the immortal words of the great philosopher George Costanza. You might recall this memorable scene from *Seinfeld* ("The Pez Dispenser" episode):

> George: No, everything is *not* going good. I'm very uncomfortable. I have no power. I mean, why should she have the upper hand. *Once* in my life I would like the upper hand. I have no hand—no hand at all. She has the hand; I have *no* hand...How do I get the hand?

Clearly, the "hand" George is referring to is POWER, or who has more influence in the relationship. In a perfect world, our partners would always share our hopes, our dreams, our wants, our viewpoints, and our needs. In that world power would be irrelevant because "What I want, you want; what I get, you get." Unfortunately, although that may be the way it works in fairy tales, not everyone is so lucky. Think about all the things that may cause tension between two people: who goes grocery shopping, who takes out the trash, should they see the latest Harry Potter movie or the recent Oscar winner on Friday night? Or perhaps you both want to go on vacation at the same time, but you want to go to the beach and your partner wants to go to New York City. You get the point: In any relationship, there are times when a little negotiation is needed. It's not unusual for two people to want different things and somebody has to win (and, by definition, somebody has to lose). Who is the winner going to be? The one with the most hand—that's who.

Where does power come from?

What determines whether one person has power over another? Researchers don't all agree on the answer to this question.[1] Some people believe that men tend to have power because society tends to give more power to men in general. Many marriage vows contain the pledge by the wife to obey the husband (and not vice versa), presumably giving him precedence when decisions are made, but times are changing, and even Kate Middleton didn't promise to obey Prince William. However, others argue that because women tend to "manage" close relationships (i.e., they're more knowledgeable about relationships), they tend to have more power in their relationships. Neither explanation captures the whole picture, because a good understanding of how power comes about should work as well for heterosexual relationships as it does for gay and lesbian relationships, where the traditional gender role explanations don't necessarily apply.

As a result, many argue that looking at the relationship itself is the best way to understand how power develops. Consider Dick and Jane (or Dick and Jack, or Diane and Jane; it doesn't matter) and their relationship. See Dick. Dick absolutely and desperately loves Jane and wants his relationship with Jane to last forever. Not only does he love Jane, but Dick doesn't want to be with anyone else (or can't imagine that anyone else would ever date him). See Jane. Jane really isn't that into her relationship with Dick (perhaps because she likes Diane, but I digress…) and believes she could find another suitable partner with little trouble. Because Dick realizes this, he tends to do whatever Jane wants in order to keep her in the relationship. In this scenario, Jane hasn't asked for or taken power from Dick. Instead, Dick *gave* power to Jane. By wanting to be in a specific relationship with someone who doesn't care about maintaining the relationship as much, Dick has given Jane hand. This is called the *principle of least interest,* and Jane is the considered the weak-link partner in the relationship.[2,3] Basically, the person who wants something *least* has the *most* power. Business negotiators know this. That's why one of the things people in negotiations have to be able to do is be prepared to always walk away. Why? Walking away shows you're less interested than the other party. As a result, you now have more power.

Leveraging your power

This is why playing hard to get might be a particularly effective dating strategy. If you show that you're undecided about pursuing a relationship with someone, you've given yourself hand in that relationship. Not only will your suitor be more attracted to you (because you want what you can't have!), but if you do decide to date the person, you've put yourself in the driver's seat. A couple words of caution about trying to leverage yourself into power, however: First, although it might seem like it's a good thing to call the shots in the relationship, research has shown that people in relationships characterized by inequalities in power may experience more negative emotions, even if they are the person with the power.[4] For example, in couples in which the partners have disparate levels of commitment (one high and the other low), *both* relationship partners tend to display and reciprocate hostile behaviors, as compared to couples in which partners have similar commitment levels, regardless of whether those partners are highly or barely committed.[5] In addition, playing hard to get runs the risk of losing that partner altogether (should he or she become discouraged and abandon pursuit of you). Or, in an ongoing relationship, threats to leave a partner will obviously upset him or her, and your partner might decide to leave you, given that you don't reciprocate his or her love. In a sense, your partner can turn the power tables on you! So, you might get to pick what movie to see, but in the end, if you're not careful, you might be watching it alone.

In a nutshell, power in relationships is determined by the wants, needs, emotions, and dependence of the two individuals involved in the relationship. Here's another way to think about it: If your relationship were to end today, who would be the most devastated? If the answer is your partner, then congratulations, you're in command of this ship! But if you can't imagine life without your partner, but can envision you partner dropping you for someone else in a heartbeat, then you may as well forget about getting your way—that is, unless your partner, in a random act of kindness, let's you have your way just to keep things interesting.

Of course, there are other things that can influence the power equation. For example, some people have specific personality characteristics that contribute to them trying to maintain power in any relationship. These folks are labeled *domineering* and are generally the people you would describe as *power hungry*. Indeed, these people try to be dominant and controlling in their relationships (all relationships, not just the romantic ones). In addition, some people are more submissive or indecisive and actually prefer handing the reigns over to their partners. Furthermore, culture plays a role as well. For example, cultures that maintain traditional patriarchal (i.e., "Man is boss") customs often give power to men in relationship, regardless of whether they need or want it.

Conclusion

Overall, then, who's the boss in relationships? The one who most looks like Tony Danza? That would make things interesting! Ultimately, people get their way in relationships for a number of reasons. They might just have the kind of personality that makes them bossy and domineering (or their partner might be submissive), they may live in a culture or society that dictates who is supposed to have power, or the specific dynamics of the relationship can dictate who has the power. However, if one person always gets his or her way, then odds are that his or her partner may be needy, clingy, and overly dependent on the relationship.

TAKE-HOME POINTS

- ♡ The person who is least dependent on the relationship for good outcomes has the most power.
- ♡ Power in relationships often carries a high price. Relationships with large power inequalities are often characterized by high levels of negative emotion and hostility.
- ♡ Unless you have a domineering personality or are in a culture where power is prescribed, power emerges from the dynamics of the relationship.

References

1. Loving, T. J., K. L. Heffner, J. K. Kiecolt-Glaser, R. Glaser, and W. B. Malarkey. 2004. "Stress Hormone Changes and Marital Conflict: Spouses' Relative Power Makes a Difference." *Journal of Marriage and the Family* 66: 595–612.
2. Attridge, M., E. Berscheid, and J. A. Simpson. 1995. "Predicting relationship stability from both partners versus one." *Journal of Personality and Social Psychology* 69: 254–268.
3. Waller, W. W., and R. Hill. 1951. *The Family: A Dynamic Interpretation*. New York: Dryden Press.
4. Le, B., and C. R. Agnew. 2001. "Need Fulfillment and Emotional Experience in Interdependent Romantic Relationships." *Journal of Social and Personal Relationships* 18: 423–440.
5. Oriña, M. M., W. A. Collins, J. A. Simpson, K. C. Haydon, J. Kim, J., and J. A. Salvatore. In Press. "Developmental and Dyadic Perspectives on Commitment in Adult Romantic Relationships." *Psychological Science*.

Dig Deeper

Huston, T. L. 1983. "Power." In *Close Relationships*, edited by H. H. Kelley Berscheid, E., Christensen, A., Harvey, J. H., et al., 169–219. New York: Freeman.

Q28: Is Fighting with My Partner a Bad Sign?

Lisa A. Neff

"The process of selecting a partner for a long-term relationship should involve the realization that you will inevitably be choosing a set of unresolvable problems that you will be grappling with for the next ten, twenty, or fifty years."

—Dan Wile, Clinical Psychologist[1]

Imagine you have been casually dating two different people, but recently you have decided you are ready to settle down and start a committed relationship with one of them. Do you choose the person who is smart, attractive, and funny, yet is a bit of a slob around the house? Or do you choose the person who is smart, attractive, and funny, yet occasionally spends money a little too frivolously? Given that both partners have the same virtues, which vice is more appealing? This may seem like an odd question, but this scenario illustrates the message of the opening quote. Namely, when you choose a relationship partner, you are also making a choice about the kinds of conflicts you will be having in the years to come. Think about it this way: When two people form a relationship, they each bring a unique set of goals, needs, and preferences to the table. As a result, partners may often find themselves in situations where they both cannot simultaneously have what they want. You may want to save money for a better place to live, but your partner wants to splurge on an awesome movie-screen-size flat-panel television (which would admittedly make your current place better). You want to spend the weekend at a local music festival, but your partner wants to go jousting at the renaissance fair. These things wouldn't be a problem if you were dating a perfect clone of yourself, but where is the fun in that? Let's face it, your partner isn't perfect, but you aren't perfect either. In any relationship between imperfect people, some amount of conflict is inevitable.

When is conflict more likely to rear its ugly head?

Interestingly, it seems couples are more likely to fight in particular locations and at specific times of the day. One study asked married couples to describe their relationship interactions every day over a two-week period.[2] Couples reported arguing more in the kitchen than in any other location. (Maybe because that's where the knives are stored?) They also reported arguing more on weekdays than on weekends. In fact, the early evening weekday hours, when partners were transitioning from work to their roles at home, seemed to be an especially turbulent period for couples. Finally, and perhaps not surprisingly, disagreements were more likely to occur on days when partners reported experiencing more life stress (e.g., work stress, sickness). We have all been there before, haven't we? You come home after a long and stressful day and all you want to do is sit in front of the TV with a bowl of your favorite cereal to unwind. Unfortunately, as you reach for your Frosted Flakes, you discover that your partner once again put an empty cereal box back in the pantry. Normally, you might shrug it off; today, however, that same behavior makes you want to scream. When couples are under greater stress, they often are more easily annoyed by each other's less-than-perfect behaviors.

The key to relationship success is lack of conflict—right?

So what does all this mean for the relationship? If you want to maintain a happy and healthy relationship, should you avoid interacting with your partner in the kitchen on weekdays just after you return home from work? Not exactly. What if you were sure to keep your pantry stocked with sugary cereals? Nope. Relationship scientists have found that the mere presence of conflict does not necessarily indicate that the relationship is in trouble. Rather, what is important for relationship success is how couples manage the conflicts that do inevitably arise. In other words, the key to a healthy relationship is learning how to discuss your differences in a way that prevents the development of negative feelings between you and your partner. For instance, suppose you find yourself in an argument with your partner about keeping the house clean. Your partner accuses you of leaving dirty dishes in the sink...again. Responding with, "Oh, yeah, well you always leave your shoes in the middle of the living room floor— who's the slob now?" is probably not the best way to resolve this issue. In fact, responding to a partner's negative behavior with further negative behavior, a process known as *negative reciprocity*, has been shown to be quite harmful. In one study, researchers brought couples into a laboratory setting and had them rate the degree to which they argued about particular topics in their relationship.[3] Next, couples picked one important problem that they would work to resolve while being videotaped. Based on researchers' *coding* (i.e., detailed observation and quantification) of the couples' verbal and nonverbal behaviors seen in the recordings, unhappy couples engaged in more negative reciprocity than happy couples. It seems that unhappy couples have a tendency to become trapped in spirals of negativity. Happy couples, however, were more likely to respond to a partner's negativity with positive and constructive behaviors like agreement, summarizing what the partner is saying, and problem solving. In this way, happy couples found ways to prevent the argument from escalating out of control. For example, instead of snapping back when your partner criticizes you, you might suggest that the two of you work together to create a household chore list.

The demand–withdraw pattern: It's particularly bad

The time has come. Your partner needs to get a job. The bills are piling up while your partner sits around the house playing Angry Birds and watching reruns of *Friends*. To provide your partner with the necessary motivation, you've decided to apply a bit of pressure by dropping not-so-subtle hints like, "I wish we had more money so that we didn't have to eat Hot Pockets every night." When that doesn't work, you resort to frequent reminders like, "Did you remember to check the job ads?" or "Did you update your resume?" At times you even criticize your partner by saying things like, "I never realized you were so lazy," or "This is great. I always wanted to live poor and pay all of the bills." Of course, you only do this out of love and to provide your partner with a source of motivation. However, your partner perceives all of this "encouragement" as nagging, annoying criticism. As a result, any time you begin to talk about jobs, your partner tunes you out, changes the subject, gives you the silent treatment, or leaves the room. This style of dealing with conflict is known as the *demand–withdraw pattern*. As one partner pushes and prods, the other partner responds by avoiding the conflict. As demand escalates, withdraw escalates. As you might expect, studies show that couples who exhibit this pattern more frequently become less satisfied in their relationships as time goes on.[4]

"It's not what you say, but how you say it."

You've probably heard this saying before. Well, there is a lot of scientific truth to that nugget of wisdom. Imagine you ask your partner what he or she wants for dinner that evening and your partner responds by saying, "Whatever you want, honey." These four simple words can have a very different meaning, depending on the speaker's tone of voice and style of delivery. If your partner responds with a smile and a lighthearted tone, these words can indicate a genuine interest in your desires. However, if your partner responds with a sneer and an eye-roll, these same words are likely to lead to an uncomfortable conversation. It turns out that the emotional tone of couples' conversations is highly predictive of relationship outcomes. Newlywed couples who exhibit more negative emotions, such as anger and contempt (e.g., eye-rolling) when discussing their problems are more likely to divorce during the first seven years of marriage.[5] However, newlyweds who express more positive affect, such as humor or affection, when talking about their issues report being happier in the marriage years later.[6] Interestingly, this last finding was true even if spouses exchanged a few harsh words, such as criticizing or blaming one's partner, during the discussion. This means you may be able to complain about how you never go out anymore, provided you do so with a bit of humor ("We should get out more—it's not okay that I'm in pajamas on the couch on Friday nights at 10 pm—although that is a whole hour past my regular bedtime!"). In other words, expressing positive emotions during conflict discussions may help protect the relationship from the effects of poor communication skills. Why would this be? When spouses use more humor in their conflict discussions, partners tend to feel closer to one another and are more likely to report that the conflict was effectively resolved.[7] When it comes to working out the differences with your partner, a little humor (which is not the same as sarcasm!) may go a long way toward reducing tension and reaffirming that you are both in it together.

Conclusion

In virtually any relationship between two people, some level of conflict is inevitable. So remember: It's not *whether* you fight, it's *how* you fight that really matters. As long as you fight fair and perhaps with a little humor, conflict won't destroy your relationship.

TAKE-HOME POINTS

♡ Conflict is most likely to occur when spouses are tired and stressed.

♡ There are good and bad ways to fight. Humor, empathy, and demonstrating listening are positive conflict tactics, whereas showing disgust and contempt are particularly negative.

♡ A pattern of conflict in which one person continually makes demands (nags) and the other responds by avoiding or with-·drawing is an especially toxic way of interacting.

References

1. Wile, D. B. 1988. *After the Honeymoon: How Conflict Can Improve Your Relationship*. New York: John Wiley and Sons, Inc.
2. Halford, W. K., F. M. Gravestock, R. Lowe, and S. Scheldt. 1992. "Toward a Behavioral Ecology of Stressful Marital Interactions." *Behavioral Assessment* 14: 199–217.
3. Gottman, J., H. Markman, and C. Notarius, C. 1977. "The Topography of Marital Conflict: A Sequential Analysis of Verbal and Nonverbal Behavior." *Journal of Marriage and the Family* 39: 461–477.
4. Heavey, C. L., A. Christensen, and N. M. Malamuth. 1995. "The Longitudinal Impact of Demand and Withdrawal during Marital Conflict." *Journal of Consulting and Clinical Psychology* 63 (5): 797–801.
5. Gottman, J., and R. Levenson. 2000. "The Timing of Divorce: Predicting When a Couple Will Divorce over a 14-Year Period." *Journal of Marriage and the Family* 62 (3): 737–745.
6. Johnson, M. D., C. L. Cohan, J. Davila, E. Lawrence, R. D. Rogge, B. R. Karney, K. T. Sullivan, and T. N. Bradbury. 2005. "Problem Solving Skills and Affective Expressions as Predictors of Change in Marital Satisfaction." *Journal of Consulting and Clinical Psychology* 73: 15–27.
7. Campbell, L., R. A. Martin, and J. R. Ward. 2008. "An Observational Study of Humor Use While Resolving Conflict in Dating Couples." *Personal Relationships* 15: 41–55.

Dig Deeper

Heffner, K. L., J. K. Kiecolt-Glaser, T. J. Loving, R. Glaser, and W. B. Malarkey. 2004. "Spousal Support Satisfaction as a Modifier of Physiological Responses to Marital Conflict in Younger and Older Couples." *Journal of Behavioral Medicine* 27 (3): 233–254.

Randall, A. K., and G. Bodenmann. 2009. "The Role of Stress on Close Relationships and Marital Satisfaction." *Clinical Psychology Review* 29 (2): 105–115.

Sullivan, K. T., L. A. Pasch, M. D. Johnson, and T. N. Bradbury. 2010. "Social Support, Problem Solving, and the Longitudinal Course of Newlywed Marriage." *Journal of Personality and Social Psychology* 98 (4): 631–644.

Q29: Should I Really "Forgive and Forget" When My Partner Isn't Perfect or Messes Up?

Nancy E. Frye

Think back to the last time when your partner really annoyed you. I mean seriously irked you. Maybe your partner neglected several of your texts, forgot to mail in the mortgage check, flirted with your best friend, forgot your anniversary, or was implicated with a call girl while serving as Attorney General of New York. If any of these ever happened, it would be nice if life was like a cartoon where you could safely smash your partner with an anvil, confident that he or she would spring back into shape. Let's face it; Your partner isn't perfect 100% of the time. The question becomes, then, what's the best way to respond when your partner shows off his or her less than perfect side?

How can forgiveness benefit the relationship?

Well, on the one hand, it seems like there's some merit to that "Turn the other cheek" way of dealing with things. First, if you tend to forgive your partner, it may be a sign of how you feel about your relationship. People who are more committed to their relationships tend to be the most willing to forgive their partners' less than desirable behaviors—and they also see those behaviors in the best possible light.[1] Did your partner put an empty milk carton in the refrigerator, leaving that bowl of cereal you just poured stranded on the counter? Surely that only happened because he or she had a rough day at work, hit traffic on the way home, or wanted to spend more time with you. (Who has time for recycling anyway?) Here, giving a little benefit of the doubt turns a potentially negative situation into something much less threatening to the relationship. So, chances are, the more forgiving you feel when your partner messes up, the more you probably want your relationship to last a long time. Even more than that, forgiveness and commitment seem to have a cyclical relationship, where commitment helps people forgive their partner, and forgiveness helps people feel more committed to their relationship.[2] So, if you're going to be in this relationship for the foreseeable future, you should forgive some of your partner's forgetful behaviors so that you can better enjoy your time together. Reciprocally, because you are forgiving, your partner may be more inclined to be committed to you, with your wonderful ability to overlook his or her peccadilloes.

Your tendency to forgive your partner's wrongdoings reflects your current relationship feelings and may also provide a glimpse into how your relationship may develop into the future. A study that tracked more than 100 married couples over a six-month period found that spouses who were initially more forgiving continued to be more forgiving six months later. Also, more-forgiving spouses tended to be more satisfied with their relationships.[3] In other words, if you hold grudges against your spouse now, you're likely to keep doing so in the future and to start feeling a bit disgruntled about your relationship. In addition to being related to later relationship feelings, forgiveness also predicts later relationship behaviors. For example, wives who were more forgiving of their husbands earlier in the relationship tended to have husbands who later reported that they, as a couple, were better able to resolve arguments and disagreements over time.[4] Thus, it seems that forgiving your partner may build up a sense of goodwill that paves the way for better conflict resolution later in your relationship.

How can forgiveness help me?

Beyond helping the relationship, forgiveness also seems to help the individual who is doing the forgiving. (Maybe this is why Mel Gibson still has friends!) Think of friends you know who tend to hold grudges. Now, think of the friends you know who tend to turn the other cheek and forgive and forget. Odds are that the second group of friends, those who forgave all of the people who made fun of them in high school for their mullet hairstyle, tend to be happier and healthier. This tendency for forgivers to be happier and healthier than non-forgivers is especially true for older people; it does not pay to carry grudges with you to your grave; doing so will only make you more likely to get there and less happy on the way.[5]

Is forgiveness always the best strategy?

When it comes to your partner's negative behavior, so far, turning the other cheek seems to make the most sense when it comes to benefitting the relationship and your own personal health and life satisfaction. Before you start looking for Hallmark's stock of "I forgive you" cards, however, there's actually a little more research on the subject of forgiveness that merits some attention.

The ability for forgiveness to influence relationship satisfaction and people's happiness with themselves tends to vary depending on the kind of partner who is the object of potential forgiveness (i.e., the *forgivee*). Imagine you're dating Sally or Sam Screw-up (think Lindsay Lohan or Charlie Sheen). First, Sally or Sam puts the empty milk carton in the refrigerator. Then, Sally or Sam forgets to come home early to let the dog out, and you come home to an unhappy dog and a messy floor. Then, Sally or Sam forgets your birthday. Again and again, you take the high road and forgive Sally or Sam because you are thinking about how forgiveness will be good for your relationship commitment, relationship satisfaction, conflict resolution, karma, and so on. Odds are that constantly turning the other cheek to your partner's transgressions will inevitably get old after a while. In fact, research that followed newlyweds during the first two years of marriage shows that the more frequently one spouse messes up, the more likely it is that the other spouse with a forgiving nature will actually become less happy over time.[6] In other words, when married to a Sally Screw-up, over time, spouses who are *less* forgiving end up happier. This is important, so it's worth stating again: Forgiving the occasional transgression—good. Forgiving the frequent transgression—bad.

Perhaps all this forgiving of your partner is encouraging his or her bad behavior to some degree. To test this, more than 100 newlyweds were followed over a seven-day period.[7] Each day participants indicated whether their partners screwed up and whether they forgave their partners. It turned out that when the partner did something wrong and was forgiven, that partner was twice as likely to do something wrong the next day compared to when a partner wasn't forgiven for negative behavior. It was almost as if forgiveness was enabling the partner's bad behavior. You could just imagine the forgiven partner thinking, "I know you'll be mad if I get home late from hanging out with my friends, but you ultimately forgive me when I'm inconsiderate, so what's the harm in doing it again?" Give them an inch, and they take your soul.

Can being too forgiving hurt me?

It turns out that feeling like you always have to forgive your partner may end up lowering your feelings of self-respect over time.[8] How many times can people forgive their partner before they start feeling like a doormat who has their good nature taken for granted? This doesn't mean that if you're with Sally or Sam Screw-up you should suddenly become Graham or Glenda Grudgekeeper, however. Again, it really depends on what your partner is like. If your partner keeps screwing up, but is at least trying to make amends, forgiveness shouldn't threaten your self-respect. Also, if your partner screws up, but you're pretty sure it's a one-time thing and not a repeat offense, your self-respect probably won't take a blow from forgiving him or her. And if your partner is repeatedly putting empty milk cartons into the fridge and you consider this a relatively minor offense (and besides, you always leave your socks on the living room floor), then forgiving is probably the right choice. In all of these cases, it may not be so bad to forgive your partner.

Conclusion

The bottom line is that turning the other cheek is usually the way to go. However, if you feel like you're turning the other cheek so often that you're getting whiplash, you may want to take a closer look at this person you're constantly forgiving. Remember, no one is perfect, and you're bound to get irked at your partner now and then. As long as your partner is earnestly trying to do better in the future, forgiveness is most likely the best policy. Just don't write a blank forgiveness check.

TAKE-HOME POINTS

♡ Forgiving minor transgressions by your partner or even major transgressions that your partner seems genuinely willing to avoid in the future strengthens your relationship and makes you happier and healthier.

♡ Forgiving a partner who continually violates your trust and who seems unwilling to change their negative behavior will likely result in you being less healthy and happy in the future.

References

1. Finkel, E. J., C. E. Rusbult, M. Kumashiro, and P. A. Hannon. 2002. "Dealing with Betrayal in Close Relationships: Does Commitment Promote Forgiveness?" *Journal of Personality and Social Psychology* 82: 956–974.
2. Karremans, J. C., P. A. M. VanLange, and R. W. Holland. 2005. "Forgiveness and Its Associations with Prosocial Thinking, Feeling, and Doing Beyond the Relationship with the Offender." *Personality and Social Psychology Bulletin* 31: 1315–1326.
3. Paleari, F. G., C. Regalia, and F. Fincham. 2005. "Marital Quality, Forgiveness, Empathy, and Rumination: A Longitudinal Analysis." *Personality and Social Psychology Bulletin* 31: 368–378.
4. Fincham, F., S. R. H. Beach, and J. Davila. 2007. "Longitudinal Relations between Forgiveness and Conflict Resolution in Marriage." *Journal of Family Psychology* 21: 542–545.
5. Toussaint, L. L., D. R. Williams, M. A. Musick, S. A. and Everson. 2001. "Forgiveness and Health: Age Differences in a U.S. Probability Sample." *Journal of Adult Development* 8: 249–257.
6. McNulty, J. K. 2008. "Forgiveness in Marriage: Putting the Benefits into Context." *Journal of Family Psychology* 22: 171–175.
7. McNulty, J. K. 2010. "Forgiveness Increases the Likelihood of Subsequent Partner Transgressions in Marriage." *Journal of Family Psychology* 24 (6): 787–790. doi:10.1037/a0021678
8. Luchies, L. B., E. J. Finkel, J. K. McNulty, and M. Kumashiro. 2010. "The Doormat Effect: When Forgiveness Erodes Self-Respect and Self-Concept Clarity." *Journal of Personality and Social Psychology* 98: 734–749.

Dig Deeper

Fincham, F. D., S. R. H. Beach. 2002. "Forgiveness in Marriage: Implications for Psychological Aggression and Constructive Communication." *Personal Relationships* 9: 239–251.
Gordon, K. C., F. M. Hughes, N. D. Tomcik, L. J. Dixon, and S. C. Litzinger. 2009. "Widening Spheres of Impact: The Role of Forgiveness in Marital and Family Functioning." *Journal of Family Psychology* 23: 1–13.
Paleari, F. G., C. Regalia, and F. D. Fincham. 2011. "Inequity in Forgiveness: Implications for Personal and Relational Well-Being." *Journal of Social and Clinical Psychology* 30: 297–324.

CHAPTER 8

Sex

"Let's talk about sex, baby. Let's talk about you and me." Thank you Salt-N-Pepa. (If you have ever heard this song it will now be stuck in your head for the rest of the day. You're welcome.) Frankly, there is a lot to talk about here, mainly because sex is a key factor that distinguishes romantic relationships from friendships. As a result, deciding when to have sex is important so that your relationship gets off on the right track. But how do you know *when* is *right*? Should you wait for love? Or does love only come after sex? Or perhaps you're waiting for marriage, but isn't that where your sex life goes to die? Or is that only true for some couples that just happen to have a direct pipeline to public opinion? If only there were statistics on people's sex lives so you could see how your sex life stacks up. Good news. We have some numbers for you. Let the comparisons begin!

Q30: How Long Should I Wait before Sleeping with My Partner?

Jennifer J. Harman

Okay, so you've met a hottie, hit it off, and are having a fantastic time. You can tell she wants you, and you're in the mood too! One thing leads to another, and before you know it, you are getting it on just like a scene from *Basic Instinct* (but without the ice pick, hopefully). Now, some of you reading this may be totally psyched and may not be thinking much of anything. Others may be thinking, "Should we be having sex? We hardly know each other! What's your name again?" or "Will she think I'm easy if we have sex?" or even,

"Does she do this on all her first dates?" (Of course not; she did say she's never done this before, right?)

Will my partner respect me if we have sex on the first date?

These questions don't come out of nowhere. How many times have you heard, "Why buy the cow when you can have the milk for free?" (Incidentally, we'd like to suggest a new saying "Why buy the diamond mine when you can get the diamonds for free?" This way no one has to be a cow; see also question 14.) Or "They won't respect you in the morning." Surprisingly, the answer to whether your partner will respect you if you give it up right away is fairly straightforward and depends on your response to one (seemingly) simple question: What do you and your partner each want? People can have many goals for a first date: having fun, getting to know the person better, impressing your friends with how hot your date is, looking for a long term relationship, having sex, and so on. You may start with one goal being more important than others, but change your priorities as the date goes on. For instance, suppose a guy asks you out and you think he is average looking, but he makes you laugh. Your intention at the beginning of the date may to just be friends and have fun, which is why you didn't bother to clean your apartment, but you may begin to really like him as the date goes on. You may even find him more sexually attractive as the hours (and tequila shots) go by. What really determines whether a date is "good" or "bad," and how you and your partner subsequently feel the next morning, is whether you had similar goals for the evening.

Do men and women have different goals for first dates?

This is the million-dollar question. Although research shows that sex is a goal more often for men than women on first dates, *both* men and women do want to get to know the other person better and see whether they might want a romantic relationship. For instance, surveys of college students[1] show that an overwhelming number of people, both men and women, go on a first date primarily to get to know another person better and to have fun (not to mention that it's usually better than getting a root canal). Less than 10% of people (although more men than women) list sex as their primary goal for the first date. In other words, men and women are surprisingly similar— most people go on a first date to figure out if it's worth pursuing a relationship with someone. You're both checking out the merchandise.

Another way to look at this question is to think about what sex means to different people. Women are more likely than are men to connect sex with love and intimacy. Across many studies, men consistently are more open-minded toward casual sex and don't think sex and intimacy have to be connected.[2] Love and marriage may go together like a horse and carriage, but sex and relationships go together like chocolate and peanut butter—sometimes they are perfect together, but sometimes chocolate is better alone. Therefore, on a first date, if the man's goals are to have sex, this goal may or may not be related to whether he wants to develop a relationship. However, for women, sex may be a way to achieve the goal of intimacy; having sex and wanting a romantic relationship are linked for women. In other words, some women believe that by having sex they might help *create* that romance. Interestingly, in this same study, as men's sexual goals increased, they actually became *less* interested in getting to know their partners! Wow.

These findings do not mean that a man would respect the woman less if she had sex with him on a first date, however. Many psychologists believe that we have *relationship scripts* that influence how, who, what, where, and when we interact with other people.[3] These are like movie scripts; they contain your expectations about the plot of the story, what is likely to happen to the characters in the story, and what the ending will be. These scripts influence how we interact with other people, including those we date. You decide if your date did or said the right things based on your expectations. Obviously, you can see how things get complicated when people have different ideas about how the story should unfold! If you are working under the "Let's get to know one another" script, and your date is working from the "Your place or mine" script, you each will have *very* different reactions to the date. Think about Ross and Rachel from *Friends*; when they first met, she was assuming that they would be friends ("Let's be friends" script) and he wanted to be dating her ("Much more than friends" script). This is where many of Ross's troubles (and much of the humor in the show) came from— they had very different goals for their relationship.

Where do expectations about sex come from?

These expectations don't appear out of nowhere; we learn them from family, friends, past experiences, romance novels, movies, and so on. In traditional American culture, women have often been seen as *loose* and *easy* if they have sex right away. This is part of a script of what is expected of women and is based in traditional gender roles. If a guy has sex on the first date, is he seen as loose or easy? Not usually! More like *stud, rock star,* or *professional athlete.* One interesting finding across many recent studies is that this sexual double standard appears to be going away.[4] For instance, more than 8,000 adults rated women with multiple sex partners very similar to men in terms of their values, popularity, and power. However, although it looks like the sexual double standard is slowly disappearing and sexual scripts are getting less traditional, it doesn't mean that *everyone* has changed their scripts. It sure would be nice to know what script your first date has ahead of time, wouldn't it?

The important part of these scripts is the settings and circumstances that lead up to the sexual encounter in question. Who asked out whom? Usually, the person who initiates the date has a clearer set of goals than the person who accepts the date. When you get asked out on a date, the person who asked you out usually sets the plans and has a clear vision for the evening. They certainly have goals for the date, and you may not have the same goals. Another thing to consider is the context in which the date occurs. Let's say you meet your date at a bar after having several martinis. What are your expectations for how this interaction will unfold? What are his expectations? Would it be different if you met at book store? Or let's say that you ask someone out on a date and find out that she is on the rebound from a really serious relationship. Although you may have at first thought that you wanted to get to know her more seriously, you realize that she is not ready for a relationship right now. Your original goal may switch to a sex goal ("rebound sex" script), or to being a friend ("not ready for anything serious" script).

If you are currently in your twenties or have seen an episode of *Jersey Shore,* you might have read this and found yourself asking, "Dating? Who dates?" One very popular script these days seems to be that of *hooking up,* which involves sexual activity but doesn't have any pretense toward romance. Hooking up typically occurs after (or during) parties or other group activities and is understood to be a solely sexual encounter (i.e., no strings attached). There are several possible reasons that the hooking-up script has become increasingly common, including the fact that the stigma attached to premarital sex has decreased greatly for women (admittedly, it was never very strong for men).[5] A recent book by two sociologists, Regnerus and Uecker,[6] suggests that hooking up may be becoming more common because college-educated women (translation: successful women) currently outnumber college-educated men (apparently being on a popular reality show also counts as success) . Why would this matter? Well, when something is a scarce resource, such as eligible and educated men, the scarce resource gets to call the sexual shots.[6] As discussed in question 31, men tend to be higher in sociosexuality, and this tendency to be more interested in sex without commitment means that when men call the shots, casual sexual encounters or hooking up is likely to become more common. Thus, if your goal is to find and develop an emotionally intimate relationship, then you might think about avoiding the hook-up scene altogether.

Conclusions

So, should you have sex on the first date, and, if you do, will he or she respect you in the morning? The trick is figuring out what script your date is working from and what his or her expectations are. But unfortunately, finding out isn't part of a normal dinner conversation. (Um, could you pass the salt and did you think we were having sex tonight and if you did, were you thinking a one-night stand or the start of something wonderful, and how are your enchiladas?) Ultimately, you have access only to the script with your lines on it. However, this doesn't mean that a little conversation and getting to know each other as the date goes on won't help you find out.

TAKE-HOME POINTS

♡ Our goals and expectations strongly influence how we interpret our dating behaviors; expectations for certain types of relationships (long-term versus short-term) can influence whether we view sex as okay when it happens early on.

♡ Men and women are found to vary on their goals for first dates, but the double standard of "early" sex has been diminishing in recent studies.

♡ Individuals higher on the sociosexuality scale are more likely to accept/engage in casual sex and engage in sexual behaviors when uncommitted.

References

1. Mongeau, P. A., M. C. M. Serewicz, and L. F. Therrien. 2004. "Goals for Cross-Sex First Dates: Identification, Measurement, and the Influence of Contextual Factors." *Communication Monographs* 71: 121–147.
2. Cohen, L. L. and R. L. Shotland. 1996. "Timing of First Sexual Intercourse in a Relationship: Expectations, Experience, and Perceptions of Others." *Journal of Sex Research* 33: 291–299.
3. Dworkin, S. L., and L. O'Sullivan. 2005. "Actual versus Desired Initiation Patterns among a Sample of College Men: Tapping Disjunctures within Traditional Male Sexual Scripts." *Journal of Sex Research* 42: 150–158.
4. Marks, M. J., and R. C. Fraley. 2005. "The Sexual Double Standard: Fact or Fiction?" *Sex Roles* 52: 175–186.
5. Bogle, K. A. 2010. "Hooking Up and Dating: A Comparison." In *Family in Transition*, 16th ed., edited by A. S. Skolnick and J. H. Skolnick, 134–154. Boston: Allyn & Bacon.
6. Regnerus, M., and J. Uecker. 2011. *Premarital Sex in America: How Young Americans Meet, Mate, and Think about Marrying.* New York: Oxford University Press.

Dig Deeper

Dworkin, S. L., and L. O'Sullivan. 2007. "'It's Less Work for Us and It Shows Us She Has Good Taste': Masculinity, Sexual Initiation, and Contemporary Sexual Scripts." In *The Sexual Self: The Construction of Sexual Scripts,* edited by M. E. Kimmel, 105–121. Nashville: Vanderbilt University Press.

Busby, D. M., J. S. Carroll, and B. J. Willoughby. 2010. "Compatibility or Restraint? The Effects of Sexual Timing on Marriage Relationships." *Journal of Family Psychology* 24: 766–774.

Sprecher, S., and K. McKinney. 1993. *Sexuality.* Newbury Park, CA: Sage.

Q31: Does Sex Lead to Love, or Does Love Lead to Sex? Is One "Direction" Better?

Jennifer J. Harman

We've all heard stories about couples having sex on their first date that then ended up happily committed or married to each other many years later. We've also heard stories of couples who waited to have sex with each other until they were in love or married, and are happily committed or married to each other years later. Indeed, the movie *He's Just Not That Into You*, based on the best-selling book of the same name, has a number of scenes in which the female characters discuss all the ways relationships can start out and end with "happy" endings of love and commitment. Although Hollywood movies and random stories of others by no means constitute data, they do provide the question: Does sex lead to love, does love lead to sex, or are both routes equally possible?

A good beginning point for addressing this question is to consider the function that sex may serve (ignoring, for now, the whole baby-making function). Sex not only motivates people to *connect* with one another (we use the term very loosely here), but it also serves as a "magnet" of sorts that keeps partners coming back until a true emotional bond can form.[1] When you have sex, the pleasure centers of your brain are stimulated in much the same way that partaking in other pleasurable experiences does (Can I PLEASE have more chocolate cake?).[2] As a result, you are likely to want to have more sex, which can eventually lead to emotionally based feelings of love. In other words, sex feels good; it leads to positive, happy, warm, tingling feelings that are very reinforcing; and these tingling feelings cause us to want to stay with the person who helps us have that experience.[3] This probably comes as no surprise, but from a scientific standpoint, it presents a bit of a "chicken and egg" issue. Do you have sex and then experience feelings that lead you to want to be with the person, or is it that wanting to be with the person, perhaps because they have a nice body (see question 1), that led you to want to have sex in the first place?

To sort this type of thing out definitively, you need a specialized situation where one group of people is purposefully led to think about sex while the other group is not (and there are all sorts of interesting ways to make sure sex *is not* on the brain, trust us). Then, you can test which group experiences more of a desire to establish a relationship. Such a design provides some information regarding whether sex *promotes* love (or attraction, anyway). Fortunately, some creative researchers did something just like this. In a set of carefully controlled experiments, participants were subliminally exposed to words and pictures that were either sexual or nonsexual in nature (let your imagination run free). When people *saw* the sexual words or erotic pictures outside of their awareness (i.e., they were exposed subliminally), they were more willing to self-disclose intimate information to a partner, they reported having more intimate thoughts, and they used more positive-conflict resolution strategies.[4] Sex, or even thoughts of sex that you don't realize you are having, make you use more relationship promotion strategies! In addition, the men (but not the women) were more willing to sacrifice important things for their partner. So, if you want your man to sacrifice his Sunday of watching football, you may want to get to work on subliminally priming sex.

Fine, but can sex lead to "love"?

The answer to this question really depends on what kind of love you are talking about. One type, *passionate love,* is the "hot-and-bothered" type of love that contains a strong sexual component.[5] Among other things, this type of love relies on feelings of strong physical attraction, arousal, and lust.[6] Provided that an individual is having lust-filled sex, it would certainly seem possible that sex can lead to feelings of passionate love. But there's a risk in letting sex play such a central role: If those lusty feelings start to go away, which is a strong possibility if partners are no longer having passionate sex, partners can start to feel like their love for each other has gone away too. In the best-case scenario, passionate love can transform into *companionate love,* which is more of a "best-friend" type of love. Of course, it may also lead to the perception that you've fallen out of love and that this isn't the relationship for you. So, sex can certainly lead to passionate love and, if you're lucky, companionate love as well.

Can love lead to sex?

Interestingly, how people define *love* determines the meaning of sex, and not the other way around.[7] Some people, for example, believe that love comes before sex (those people are generally women), whereas others may not (those people are generally men). It turns out that there may be some truth to the common perception that men need to have sex to fall in love, whereas women need to fall in love to have sex. Love within an emotionally bonded relationship is often the primary reason that women have sex for the first time,[8] whereas being sexually aroused or curious about sex is the primary reason men have sex for the first time.[9] Now, before we give too much credit or blame to men or women, it is important to point out that there is a psychological construct that may provide a better explanation. *Sociosexuality* is a person's inclination toward separating the experiences of love and sex.[10] A person high in sociosexuality, or someone referred to as *unrestricted*, is more likely to believe that sex without love is okay. It should come as no surprise that unrestricted people are more likely to enjoy casual sex. Whereas it is true that men are more likely to be unrestricted, individuals high in sociosexuality, regardless of gender, are more likely to have sex without requiring the experience of love.

Which path is better—Love first or sex first?

The answer to this question really depends on your expectations. If you believe that sex should only happen after both partners love each other, but you go out and have sex after a first date, for example, you will probably feel regret. These feelings of regret can contribute to lower levels of satisfaction and commitment to any relationship that may result, especially for women.[11] Some of the emotional reactions to sex depend on what precedes the sex. If couples express love before they have sex, the perception will likely become that the sexual act is an expression of love and commitment. But if lust, rather than love, is expressed before sex, then the sexual act would likely be interpreted as just a sexual act. Of course, as discussed earlier, even these sexual acts can eventually lead to feelings of love. In short, the answer to the question of which *should* come first is: *neither* direction is "best" for everyone. Much depends on what you personally want and expect from the sexual experience, and what the experience ultimately means for the relationship that you want to have with the person.

TAKE-HOME POINTS

♡ Positive outcomes associated with sexual behavior (i.e., pleasure) are reinforcing and make us want to repeat the behavior; this leads to greater likelihood of emotional attachment (i.e., love).

♡ People differ in their beliefs about what *sex* means; some equate sex with love, and others do not.

♡ Sex can sometimes lead to passionate love, which can lead to more stable companionate love; there is not however, evidence pointing to a correct ordering of these experiences.

References

1. Hazan, C., and D. Zeifman. 1994. "Sex and the Psychological Tether." In *Attachment Processes in Adulthood,* edited by K. Bartholomew and D. Perlman, 151–178. London: Jessica Kingsley.
2. Szechtman, H., M. Hershkowitz, and R. Simantov. 1981. "Sexual Behavior Decreases Pain Sensitivity and Stimulated Endogenous Opioids in Male Rats." *European Journal of Pharmacology* 70: 279–285.
3. Young, L. J., and Z. Wang. 2004. "The Neurobiology of Pair-Bonding." *Nature Neuroscience* 7: 1048–1054.
4. Gillath, O., M. Mikulincer, G. E. Birnbaum, and P. R. Shaver. 2008. "When Sex Primes Love: Subliminal Sexual Priming Motivates Relationship Goal Pursuit." *Personality and Social Psychology Bulletin* 34: 1057–1069.
5. Walster, E., and E. Berschied. 1971. "Adrenaline Makes the Heart Grow Fonder." *Psychology Today* 5: 47–62.
6. Regan, P. C. 2004. "Sex and the attraction process: Lesson from science (and Shakespeare) on lust, love, chastity, and fidelity." In *The Handbook of Sexuality in Close Relationships,* edited by J. H. Harvey, A. Wenzel, and S. Sprecher, 115–133. Mahwah NJ: Lawrence Erlbaum Associates.
7. Hendrick, S. S., and C. Hendrick. 2002. "Linking Romantic Love with Sex: Development of the Perceptions of Love and Sex Scale." *Journal of Social and Personal Relationships* 19: 361–378.
8. Christopher, F. S., and R. M. Cate. 1985. "Factors Involved in Premaraital Sexual Decision-Making." *Journal of Sex Research* 20: 363–376.
9. Laumann, E. O., J. H. Gagnon, R. T. Michael, and S. Michaels. 1994. *The Social Organization of Sexuality: Sexual Practices in the United States.* Chicago: University of Chicago Press.

10. Simpson, J. A., and S. W. Gangestad. 1991. "Individual Differences in Sociosexuality: Evidence for Convergent and Discriminant Validity." *Journal of Personality and Social Psychology* 60 (6): 870-883. doi:10.1037/0022-3514.60.6.870

11. Metts, S. 2004. "First Sexual Involvement in Romantic Relationships: An Empirical Investigation of Communicative Framing, Romantic Beliefs, and Attachment Orientation in the Passion Turning Point." In *The Handbook of Sexuality in Close Relationships*, edited by J. H. Harvey, A. Wenzel, and S. Sprecher, 135–158. Mahwah NJ: Lawrence Erlbaum Associates.

Dig Deeper

Baumeister, R. F., and D. M. Tice. 2001. *The Social Dimension of Sex*. Boston: Allyn & Bacon.

Sprecher, S. 2002. "Sexual Satisfaction in Premarital Relationships: Associations with Satisfaction, Commitment, and Stability." *The Journal of Sex Research* 2: 1–7.

Q32: WILL WE STOP HAVING SEX ONCE WE ARE MARRIED?

Jennifer J. Harman

In the Academy Award–winning film *Annie Hall*,[1] Woody Allen (Alvy) and Diane Keaton (Annie) spend one evening discussing why their sex life has changed so dramatically since they first started dating:

ALVY: It's always some kind of an excuse. It's—You know, you used to think that I was very sexy. What ... When we first started going out, we had sex constantly ... We're—we're probably listed in the Guinness Book of World Records.

ANNIE (Patting Alvy's hand solicitously): I know. Well, Alvy, it'll pass, it'll pass, it's just that I'm going through a phase, that's all.

ALVY: M'm.

ANNIE: I mean, you've been married before, you know how things can get. You were very hot for Allison at first.

Sex and marital status

Does sex change after people get married or have been a relationship for a long time? Does the "thrill" really go away? Could it be that simply living together takes away some of the romance, which results in less sexual desire for one's partner? I mean, is it really sexy to watch your partner brush their teeth or use the bathroom with the door open? But wait, cohabiting, unmarried couples report having sex more often than married couples.[2] A-ha! This must mean that it really is marriage that undermines sex. No, it isn't that simple either! Married people have more sex than single people.[3] Okay, married > single, but married < cohabitation. What's going on?

One explanation is that frequency of sex declines as the duration of the relationships increase (and people get older).[4] You might not be setting the bed on fire after marriage, but any changes in sexual frequency may not have much, if anything, to do with marital status and has more to do with marriage being a longer-term relationship between two people who are older. For example, relationships that have stood the test of time long enough to lead to marriage are the result of partners' commitment to each other. In fact, research shows that couples' level of psychological commitment to each other seems to matter most in making couples satisfied with their sexual relationship.[5] The connection between commitment and sexual satisfaction is also true in contexts other than marriage. For example, sexual satisfaction is high for non-married women who believe that their relationships will last forever and lowest when they believe their relationships are more temporary.[6]

It's important to note that you need to be careful when considering a category like marital status. Sure, you'll see research findings comparing married to non-married, or married to cohabitating, but always keep in mind that anything focusing too much on marital status is an oversimplification. What we mean here is that if you take a couple and look at them the day before they are married and compare them to the day after they are married, you likely won't see any big differences. The simple act of marriage doesn't change people much. Instead, there are other underlying psychological factors that are a little harder to see that ultimately account for the difference.

What leads to the perception that marriage destroys your sex life?

Where does the belief that marriage torpedoes your sex life come from? For one thing, relationships develop over time.[7] In the beginning, couples experience a *honeymoon phase*, a magical time when one's partner is novel and exciting; there is lots of sex and passion, experimentation, and intimacy.[8] This is the time when you become excited daydreaming about your partner, you think they're hot, the sight of them makes you feel tingly and your heart feel fluttery, and you may even obsessively write your partner's name repeatedly in your notebook. Unfortunately, this does not last forever. As partners and relationships mature, a working/responsibility phase begins, where the practical demands of life affect the amount of time partners can spend together, which in turn influences their sexual relationship.[9] In other words, time is a zero-sum game; work, family, and kids can all cut into the amount of time available to have sex. Life may also get in the way by creating extra stress that can inhibit the enjoyment of sex. For example, women report less sex during pregnancy,[2] with declines being most evident toward their last trimester.[10] Many studies also find a decline in satisfaction following the birth of a baby—a time when a crying baby, sleep deprivation, and diaper changes all influence how likely it is for partners to want to initiate and receive sexual advances from their partners.[10] The good news is that at retirement, many couples have more time for each other and sometimes report "rediscovering" their love for each other again, and this can result in a rekindled sexual relationship.[8]

What determines sexual satisfaction?

ALVY'S PSYCHIATRIST: How often do you sleep together?

ANNIE'S PSYCHIATRIST: Do you have sex often?

ALVY: Hardly ever. Maybe three times a week.

ANNIE: Constantly! I'd say three times a week.

Alvy and Annie agree about the amount of sex they are having, which is good sign because they are having it with each other. But having sex three times a week means different things to each partner, and this leads to very different feelings of (dis)satisfaction. Annie and Alvy may both be a bit unhappy, but the fact of the matter is that they have sex more often than most married couples, who average about 6.3 times a month, or a bit over 1.5 times per week.[2] This also highlights a funny thing about individuals' abilities to perceive the exact same situation in different ways. Alvy and Annie both agree on the objective reality of their relationship, but subjectively perceive that reality very differently. When you scrutinize the statistics, Alvy is having twice as much sex as the average husband, yet he isn't twice as happy. As you can see, sexual frequency may not be the best way to determine sexual satisfaction, because one person's definition of *a lot of sex* may vary considerably from another person's.

If sexual satisfaction isn't really about how often you crank up the Barry White tunes, there must be other factors that contribute. Such factors include things like whether orgasm is achieved, as well as individuals' general positive feelings about the experience. Often people mistakenly believe frequency matters the most for relationships because it's the easiest thing to quantify. However, *sexual satisfaction*, or how happy you are with your sexual experiences in your relationship, is a better predictor of relationship satisfaction.[6]

In fact, when partners report feeling sexually satisfied, they also are likely to report high relationship satisfaction (and vice versa).

So does being married make people less satisfied with their sex life? For most, the answer is no. When researchers asked people across the United States about their sex life, 88% of married individuals considered themselves "extremely" or "very" pleased with the sex in their relationships, even more so than couples who were just cohabitating or dating.[3] Such findings highlight the importance of quality over quantity. You may have sex less often after getting married or after being in a relationship for a long time, but when you do have sex, it may be better, more satisfying sex. Really, it comes down to a choice: Would you rather guzzle a liter of boxed wine, or enjoy the aromas and complexity of a finely aged glass of Bordeaux? So, even if you are married, both have full time jobs, with kids and a mortgage, the right combination of communication, commitment, love, and dedication to make time for each other can better ensure that you will be like the majority of married people: quite satisfied with your sex life.

Conclusion

Will you stop having sex once you're married? Not necessarily, but you will very likely stop having sex as much as you did before you were married. However, you won't necessarily be unhappy with your sex life. Part of a healthy sexual relationship is learning each other's turn-ons and turn-offs. That's a far easier task in a long-term relationship.

TAKE-HOME POINTS

♡ The demands of life (e.g., kids, work, illness) can interfere with sexual frequency dramatically, so it is not marital or relationship status per se that predicts this decline.

♡ Sexual satisfaction is more closely linked to quality rather than quantity. Fortunately, only frequency typically declines in longer-term relationships over time.

♡ Sexual satisfaction is strongly related to overall relationship satisfaction, so a focus on quality of each interaction rather than frequency is the way to go.

References

1. Allen, W., and M. Brickman. 1977 *Annie Hall*. Retrieved on December 6, 2010, from http://www.awesomefilm.com/script/anniehall.txt
2. Call, V., S. Sprecher, and P. Schwartz. 1995. "The Incidence and Frequency of Marital Sex in a National Sample." *Journal of Marriage and the Family* 57: 639–652.
3. Laumann, E. O., J. H. Gagnon, R. T. Michael, and S. Michaels. 1994. *The Social Organization of Sexuality: Sexual Practices in the United States.* Chicago: University of Chicago Press.
4. Blumstein, P., and P. Schwartz. 1983. *American Couples.* New York: Simon & Schuster.
5. Waite, L. J., and K. Joyner. 2001. "Emotional Satisfaction and Physical Pleasure in Sexual Unions: Time Horizon, Sexual Behavior, and Sexual Exclusivity." *Journal of Marriage and the Family* 63: 247–264.
6. Sprecher, S., and R. M. Cate. 2004. "Sexual Satisfaction and Sexual Expression as Predictors of Relationship Satisfaction and Stability." In *The Handbook of Sexuality in Close Relationships,* edited by J. H. Harvey, A. Wenzel, and S. Sprecher, 235–256. Mahwah NJ: Lawrence Erlbaum Associates.
7. Havinghurst, R. J. 1981. "Personality and Patterns of Aging." In *The Life Cycle,* edited by L. D. Steinberg, 341–348. New York: Columbia University Press.
8. Aubin, S., and Heiman, J. R. 2004. "Sexual dysfunction from a relationship perspective." In *The Handbook of Sexuality in Close Relationships,* edited by J. H. Harvey, A. Wenzel, and S. Sprecher, 477–517. Mahwah NJ: Lawrence Erlbaum Associates
9. Shibley-Hyde, J., J. D. DeLamater, and A. M. Durik. 2001. "Sexuality and Dual-Earner Couple, Part II: Beyond the Baby Years." *Journal of Sex Research* 38: 10–23.
10. Haugen, E. N., P. A. Schmutzer, and A. Wenzel. 2004. "Sexuality and the partner relationship during pregnancy and the post-partum period." In *The Handbook of Sexuality in Close Relationships,* edited by J. H. Harvey, A. Wenzel, and S. Sprecher, 411–435. Mahwah NJ: Lawrence Erlbaum Associates

Dig Deeper

Ahlborg, T., K. Rudeblad, S. Linnér, and S. Linton. 2008. "Sensual and Sexual Marital Contentment in Parents of Small Children—A Follow-Up Study When the First Child Is Four Years Old." *Journal of Sex Research* 45: 295–304.

Yabiku, S. T., and C. T. Gager. 2009. "Sexual Frequency and the Stability of Marital and Cohabiting Unions." *Journal of Marriage and Family* 71: 983–1000.

Q33: HOW DOES MY SEX LIFE STACK UP TO OTHERS?

Benjamin Le

First things' first: There is tremendous amount of variety in the sexual behaviors of Americans and people all over the world, so you should be careful in making evaluations about your sex life in comparison to others. The range of things that are *normal* is large; don't despair if you stack up unfavorably to the numbers reported here. Chances are that you will be above average in some ways, and below average in others. What's important is your level of sexual satisfaction (or dissatisfaction) prior to reading this chapter. If you are already perfectly happy with your sex life, don't let these statistics spoil your fun; but if you are currently dissatisfied with your life between the sheets, the numbers might provide some insight into why that's the case.

A brief history of sex research

The first research on sexual behavior in United States traces back to Alfred Kinsey,[1,2] who, in the late 1940s and early 1950s, began collecting statistical data on human sexuality and sexual practices via intensive interviews. Shortly thereafter, Masters and Johnson[3] began their studies on the physiological and psychological mechanisms involved in sexual behavior (i.e., detailed laboratory observation of research participants' sexual arousal, intercourse, and masturbation—where do I sign up?!). Although it is certainly sexy research (pardon the pun), it has less bearing on the question of what constitutes a "normal" sex life than does Kinsey's research. However, we won't directly discuss Kinsey's findings because they are now more than half a century old. Kinsey's data also were not entirely scientific because they were generated from a non-random sample (i.e., people who were willing to be interviewed about sex during that relatively conservative time period, at least by today's standards) that might not be representative of the American population.

Current sex research

Recent studies have done a better job gathering representative samples, including the *National Health and Social Life Survey*[4] (NHSLS); the *General Social Survey*[5] (GSS); and most recently, the *National Survey on Family Growth*[6] (NSFG) conducted between 2006 and 2008. Data from the NSFG were collected from nearly 13,500 people across the United States who ranged in age from teenagers through middle age (15–44 years old). Think of these studies as the scientific version of the sex polls you might see in magazines like *Cosmopolitan* or *Men's Health*.

The information that follows is intended as a quick look at some of the numbers; it's not meant to be comprehensive. Also, because the numbers largely speak for themselves, we are taking a bit of a *Dragnet* ("Just the facts") approach. Think of these numbers as your way of peeking in on your neighbors' sex lives in a socially acceptable way that avoids the hassle of hiding in bushes under a window. Note that these data are all self-reported; keep in mind that respondents may not have been completely honest (either overstating or understating their experience because of social desirability concerns). Unless otherwise noted, the following data are from the NSFG (not to be confused with NSFW).

Sexual attraction and sexual orientation

♡ 83% of women were attracted only to men, slightly less than 1% were attracted only to women, and 15% expressed some level of attraction to both sexes; 94% of women self-identify as heterosexual, 1% as homosexual/gay/lesbian, and 4% as bisexual.

♡ 94% of men were attracted only to women, slightly more than 1% were attracted only to men, and 5% expressed some level of attraction to both sexes; 96% of men self-identify as heterosexual, 2% as homosexual/gay, and 1% as bisexual.

Types of sexual activity

♡ For people between the ages of 25 and 44, 97% of men and 98% of women have engaged in (vaginal) intercourse, 90% of men and 89% of women have had oral sex with an opposite-sex partner, and 44% of men and 36% of women reported having heterosexual anal sex at some point in their lives.

♡ Among 25- to 44-year-olds, 6% of men and 12% of women have had some level of same-sex sexual contact in their lifetimes.

Age and number of sexual partners

Men typically engaged in sexual intercourse for the first time at age 16, whereas for women it was age 17 (NHSLS); by age 18, more than half of males and nearly two-thirds of females have had intercourse.[7]

♡ Across all ages, in the previous year, 16% of females had no sexual partners, 12% had at least one same-sex partner, 61% had one opposite-sex partner, and 9% had two or more opposite-sex partners. Among 20- to 24-year-old women, the numbers are 16% (no partners), 15% (same sex), 50% (one partner), 18% (two or more), respectively.

♡ Across all ages, in the previous year, 16% of males had no sexual partners, 4% had at least one same-sex partner, 60% had one opposite-sex partner, and 18% had two or more opposite-sex partners. For 20- to 24-year-old men, the numbers are 18% (no partners), 5% (same sex), 48% (one partner), 27% (two or more), respectively.

♡ Women 15 to 44 years old typically had 3.2 heterosexual partners in their lifetime. This is a large age range, with lifetime partners differing depending on age. For example, 15- to 19-year-olds average 1.4 partners (although 48% have had no partners), 20- to 24-year-olds average 2.6 partners (13% have had no partners), and 25- to 44-year-olds average 3.6 partners (1.6% none).

♡ Men 15 to 44 years old typically had 5.1 heterosexual partners in their lifetime. Among 15- to 19-year-olds, the average is 1.8 partners (43% have had no partners), 20- to 24-year-olds average 4.1 partners (14% have had no partners), and 25- to 44-year-olds average 6.1 partners (2.4% none—so there may be a few 40-year-old virgins after all).

♡ From the GSS, which includes a larger age range than the NSFG, women averaged 4 sexual partners, whereas men averaged 12, with an overall average of 7.[8]

Sex differences in number of partners

One thing that you might have noticed is that the average number of sexual partners for men and women are not the same. Although the actual numbers reported vary among samples, a consistent finding is that men report having more partners in their lifetimes than do women. If men and women are having sex with each other, shouldn't these numbers be the same? There are a few explanations for this difference in reports of number of sex partners[5]:

♡ Not all sex occurs between men and women. However, the rates of male–male sex would have to be very high (much higher than is found in studies of homosexual activity) compared to female–female sex and heterosexual sex to account for the difference in male and female reports of number of partners.

♡ There is a small population of women (e.g., prostitutes) who are having a lot of sex with men who are not included in these studies. This makes some sense, but estimates of rates of prostitution probably don't fully account for the difference.

♡ Men and women may define *sex* differently, with men being much more inclusive when thinking about what counts as sex and women using a more narrow definition (with Bill Clinton, who "did not have sex with that woman," being the notable exception to this explanation).

♡ Men may exaggerate their numbers to seem more cool or macho, whereas women may underreport their sexual activity to seem more chaste. This explanation seems to have the most support, which suggests that any time a person gives you their "number" of sexual partners, it may be necessary to adjust based on that person's sex (i.e., male vs. female).

Frequency and timing of sex

♡ Overall, married couples (NSFH data from 1987–1988) report having sex 6.3 times per month, on average. However, in what may be the only benefit of marrying younger, married couples under the age of 24 reported nearly double that frequency (11.7 times/month).[9]

♡ Married couples' frequency of sex declines both as a function of age of the husbands and wives, and as the relationships duration increases.

♡ Non-married couples who cohabit report having sex more frequently than similarly aged married couples.[9]

♡ Data on frequency of sex in dating relationships is surprisingly difficult to obtain, but it is undoubtedly quite variable given the diversity in the types of premarital relationships (i.e., casually dating vs. engagement), different contexts (e.g., being at college vs. living at home), physical distance (i.e., proximal vs. long-distance), and beliefs (i.e., acceptability of premarital sex) that are at play in dating.

♡ In premarital relationships,[10] less than 10% had sex on the first date, but by "a few weeks" nearly 40% have been sexually intimate. Within two months of beginning the relationship, more than half of all couples have engaged in sexual activity, and by one year, three out of four dating couples are having sex.

♡ Approximately 17% of couples do not have sex until after marriage; only a very small number of couples (5%) have premarital sex for the first time after one year of dating (i.e., if you haven't done it by one year, you're probably going to have to tie the knot before getting any lovin').

Rates of extradyadic sex

♡ Overall, the rates of extramarital sex (i.e., cheating on a spouse) are higher for men than women; 22%–25% of men (from the GSS and NHSLS, respectively) reported they had cheated on their spouses, whereas these numbers are 13%–15% for women.

♡ However, this sex difference in reports of cheating seems partially to be a function of age. With older samples, men are more likely to report cheating, but with younger samples, the rates for men and women are about the same.

♡ Cohabitating couples have higher rates (33%) of extradyadic sex than married couples.[11]

Hooking up

It probably doesn't surprise you that "hooking up" is quite common among college students. In one study, *hooking up* was defined as a range of sexual behaviors, including kissing (25%), manual stimulation (27%), oral sex (10%), and sexual intercourse (41%).[12]

Approximately 70% of college students reported having at least one hook up, with 55% of those encounters being with someone they did not know previously. Overall, the average number of hookups in this college sample was approximately 10 encounters per person.

Conclusions

By this point, 100% of the readers of this chapter have compared a statistic to their own experiences to see how their sex life stacks up to others. To reinforce a point we made at the beginning of this answer: The numbers presented here simply represent national averages; they do not encompass the wide variety of sexual behaviors that Americans engage in. And just because a lot of people are (or are not) doing something, it doesn't mean it's the right thing for you and your partner. The best advice is to talk openly about what you'd like to be doing in the bedroom (or in the kitchen, if that's your thing) and figure out what you're both comfortable with.

TAKE-HOME POINTS

♡ Married couples, on average, have sex once or twice a week, with frequency decreasing over the course of the relationship.

♡ Women report having three to four sexual partners, whereas men report somewhat higher numbers. This difference is likely due to different definitions of what "counts" as sex between men and women, and also biases in self-reports.

♡ Rates of cheating are in the 15% to 25% range.

References

1. Kinsey, A. C., W. B. Pomeroy, and C. E. Martin. 1948. *Sexual Behavior in the Human Male*. Philadelphia: Saunders.
2. Kinsey, A. C., W. B. Pomeroy, C. E. Martin, and P. H. Gebhard. 1953. *Sexual Behavior in the Human Female*. Philadelphia: Saunders.
3. Masters, W. H., and V. E. Johnson. 1966. *Human Sexual Response*. New York: Bantam Books.
4. Lauman, E. O., J. H. Gagnon, R. T. Michael, and S. Michaels. 1994. *The Social Organization of Sexuality. Sexual Practices in the United States*. Chicago: The University of Chicago Press.

5. Willetts, M. C., S. Sprecher, and F. D. Beck. 2004. "Overview of Sexual Practices and Attitudes within Relational Contexts." In *Handbook of Sexuality in Close Relationships,* edited by J. Harvey, A. Wenzel, and S. Sprecher, 57–85. Mahwah NJ: Erlbaum.
6. Chandra, A., W. D. Mosher, and C. Copen. 2011. *Sexual Behavior, Sexual Attraction, and Sexual Identity in the United States: Data from the 2006–2008 National Survey of Family Growth.* Retrieved from http://www.cdc.gov/nchs/data/nhsr/nhsr036.pdf.
7. Carver, K., K. Joyner, and J. R. Udry. 2003. "National Estimates of Adolescent Romantic Relationships." In *Adolescent Romantic Relations and Sexual Behavior,* edited by P. Florsheim, 23–56. Mahwah NJ: Erlbaum.
8. Smith, T. W. 1998. "American Sexual Behavior: Trends, Socio-Demographic Differences, and Risk Behavior." *GSS Topical Report No. 25.* Chicago: National Opinion Research Center University of Chicago.
9. Call, V., S. Sprecher, and P. Schwartz. 1995. "Marital Sexual Intercourse Frequency in a National Sample." *Journal of Marriage and the Family* 57: 639–652.
10. Busby, D. M., J. S. Carroll, and B. J. Willoughby. 2010. "Compatibility or Restraint? The Effects of Sexual Timing on Marriage Relationships." *Journal of Family Psychology* 24: 766–774.
11. Blumstein, P., and P. Schwartz. 1983. *American Couples: Money, Work, Sex.* New York: Morrow.
12. Paul, E. L., and K. A. Hayes. 2002. "The Casualties of 'Casual' Sex: A Qualitative Exploration of the Phenomenology of College Students' Hookup." *Journal of Social and Personal Relationships* 19: 639–661.

Dig Deeper

If there was something we didn't report that you're interested in, you can download the report here: http://www.cdc.gov/nchs/data/nhsr/nhsr036.pdf.
Another good resource is the *National Survey of Sexual Health and Behavior* (NSSHB): http://www.nationalsexstudy.indiana.edu.

CHAPTER 9

Expanding the Family

*K*ids. The other four-letter word. Love them or hate them, our society demands that you either embrace the world of sleepless nights and loss of independence, or open yourself up to less-than-flattering judgments and public shame. Sorry, there is no more appealing third option. Given the pros and cons on both sides of the have-kids-or-not coin, decisions about whether to have kids, and when and how you plan to do so if you venture down that road, is a highly personal decision worthy of careful analysis. Choose wisely, my friend.

Q34: AM I WRONG FOR NOT WANTING TO HAVE KIDS?

Timothy J. Loving

No, you are not wrong for not wanting to have kids, but that doesn't mean you won't be made to feel like you're wrong, especially if you are a woman.[1] For all practical purposes, we live in a *pronatalist* or *prochildbearing* society that "encourages reproduction and exalts the role of parenthood."[2] This pronatalism starts very early and can be found reflected in children's toys (baby dolls), books (e.g., a Little Golden Book's "Little Mommy"), and nursery rhymes ("…and then comes YOU with the baby carriage"). I still remember vividly the comment my then new mother-in-law made to my wife and me the morning after we were married. We were opening wedding gifts, and not five minutes into the extravaganza my M.I.L. proclaimed, "Next time you'll be opening baby shower gifts." No pressure there, eh?

Because of these very strong pronatalist attitudes in Western society, which are apparent in other cultures as well,[3] people often perceive those choosing to not have children negatively, including seeing them as less happy, sensitive, and loving, and more selfish.[2,4,5] A large amount of the research on the topic makes use of hypothetical vignettes, where study participants (typically undergraduate students) read about people in which the only differences are whether the individual described has or does not have children (or wants versus does not want children). In some cases, the researchers manipulate whether the person described deliberately chooses to not have kids (i.e., *childfree*, or voluntarily childfree/childless), is not able to have kids because of fertility issues (i.e., involuntarily childless), and so on. Other work has asked individuals to rank order various lifestyle options, such as having an egalitarian marriage, being married without kids, or, for example, living on a rural commune with shared sex (no really, we aren't making that up—swingers, baby!).[6] In this work, participants prefer childfree marriages less than egalitarian marriages, long-term cohabitation relationships (see question 14), traditional marriages, and relationships in which there is an evaluation of whether to continue the relationship every five years (sort of a "pay as you go" model). Interestingly, but perhaps not surprisingly, the undergraduate men in this sample even preferred the rural "rampant sex" commune situation over a childfree marriage (women did not; see question 30 for potential insight). It is likely that the younger, hormone-driven sample biased the results.

Despite these apparent stigmas, which may be decreasing (more on that later), consciously choosing to not have kids is an increasingly common choice made by both women and men.[4] The increased incidence in deliberate childfreeness for women is particularly striking, in light of the fact that society generally considers childbearing to be a core part of the female experience.[7] Many factors contribute to somebody's decision to not have kids: concerns about work–family balance, financial considerations, poor parenting models in one's past, a general lack of basic interest in children, and worries that one's personality is incompatible with childrearing contributing heavily to the Con column.[8] In other words, choosing to have or not have kids can be a rational decision, and one that comes with enormous implications. There are very logical reasons someone would choose to forego parenthood,[9] and it very much is and should be an individual (or couple-level) decision.

As noted at the outset, however, your rational choice to remain childfree does not protect you from the attitudes and opinions of others. Although childfree couples often report better marital quality than do married couples with kids, that doesn't stop friends and family from doling out the pressure. First comes love, then comes marriage, then comes incessant nagging about the whereabouts of impending grandchildren. To make matters worse, that pressure often tends to be mixed, with the childfree hearing from some family and friends that they should definitely procreate, whereas others in their social network might say they're not ready.[10] Fortunately, there is some evidence that younger generations are more accepting of the decision to avoid sleepless nights, messy diapers, snotty noses, whining, and so on. It is hard to imagine why, especially when it sounds so blissful, eh? For example, in another vignette study, participants rated childfree women more positively than unhappy pregnant women (who, presumably, violated the social norm that pregnancy is bliss),[5] and other more recent studies reveal similar findings.[1] Yet, couples who go childfree still report feeling stigmatized.[11] What's going on here? It very well may be a function of the methods employed. Remember that a lot of these studies use vignettes in which undergraduate students are asked to indicate feelings about people described as childfree versus not. It's not hard to imagine that an 18-year-old has no problems with somebody choosing to not have kids, but their attitudes may change over time as they transition into serious relationships and thoughts of parenthood become more salient.

Conclusion

So, are you wrong for not wanting to have kids? Not at all. Parenthood is certainly very fulfilling and satisfying for some, but it's not for everyone[12] (see also questions 33 and 34). As long as you're willing to weather the stigma, which may get worse as you get older, you are likely to live a very satisfying childfree life.

TAKE-HOME POINTS

♡ We live in a pronatalist society.
♡ Although choosing to have kids or not is a personal decision, many people still feel stigmatized when they go against society's pronatalism.

♡ There is some indication that younger generations are more open to childfreeness, but it's not clear that acceptance holds as individuals get older.

♡ There are pros and cons to having children that should be weighed carefully.

References

1. Koropeckyj-Cox, T., V. Romano, and A. Moras. 2007. "Through the Lenses of Gender, Race, and Class: Students' Perceptions of Childless/Childfree individuals and Couples." *Sex Roles* 56 (7–8): 415–428.
2. Jamison, P .H., L. R. Franzini, and R. M. Kaplan 1979. "Some Assumed Characteristics of Voluntarily Childfree Women and Men." *Psychology of Women Quarterly* 4 (2): 266–273.
3. Rowlands, I., and C. Lee. 2006. "Choosing to Have Children or Choosing to Be Childfree: Australian Students' Attitudes towards the Decisions of Heterosexual and Lesbian Women." *Australian Psychologist* 41 (1): 55–59.
4. Hoffman, S. R., and R. F. Levant. 1985. "A Comparison of Childfree and Child-Anticipated Married Couples." *Family Relations* 34(2): 197–203.
5. Shields, S. A. and E. Cooper. 1983. "Stereotypes of Traditional and Nontraditional Childbearing Roles." *Sex Roles* 9 (3): 363–376.
6. Strong, L. D. 1978. "Alternative Marital and Family Forms: Their Relative Attractiveness to College Students and Correlates of Willingness to Participate in Nontraditional Forms." *Journal of Marriage and the Family* 40 (3): 493–503.
7. Ory, M. G. 1978. "The Decision to Parent or Not: Normative and Structural Components." *Journal of Marriage and the Family* 40 (3): 531–539.
8. Park, K. 2005. "Choosing Childlessness: Weber's Typology of Action and Motives of the Voluntarily Childless." *Sociological Inquiry* 75 (3): 372–402.
9. Seccombe, K. 1991. "Assessing the Costs and Benefits of Children: Gender Comparisons among Childfree Husbands and Wives." *Journal of Marriage and the Family* 53 (1): 191–202.
10. Fried, E. S., and J. R. Udry. 1980. "Normative Pressures on Fertility Planning." *Population and Environment: Behavioral and Social Issues* 3 (3–4): 199–209.
11. Somers, M. D. 1993. "A Comparison of Voluntarily Childfree Adults and Parents." *Journal of Marriage and the Family* 55 (3): 643–650.
12. Galatzer-Levy, I. R., H. Mazursky, A. D. Mancini, and G. A. Bonano. 2011. "What We Don't Expect When Expecting: Evidence for Heterogeneity in Subjective Well-Being in Response to Parenthood." *Journal of Family Psychology* 25 (3): 384–392.

Dig Deeper

Gold, J. M., and J. S. Wilson. 2002. "Legitimizing the Child-Free Family: The Role of the Family Counselor." *Family Journal: Counseling and Therapy for Couples and Families* 10: 70–74.

Burkett, E. 2000. *The Baby Boon: How Family-Friendly America Cheats the Childless.* New York: Free Press.

Q35: WHAT WILL HAPPEN TO US IF MY PARTNER AND I ARE UNABLE TO HAVE KIDS?

Marci E. J. Gleason

There may come a time when you finally decide you are ready to plunge into parenthood (see question 37) only to find that the stork has seemingly misplaced your order. First, let's get specific: What does it mean to be infertile? The standard medical definition of *infertility* is based on women of reproductive age (ages 15–44) having unprotected heterosexual sex for a year without becoming pregnant (or for 6 months for those 35 and older). Rates of infertility typically do not include cases in which either partner is infertile due to a surgical procedure (e.g., removal of the ovaries due to ovarian cancer) or individuals who are unable to carry a pregnancy to term (e.g., suffering multiple miscarriages). Unfortunately, according to a representative sample of women, many couples face this dilemma: approximately 7.4% of married or cohabiting women in the United States reported experiencing infertility in a five-year period.[1] When considering all types of infertility across the lifespan, the rate of infertility is much higher—at least 17% of couples struggle to start a family once they begin trying.[2]

Will infertility destroy your relationship?

Infertility is indeed a significant stressor in relationships, and as we know, stress is not easy on relationships (see question 28). Many people experience infertility due to health problems, and the treatment of infertility can lead to both mental distress and unpleasant physical symptoms for both men and women, all of which are documented stressors on relationships. In addition, almost all treatment for infertility is expensive, including adoption, and health insurance in the United States rarely covers the more expensive procedures (and as discussed in question 25, money is a common source of conflict in relationships). Not surprisingly, both couple members tend to show increased distress during infertility treatment, and a lack of successful treatment can result in decreased relationship satisfaction and increased anxiety and depression, particularly among infertile women.[4] Women, more so than men, may be particularly vulnerable to depression and anxiety after a diagnosis of infertility for two reasons: First, the importance of being a mother is often felt more strongly among women than being a father is by men; a belief that society reinforces. Second, the burden of infertility treatment (e.g., men might have to "provide some samples" whereas it may be necessary for women to get a series of shots and far more tests than men) is far greater for women, regardless of the cause of the infertility (actually much like the burden of pregnancy is on women, but in that case it is more likely to be considered a positive, role-fulfilling event).[3]

So if you can't have children, will you be depressed and be at risk for divorce? Not necessarily; there is also compelling evidence that couples who have experienced infertility can actually benefit from the experience. In a survey of 2250 individuals being treated for infertility, the majority (more than 60% of women and nearly as many men) reported that their marriages improved and that the inability to have a child had brought them closer together; less than 10% thought that it had hurt the level of closeness that they felt with their partner.[5] Furthermore, men were more likely to experience marital benefit when they were open about the infertility and discussed it with their partner. Again, open communication among couple members seems to be important (see question 16). In particular, couples who eventually have children, through successful treatment or adoption, appear very similar in satisfaction to couples who had no trouble getting pregnant.

Having a baby the not-so-old fashioned way

There are many ways to start a family that don't involve the traditional meet-and-greet in the master bedroom or backseat of a car. These fall into three main camps: adoption, infertility treatment, and surrogacy. Adoption has been a common practice throughout history and there are many ways to adopt children in the United States.[6] The *traditional adoption,* which still exists today, is that of a closed infant adoption wherein adoptive parents receive the baby shortly after birth, and neither they nor the birth parents have any knowledge of each other. *International adoption* (adopting children from other countries, a la Angelina Jolie and Brad Pitt) and *open adoption* (adopting a child while having contact with the child's birth family) are becoming increasingly more common than the traditional method.[8] Adoption can be a wonderful way to start a family, and longitudinal studies of adopted children suggest that they are likely to be well adjusted and the families formed through adoption are cohesive.[8] Yet another type of adoption is through the foster care system, which differs in key ways from those listed earlier: children adopted through foster care are often older, have memories and ongoing relationships with their birth parents, are more likely to have been victims of abuse, and are more likely to have behavioral issues.[7] It is important to note that children who have been abused or neglected prior to adoption are more likely to have behavioral problems in the future, but this tendency can be avoided through effective parenting.

Increasingly, infertile couples are turning to medical procedures to become parents. Medical infertility treatments have greatly improved and involve everything from drug therapy to surgery to in vitro fertilization (IVF—the children of this procedure were commonly referred to in the past as *test tube babies*).[9] These medical procedures, along with donor-assisted reproduction (where sperm, eggs, or both are acquired from an outside party in order to achieve pregnancy) and surrogacy (where another woman carries and gives birth to the child) are making it possible for increasingly more infertile couples to have children. (More information about these procedures is readily available and suggestions for reading can be found in the "Dig Deeper" section.) Researchers have found that women who have children through fertility treatments are likely to experience more complications during pregnancy and at birth, but actually reported fewer symptoms of anxiety and depression in the first few months of motherhood than women who got pregnant without medical intervention.[10] Parents of infants conceived through donation (of either egg or sperm) have warmer relationships with their infants compared to parents of naturally conceived children.[11] These studies suggest that there might be something about either the process of infertility treatment or about couples who decide to undergo the difficult and expensive procedures that lead to positive parenting outcomes. However, as many of these procedures are new, this area of study is also in its infancy, and a true consensus in the field about the long-term effects of fertility treatment has not been reached.

Conclusions

If the stork fails to visit you and your partner when you decide you are ready, there are many options. However, before you decide you are infertile, be sure to practice evidence-based strategies for getting pregnant: learn when female ovulation occurs and have sex a few days before and after that time.[12] Many doctors recommend having sex every other day in order to insure you hit those peak fertility days ("Have lots of sex"—talk about the greatest medical advice ever!). Also heartening is the fact that there is a good chance that even if you don't conceive naturally and you want children, you will, one day, have one. For instance, in a longitudinal study of women who had undergone IVF, researchers found that 82% were parents 10 years later, either through assisted reproductive procedures, spontaneous pregnancy (suggesting even when diagnosed with infertility, one shouldn't stop trying), adoption, fostering, or step-parenting.[13] Finally, individuals who either choose to remain childfree or embrace being childless (see question 34), not surprisingly, can lead rich and satisfying lives.[14]

TAKE-HOME POINTS

♡ Infertility is a relatively common dilemma faced by couples.
♡ Although infertility is stressful and is associated with stress for both members of the couple, many couples actually report that it strengthened their relationship.
♡ There are many ways to start a family and very little to suggest that being unable to conceive naturally will negatively affect your relationship or your parenting.

References

1. Chandra, A., G. M. Martinez, W. D. Mosher, J. C. Abma, and J. Jones. 2005. "Fertility, Family Planning, and Reproductive Health of U.S. Women: Data from the 2002 National Survey of Family Growth." *Vital and Health Statistics. Series 23, Data from the National Survey of Family Growth* (25): 1–160.
2. Steuber, K. R., and D. H. Solomon. 2008. "Relational Uncertainty, Partner Interference, and Infertility: A Qualitative Study of Discourse within Online Forums." *Journal of Social and Personal Relationships* 25: 831–855.

3. Nelson, C. J., A. W. Shindel, C. K. Naughton, M. Ohebshalom, and J. P. Mulhall. 2008. "Prevalence and Predictors of Sexual Problems, Relationship Stress, and Depression in Female Partners of Infertile Couples." *The Journal of Sexual Medicine* 5: 1907–1914.

4. Greil, A. L., and K. Slauson-blevins. 2010. Review article. "The Experience of Infertility: A Review of Recent Literature." *Sociology of Health and Illness* 32 (1): 140–162. doi: 10.1111/j.1467-9566.2009.01213.x

5. Schmidt, L., B. Holstein, U. Christensen, and J. Boivin. 2005. "Does Infertility Cause Marital Benefit? An Epidemiological Study of 2250 Women and Men in Fertility Treatment." *Patient Education and Counseling* 59: 244–51.

6. http://www.adoption.org

7. Simmel, C. 2007. "Risk and Protective Factors Contributing to the Longitudinal Psychosocial Well-Being of Adopted Foster Children." *Journal of Emotional and Behavioral Disorders* 15: 237–249.

8. Howard, J. 2009. "Adoption." In *The Encyclopedia of Human Relationships,* edited by H. T. Reis and S. Sprecher, 30–34. Thousand Oaks CA: Sage.

9. http://www.resolve.org

10. Punamäki, R.-L., L. Repokari, S. Vilska, et al. 2006. "Maternal Mental Health and Medical Predictors of Infant Developmental and Health Problems from Pregnancy to One Year: Does Former Infertility Matter?" *Infant Behavior and Development* 29: 230–42.

11. Golombok, S., E. Lycett, F. MacCallum, et al. 2004. "Parenting Infants Conceived by Gamete Donation." *Journal of Family Psychology* 18: 443–52.

12. Twenge, J. M. 2012. *The Impatient Woman's Guide to Getting Pregnant.* New York: Free Press.

13. Sundby, J., L. Schmidt, K. Heldaas, S. Bugge, and T. Tanbo. 2007. "Consequences of IVF among Women: 10 Years Post-Treatment." *Journal of Psychosomatic Obstetrics and Gynecology* 28: 115–20.

14. Jeffries, S., and C. Konnert. 2002. "Regret and Psychological Well-Being among Voluntarily and Involuntarily Childless Women and Mothers." *The International Journal of Aging and Human Development* 54: 89–106.

Dig Deeper

Savage, D. 2000. *The Kid: What Happened after My Boyfriend and I Decided to Go Get Pregnant.* New York: Plume.

Sher, G., V. M. Davis, and J. Stoess J. 2005. *In Vitro Fertilization: The A.R.T. of Making Babies (Assisted Reproductive Technology).* New York: Facts on File, Inc.

Q36: WILL HAVING KIDS RUIN OUR RELATIONSHIP?

Jody L. Davis

Over the course of long-term romantic relationships, couples inevitably experience major life events such as moving to a new city, beginning a new job, or having a child. (Although ideally, these will not all occur during the same year!) This last event—having a child—ranks right up there as one of life's biggest moments, affecting parents' identity, life-satisfaction, bank account, social relationships, and emotional well-being. (If you're old enough to recall those "Calgon, take me away!" commercials, it's no coincidence that they always involved screaming children.) Having children also can transform your relationship with your partner. Have you ever heard people say that having a child will bring a couple closer together? Perhaps it works that way for some, but there is wide variation in how successfully people (and couples) transition to parenthood.

Does having kids keep relationships together?

The majority of married couples will have children (e.g., 88% of ever-married women have a child by the age of 44). Thus, it would be fair to think that researchers should have a clear idea of how having children affects romantic relationships.[1] And there are consistent research findings on one issue: Married couples with children—at least, those who have toddler-age children—are less likely to divorce compared to those who do not have children.[2] But don't be fooled by this statistic. Kids are an enormous investment, and they may keep a couple together, but that doesn't necessarily mean the couple is happier because of having kids.[3] There's a big difference between being happily married and not getting divorced! Research findings are surprisingly mixed on the topic of how having children affects relationship *satisfaction*, possibly in part due to differing methodologies.[3]

Before turning to what we do know, let's put this research in context. Without access to a cloned relationship that exists in an alternate universe, it's impossible to study the following question directly: *What would a given couple's relationship have been like over time if they had not had children?* In other words, researchers are not able to take a group of 100 couples, all of whom are capable of having kids and all of whom want them, choose 50 of them at random and tell them they cannot have kids, and then see what happens. Instead, researchers often use cross-sectional studies that compare couples with and without children at a single point in time because such studies are easier to conduct (by *easy*, we mean *ethical and possible*). When researchers examine couples over time, or *longitudinally*, they most often follow couples from late pregnancy through a year or so after birth. Ideally, we would be able to draw conclusions from multiple longitudinal studies that last several years (just in case relationship satisfaction with infants is different than with older children), begin pre-pregnancy for a couple's first child (in case relationship processes are different during pregnancy than before pregnancy), and include childless-couple comparison groups.[4] While we're at it, we'd also like to request studies that cure cancer, solve world hunger, and teach politicians to get along! Why do we need such complex studies? As you know from the section on "Are people less happy after they get married?" (question 15), there are predictable changes over time in all couples. Researchers' ongoing task is to separate which of those changes are unique to couples with children. Unfortunately, the ideal research designs are time-consuming and expensive, which contributes to the lack of definitive answers.

How does having kids affect marital satisfaction?

Some studies show a decline in marital satisfaction that is uniquely associated with the transition to parenthood, whereas other studies do not. A recent *meta-analysis* (science jargon for a study that synthesizes results from many previous studies) of 41 longitudinal studies (some of which began during pregnancy and some of which began before pregnancy) concluded that couples with and without children experience similar decreases in satisfaction over comparable amounts of time.[5] For example, in an 8-year longitudinal study including a childfree-couple control group, couples with or without children experienced similar declines in marital satisfaction, but the decline occurred more suddenly—following the birth of a child— among couples with children.[3] Thus, having kids gives the typical drop in marital satisfaction a bit of a turbo-boost—lack of sleep and dirty diapers can do that! In many ways, the more interesting issue is whether we can predict which couples are most likely to experience such steep declines.

Some couples will be affected more than others

Studies testing a number of different possibilities indicate that there are certain pre-baby features of individuals and relationships that may be useful for predicting shifts in relationship satisfaction after birth. Decreases in relationship satisfaction are magnified among partners who, before having a baby, were depressed, had unrealistically high expectations about parenthood (that were later unfulfilled), or had poor problem-solving skills.[3,4,6] These findings make intuitive sense. Imagine that you expect your partner to share equally in caring for an infant, but when the baby arrives, your partner instead withdraws from the family and spends extra time at work; clearly, you would feel disappointed! Interestingly, some variables have affected relationship satisfaction in both directions, depending on which study you examine. On the one hand, most studies report the intuitive finding that couples with higher relationship satisfaction pre-baby are buffered from drops in satisfaction during the transition to parenthood.[4,6] On the other hand, some studies report that those with higher levels of relationship satisfaction pre-baby experience greater drops in satisfaction during the transition to parenthood, perhaps because they are more likely to have unrealistically high expectations (see also question 9). Results are similarly mixed for associations with couples' income levels. Sometimes more money helps, but other times, "Mo' money, mo' problems." In addition, some studies show an effect and some show no effect for topics such as whether couples planned to have a child (it may depend on whether the couple thinks of the baby as a happy surprise or a stressful accident), whether couples had been married a shorter amount of time before having a child, and whether partners came from families with poor-quality parental relationships.[3,4] Researchers are still accumulating evidence that will allow us to identify factors that protect new parents from a relationship satisfaction decline (or even lead to an increase, in a small minority of relationships).

Are there post-baby factors that influence the transition?

Yes, but the funny (or not so funny) thing is that because they are post-baby, you won't know about them until after a baby arrives. Decreases in relationship satisfaction are magnified among couples who show more negative emotion during marital conflicts and among couples who have female babies (possibly because fathers are less involved with female versus male infants), and there are mixed results on the effect of having infants with difficult temperaments (e.g., babies who are difficult to soothe).[3,4] In addition, longitudinal studies beginning during pregnancy have demonstrated that after having a child, wives are likely to take on a disproportionate amount of the childcare and household responsibilities. This increasing asymmetry in division of labor precipitates a drop in relationship satisfaction, particularly for women.[4] Moreover, during the transition to parenthood, there are likely to be increases in conflict, greater negative communication or emotion, and decreases in conflict management, all of which may decrease relationship satisfaction.[3,4] And let's not underestimate the role that late-night feedings and extra visits from the in-laws may play!

Avoiding these negative outcomes

Are there ways to decrease the odds of experiencing a nose-dive in relationship satisfaction after the birth of a child? Certainly! Interestingly, a small number of people do not experience a decline, and some even experience a gain in relationship satisfaction; those lucky folks can rest easy and bask in the glow of parenthood.[3,4,7] For everyone else, it may be useful to consider interventions designed to strengthen relationship satisfaction during the transition to parenthood. Strengthening relationships after the birth of a child is important not only for the parents' well-being, but also for the child's well-being—poor parental relationship quality is associated with negative outcomes for children. Children experience better outcomes when parents have greater involvement in childrearing, and marital quality appears to be an especially strong predictor of fathers' involvement with their children.[7]

Having unrealistically positive expectations seems to be a reliably strong risk factor for declines in relationship satisfaction. It may be helpful to learn about the hard work and sacrifice involved in parenting. We recommend staying up for 48 hours straight while listening to a baby cry, assembling dozens of toys, and chauffeuring kids all around town to properly calibrate your expectations. Sound too intense? Just spending some time babysitting other people's children may be helpful. Fortunately, there are a handful of interventions (that don't involve these trial-by-fire types of experiences) that can help couples maintain healthy relationships as they transition to parenthood.[8] In one study beginning three months before birth, couples who were randomly assigned to attend weekly workshops for six months on topics such as division of family labor and problem-solving strategies experienced a smaller decline in satisfaction over the next five years compared to those who did not attend the workshops. Increased relationship satisfaction may then have spillover effects, such as increasing parents' involvement with their children.[7] Although you may not have time or access to participate in a structured workshop like this, it does make sense to talk with your partner about common issues before you begin the hazing process that comes with the arrival of a child.

Conclusion

Overall, we can put to rest any fanciful idea that having children is likely to create marital bliss where it has thus far been lacking. Instead, it appears that the transition to parenthood often accelerates what appear to be typical drops in marital satisfaction. So, should you decide not to have kids because of concern over how it will change your relationship? Probably not; there are plenty of other reasons not to have kids (just kidding)! Declines in relationship satisfaction during the initial transition to parenthood are modest and varied, and there are still several questions left unanswered. For example, little is known about the *long-term* impacts of having a child on relationship quality (when children are older, or out of the house). But be aware that the transition to parenthood may be a vulnerable time for your relationship. When going through a difficult transition, it can be comforting to know that other couples experience similar challenges, and that strategies such as calibrating your expectations to match the realities of parenting may be helpful. A common tendency is to underestimate the impact of life events on relationship processes. Attributing relationship problems to a stressful situation instead of to your partner may lead you to feel better about your relationship (e.g., "My partner didn't snap at me because he doesn't love me; he did it because our son just peed on him!"). Having to navigate through major life events is unavoidable; the manner in which you and your partner do so will determine your well-being.

TAKE-HOME POINTS

♡ It is challenging to design and conduct studies that examine shifts in relationship satisfaction during the transition to parenthood.

♡ During the transition to parenthood, many couples experience a more rapid decline in relationship satisfaction than they otherwise would have.

♡ Individuals who are not depressed, have realistic expectations, and have good problem-solving skills experience less of a decline in relationship satisfaction post-baby.

♡ After having a child, couples with more equitable division of labor, less conflict, and less negative emotion experience less of a decline in relationship satisfaction.

References

1. United States Census Bureau. 2010. "Distribution of Women 40 to 44 Years Old by Number of Children Ever Born and Marital Status." *Current Population Survey*, June 1976–2008. Retrieved from http://www.census.gov/population/socdemo/fertility/cps2008/SupFert-Tab2.xls

2. White, L. K., and A. Booth. 1985. "Transition to Parenthood and Marital Quality." *Journal of Family Issues* 6: 435–449.

3. Doss, B. D., G. K. Rhoades, S. M. Stanley, and H. J. Markman. 2009. "The Effect of The Transition to Parenthood on Relationship Quality: An 8-Year Prospective Study." *Journal of Personality and Social Psychology* 96: 601–619.

4. Lawrence, E., A. D. Rothman, R. J. Cobb, and T. N. Bradbury. 2010. "Marital Satisfaction across the Transition to Parenthood: Three Eras of Research." In *Strengthening Couple Relationships for Optimal Child Development: Lessons from Research and Intervention*, edited by

M. S. Schulz, M. K. Pruett, and P. K. Kerig, 97–114. Washington DC: American Psychological Association.

5. Mitnick, D. M., R. E. Heyman, and A. M. Smith Slep. 2009. "Changes in Relationship Satisfaction across the Transition to Parenthood: A Meta-Analysis." *Journal of Family Psychology* 23: 848–852.

6. Goldberg, A. E., J. Z. Smith, and D. A. Kashy. 2010. "Preadoptive Factors Predicting Lesbian, Gay, and Heterosexual Couples' Relationship Quality across the Transition to Parenthood." *Journal of Family Psychology* 24: 221–232.

7. Schulz, M. S., C. P. Cowan, and P. A. Cowan. 2006. "Promoting Healthy Beginnings: A Randomized Controlled Trial of a Preventative Intervention to Preserve Marital Quality during the Transition to Parenthood." *Journal of Consulting and Clinical Psychology* 74: 20–31.

8. Pinquart, M., and D. Teubert. 2010. "Effects of Parenting Education with Expectant and New Parents: A Meta-Analysis." *Journal of Family Psychology* 24: 316–327.

Dig Deeper

Cowan, C. P., and P. A. Cowan. 2000. *When Partners Become Parents: The Big Life Change for Couples.* Mahwah NJ: Erlbaum.

Huston, T. L., and E. K. Holmes. 2004. "Becoming parents." In *Handbook of Family Communication,* edited by A. Vangelisti, 105–133. Mahwah NJ: Erlbaum.

Levy-Shiff, R. 1994. "Individual and Contextual Correlates of Marital Change Across the Transition to Parenthood." *Developmental Psychology* 30: 591–601.

Q37: Is There a "Good" Time to Have Kids?

Jody L. Davis

First comes love, then comes marriage, then comes baby in the baby carriage. Is that the way it should happen? This normative course may characterize some couples, but there are many paths to parenthood. These days there are effective birth control options, and more people are electing to delay parenthood than ever before: between 1990 and 2008, the birth rate for women younger than 35 declined 9%, but the birth rate for women older than 35 increased 19%.[1] In 2006, the average age when a woman had her first child was about 25, but in 1970 it was about 21.[2] In addition, it is becoming more common for people to have children without being married; in 1960, only 5% of births were to unmarried women, but by 2008, the number had grown to 41%.[3] With the timing of parenthood largely under your control (aside from the "biological clock"), you may be wondering when the optimal timing is for having kids. We'll address this question by (1) identifying a few predictable outcomes of having children (that could influence your choice of timing), and (2) presenting evidence about a range of factors that affect parent or child well-being.

Life will change

There are various predictable changes that take place after having kids that generally occur no matter when you take the plunge into parenthood. So, whenever you areprepared (or at least willing) to experience such changes, it could be good timing for you! First, you may wonder whether having children may affect the likelihood that you will complete your college education. The answer is a conditional "yes"—those who have children *and* work full-time are more likely to attend college part-time or delay their enrollment.[4] Second, what you do for leisure activities will be affected, although results on this topic are mixed. Obviously, certain activities can become difficult (or at least different!) with a toddler in tow, so if you have a short-term goal of doing something dramatic like sailing around the world, it would be easier to do so pre-baby. However, in a longitudinal, national U.S. sample, new parents reported more frequent social interaction with relatives, friends, and neighbors compared to couples without children.[5] Thus, you may be less likely to engage in certain activities, but such losses may be offset to a degree by increased social connections (although perhaps not completely offset until you make it out of the "frequent vomiting" stage of infancy). Third, there are specific personality changes that are likely to follow the birth of a child. For example, parents of young children increased in emotionality (i.e., were more likely to experience negative emotions) after parenthood (especially if they were high in emotionality to begin with and especially when they had two or more kids). Although it may be surprising that personality traits can shift, one theory is that existing traits may become more extreme after experiencing some life events. For example, after parenthood, highly sociable men became more sociable, whereas less sociable men became less sociable.[6] Fourth, according to a nationally representative U.S. sample, having children affects parents' well-being differently depending on marital status and gender. For example, among married women, parenthood was associated with increases in housework but less depression; among unmarried men, parenthood was associated with greater depression.[5] Finally, children cost money—*lots* of money. In 2009, people with household incomes from about $56,000 to $98,000 spent about $12,600 per year on each child from birth to age 17 (before sending them to college!); housing costs (additional bedrooms) accounted for up to a third of the expense.[7] So, it makes sense to evaluate your ability to spend a great deal of money on kids. Collectively, these types of findings provide some information on when it may be most opportune to have (or not have) kids. Specifically, if you can control it, have kids when you are comfortable with a change in leisure activities, you like your friends and family enough to put up with them more, you and your loved ones are prepared for your personality to become stronger, and you're stinking rich. Easy, huh?

Age matters

In addition, there are specific factors that set the stage for the transition to parenthood; these circumstances may or may not be under your control. For example, there is fascinating research on the topic of whether there is an ideal age for a woman to get pregnant. The medical and social risks associated with teen pregnancy are well documented; it's easy to rule out the teenage years as an optimal time to have children. Beyond the adolescent years, however, there are a couple of timing possibilities depending on the criteria used to evaluate the options. If the standard is ease of pregnancy and childbirth, then it would be best to have children around age 20, before women experience declines in fertility and increases in pregnancy and birth complications. But if the standard is the long-term health of infant and mother, then it would be best to delay parenthood for as long as possible. You may find it somewhat surprising that these two things don't go together (i.e., that the best age for good health post-birth is different than the best age for fertility). An operative issue at play here is the extent to which the woman is in a good place in life to provide the best possible care for her child. But you can't entirely leave fertility-related issues out of the equation. Thus, in research using a national sample from the United States, it turns out that the optimal age range for childbirth, taking into account both criteria, may be the early to mid-thirties.[8] Giving birth during this time yields positive outcomes for long-term infant and mother health and mortality risk, likely due to social and economic resources that people are more likely to attain later in life that benefit health. Moreover, there is evidence that older parents provide more skilled parenting, even when controlling for variables such as parents' education level (an effect that seems to level off after age 30).[9] Given that the average age of parents is climbing, this is reassuring news.

Balancing work and family

You may also be wondering how maternal employment affects children. In 2008, 71% of mothers—60% of those with children age 3 or under—were working (up from 47% and 34%, respectively in 1975).[3] According to a recent meta-analysis, whether or not mothers of young children were employed largely had no effect on children's later achievement or behavioral problems, but there were some interesting small effects for achievement. For example, when mothers were employed during the toddler years, children's school achievement tended to be slightly greater (but when mothers were employed—especially full-time—during children's first year of life, achievement tended to be slightly lower); whether mothers were employed during years 3–6 had no effect on their children's achievement.[10] Overall then, there are small effects for mothers' employment, and they seem to depend on other factors. In addition, studies on this topic are *correlational,* which means that we do not know what the causal relationships are. It could be that mothers who are able to stay home for a year have greater resources that allow them to stay home (nice how that works), and that those greater resources are the reason that their children's achievement is greater (because the resources buy not only more one-on-one time with mom, but also things like healthier foods, better medical care, and less stress for the whole family). The only definitive way to claim that mothers' work affects children's outcomes would be to study the topic using the experimental method by randomly assigning groups of mothers to either work or stay home for a year. Wouldn't you like to be in that study?

Notice the focus on how having a mother who works affects children, but not on how having a father who works affects children. Much of the research that has examined the impact of fathers' work on children has focused on the nature of the work (blue-collar versus white-collar professions) rather than whether the father is working.[11] For mothers, the question often asked is whether working hurts children; but for fathers, the question often asked is whether the nature of their work affects children. This inconsistency reflects reality—women are more likely to be the primary caretakers of young children—but also perpetuates the idea that mothers, not mothers and fathers, are responsible for how young children are raised.

Conclusion

A converging message seems to be that delaying parenthood is desirable in various ways, both for parent and child.[6,8,9] Rather than being a "selfish" decision, delaying parenthood is likely to benefit children. One decided drawback of planning to start a family later in life is reduced fertility, but these days there are many ways to start a family (see question 35). Some reassuring news is that no matter what timing you decide on, you are likely to rationalize your choice by focusing on the benefits of your timing and drawbacks of other possible timings you could have chosen! In other words, the best time could be the time that you've determined is best for you. Just be prepared for a few bumps in the road.

TAKE-HOME POINTS

♡ New parents are likely to experience changes in their social lives, personalities, and finances.

♡ There are a range of benefits to parents and children when parenthood is delayed.

♡ Parents' employment has modest associations with children's outcomes.

References

1. Pew Research Center. 2010. "The New Demography of American Motherhood." Retrieved from http://pewsocialtrends.org/files/2010/10/754-new-demography-of-motherhood.pdf

2. Mathews, T. J. and B. E. Hamilton. 2009. "Delayed Childbearing: More Women Having Their First Child Later in Life." National Center for Health Statistics Data Brief 21 1–8. Retrieved from http://www.cdc.gov/nchs/data/databriefs/db21.pdf

3. Pew Research Center. 2010. "The Decline of Marriage and Rise of New Families." Retrieved from http://pewsocialtrends.org/2010/11/18/the-decline-of-marriage-and-rise-of-new-families

4. National Center for Education Statistics. 2002. "Nontraditional Undergraduates." Retrieved from http://nces.ed.gov/pubs2002/2002012.pdf

5. Nomaguchi, K. M., and M. A. Milkie. 2003. "Costs and Rewards of Children: The Effects of Becoming a Parent on Adults' Lives." *Journal of Marriage and Family* 65: 356–374.

6. Jokela, M., M. Kivimaki, M. Elovainio, and L. Keltikangas-Jarvinen. 2009. "Personality and Having Children: A Two-Way Relationship." *Journal of Personality and Social Psychology* 96: 218–230.

7. Lino, M. 2010. "Expenditures on Children by Families, 2009." United States Department of Agriculture, Center for Nutrition Policy and Promotion. Miscellaneous Publication No. 1528-2009. Retrieved from http://www.cnpp.usda.gov/publications/crc/crc2009.Pdf.

8. Mirowsky, J. 2005. "Age at First Birth, Health, and Mortality." *Journal of Health and Social Behavior* 46: 32–50.

9. Bornstein, M. H., D. L. Putnick, J. T. D. Suwalsky, and M. Gini. 2006. "Maternal Chronological Age, Prenatal and Perinatal History, Social Support, and Parenting of Infants." *Child Development* 77: 875–892.

10. Lucas-Thompson, R. G., W. A. Goldberg, and J. Prause. 2010. "Maternal Work Early in the Lives of Children and Its Distal Associations with Achievement and Behavior Problems: A Meta-Analysis." *Psychological Bulletin* 136: 915–942.

11. Hart, M. S., and M. L. Kelly. 2006. "Fathers' and Mothers' Work and Family Issues as Related to Internalizing and Externalizing Behavior of Children Attending Day Care." *Journal of Family Issues* 27: 252–270.

Dig Deeper

Boivin, J., F. Rice, D. Hay, G. Harold, A. Lewis, M. M. B. van den Bree, and A. Thapar. 2009. "Associations between Maternal Older Age, Family Environment and Parent and Child Well-Being in Families Using Assisted Reproductive Techniques to Conceive." *Social Sciences and Medicine* 68: 1948–1955.

Claxton, A., and M. Perry-Jenkins. 2008. "No Fun Anymore: Leisure and Marital Quality across the Transition to Parenthood." *Journal of Marriage and Family* 70: 28–43.

Knoester, C., and D. J. Eggebeen. 2006. "The Effects of the Transition to Parenthood and Subsequent Children on Men's Well-Being and Social Participation." *Journal of Family Issues* 27: 1532–1560.

Rholes, W. S., J. A. Simpson, J. L. Kohn, C. L. Wilson, A. M. Martin III, S. Tran, S. and D. A. Kashy. 2011. "Attachment Orientations and Depression: A Longitudinal Study of New Parents." *Journal of Personality and Social Psychology* 100: 567–586.

Twenge, J. M. 2012. *The Impatient Woman's Guide to Getting Pregnant.* New York: Free Press.

CHAPTER 10

Parenting

John Watson, the famous psychologist, once said, "Give me a dozen healthy infants, well-formed, and my own specified world to bring them up in and I'll guarantee to take any one at random and train him to become any type of specialist I might select…" Watson was clearly the modest type. The basic idea here is that how we reward and punish children has a profound impact on who and what they become. Although Watson's claim was more than a bit grandiose, the general idea that caregivers influence how a child turns out is indisputable. And with great power comes great responsibility. In this chapter, we cover the basic qualities of what makes a "good" parent and hopefully shed a little light on two topics about which people tend to have very strong opinions (that are often in direct opposition to scientific data).

Q38: WHAT MAKES A PARENT A "GOOD" PARENT?

M. Minda Oriña

In February 2006, Britney "Hit Me Baby One More Time" Spears was photographed driving her SUV while holding her baby, Sean, in her lap. The incident made headlines immediately and prompted a backlash of negative public opinion. It wasn't long before the media-fueled craze resulted in Spears being labeled as one of the world's worst moms (right up there with Joan Crawford's character in *Mommy Dearest*). Obviously, not strapping a kid into a car seat is inexcusable, but the response highlights the strong and ingrained ideas the public has about what makes a parent good versus bad. In fact, a quick Google search on "good parenting" brings up lists of behaviors that parents should do to become "good parents." Are these lists accurate? Can we guarantee that performing a checklist of certain behaviors will ensure that children become well-adjusted, successful, and happy adults? Of course not. It is also important to point out that people generally use the term *good* as a value judgment (what is good for them, may not be good for you) and their recommendations are not always based on the most current scientific data. But we can highlight which parenting styles are associated with the best (i.e., good) outcomes in terms of cognitive, social, and emotional development of children, and we can use scientific data to warn you about what parents should absolutely avoid doing.

What types of parent behavior are best for kids?

Researchers have found that *specific* parenting behaviors (e.g., having an early vs. late bedtime) don't predict specific child outcomes (e.g., getting along with others, high self-esteem) as well as *broad* patterns of parenting. In particular, according to considerable research by Diana Baumrind, the extent to which parents provide warmth, nurturance, expectations, and guidance, and the extent to which they communicate with their children and discipline their children when needed is associated with important child outcomes.[1] These behaviors can be distilled in two primary dimensions, termed *responsiveness* and *demandingness,* to create four distinct styles of parenting.

Parental responsiveness captures the extent to which parents attempt to socialize their children by being particularly attuned to their child's specific developmental needs; such efforts help teach their children to control their emotions and behavior. Parental demandingness captures the extent to which parents set expectations regarding behavior and make use of developmentally appropriate discipline techniques when children are disobedient. *Authoritative parents*, who are high on both responsiveness and demandingness, set clear expectations and limits for their children's behaviors ("I'd like you to clean up around the house today"), but they are also warm and responsive to their children's needs and are supportive in their discipline attempts ("If you have school work to do today, then the chores must be done tomorrow"). Although they do set expectations, authoritative parents listen to their children and provide reasons for their expectations ("Being tidy around the house shows respect for those whom you live with"). *Authoritarian parents* also set clear expectations for their children, but not necessarily in a warm and fuzzy way. Such parents demand and expect obedience ("You WILL be home by 10 pm"), provide no explanations for their demands (Why? "Because I said so"), and tend to be punitive when their children disobey ("You're grounded for a week for every minute you're late"). In other words, authoritarian parents attempt to control their children through the use or threat of punishment. *Indulgent* or *permissive parents* are highly responsive but do not set expectations or boundaries for their children's behaviors. Such parents are considered loving but lenient, and do not place demands on children to self-regulate ("You feel better when you scream in the house? Okay, scream away!"). Finally, *uninvolved parents*, while providing for children's basic needs, are not responsive or demanding ("Do whatever you want") and have more of a "Wake me when you're 18 and out of the house" approach.

How do parenting styles influence children's outcomes?

Most of the time, psychological research yields complicated answers for our questions. For example, you might expect to find that a particular parenting style improves some child outcomes, but is detrimental for other child outcomes. Or we might find that good outcomes only occur in some cultural contexts and not in others. Consequently, we often have to put strong qualifiers in the advice we give. However, in the case of parenting styles, there are consistent findings showing that *authoritative parenting* uniformly produces positive child outcomes, cognitively, socially, and emotionally, and these findings are consistent across cultures; that is, children from authoritative families tend to be well adjusted, happy, and successful.[2,3] In addition, we find that parent-report, child-report, and objective measures all agree![4,5]

The other styles of parenting have mixed outcomes. In general, high parental responsiveness tends to be associated with psychosocial outcomes (Do the children feel good about themselves, and do they interact well with others?), and high parental demandingness is associated with behavioral control and instrumental competence (Do the children do well in school and do they have self-control?).

Consequently, children with authoritarian parents (high demand-ingness and low responsiveness) perform well in school (although not as well as children with authoritative parenting) and don't ex-hibit problem behaviors (perhaps because they worry about getting in trouble at home). However, these children do tend to have prob-lems socially, have poor self-esteem, and are more likely to suffer from depression. Children from indulgent families (high respon-siveness and low demandingness) are socially competent, have high self-esteem, and do not suffer from depression. Yet, children from indulgent families tend to engage in problem behaviors and do not perform as well academically.[4,5] It is *uninvolved parenting* that pro-duces the poorest outcomes across the board, and it doesn't matter who is judging the children's outcomes (the child, the parent, or observers).

Can parents influence their children's attachment style?

Finally, attachment theory (see question 8) also suggests that the manner in which parents respond when their children are distressed has consequences for how children see themselves and important others. Specifically, by providing sensitive and responsive caregiving, particularly during times when the child is distressed, parents can help their children develop a secure attachment, which promotes positive outcomes across many aspects of life. For example, children who are securely attached in infancy are more likely to become good problem solvers when they are two years old, display more positive and less negative emotions in toddlerhood, become social leaders in nursery school, and have more close friends in adolescence.[6] Basi-cally, they are the coolest kids on the playground.

How do "security-promoting" parents behave? Generally speaking, they provide sensitive caregiving by not being smother-ing, intrusive, controlling, unresponsive, underinvolved, or rejecting. Such care involves giving *contingent* care by reading kids' signals, providing appropriate stimulation, and being prompt and respon-sive when a child is distressed, sick, or feeling threatened. These types of parental behaviors foster autonomy by allowing their chil-dren to safely explore their world, because the kids know that they can always count on mom (or dad) to be there when the kids are fearful or distressed.

Conclusions

Because each child differs in terms of their temperament and needs, and because the range of tricks good parents have in their toolbags is incredibly varied, it's difficult to provide global lists of behaviors that make someone a good parent. What we can say is that educating yourself about your child's developmental needs and capabilities, being responsive (but not smothering), setting realistic and consistent boundaries and expectations, and communicating your wishes and the underlying rationale for them will get your kids off to an outstanding start in life. That doesn't mean they will be perfect; they will make mistakes (and so will you). But those mistakes won't crush their self-esteem, and they'll always be comfortable talking to you about those mistakes.

TAKE-HOME POINTS

- ♡ Set boundaries and expectations for your children, and be attuned to your children's needs!
- ♡ Provide the underlying rationale for your boundaries and expectations for your children.
- ♡ Be responsive to your child *when* your child needs it. Overly responsive and under responsive caregiving are both associated with poor outcomes.

References

1. Baumrind, D. 1991. "The Influence of Parenting Style on Adolescent Competence and Substance Use." *Journal of Early Adolescence* 11 (1): 56–95.
2. Maccoby, E. E. 1992. "The Role of Parents in the Socialization of Children: An Historical Overview." *Developmental Psychology* 28: 1006–1017.
3. Hill, N. E., and K. R. Bush. 2001. "Relationships between Parenting Environment and Children's Mental Health among African American Mothers and Children." *Journal of Marriage and the Family* 63: 954–966.
4. Weiss, L. H., and J. C. Schwarz. 1996. "The Relationship between Parenting Types and Older Adolescents' Personality, Academic Achievement, Adjustment, and Substance Use." *Child Development* 67 (5): 2101–2114.

5. Miller, N. B., P. A. Cowan, C. P. Cowan, and E. M. Hethering-ton. 1993. "Externalizing in Preschoolers and Early Adolescents: A Cross-Study Replication of a Family Model." *Developmental Psychology* 29 (1): 3–18.

6. Sroufe, L. A., B. Egeland, E. Carlson, and W. A. Collins. 2005. *The Development of the Person: The Minnesota Study of Risk and Adaptation from Birth to Adulthood.* New York: Guilford Press.

Dig Deeper

Sroufe, L. A., B. Egeland, E. Carlson, and W. A. Collins. 2005. *The Development of the Person: The Minnesota Study of Risk and Adaptation from Birth to Adulthood.* New York: Guilford Press.

Q39: Is There a Best Way to Discipline My Kids?

Timothy J. Loving

No matter how skilled at parenting you are (see question 38), you will undoubtedly find yourself having to dip into the proverbial parenting toolbox in hopes of coming up with an effective means for shaping your child's behavior after they have violated or otherwise disobeyed your expectations of acceptable behavior. Hopefully, you have more tools at your disposal than brandishing a wire clothes hanger and berating your kid! (R.I.P. Joan Crawford!) Interestingly, despite the universal need for discipline techniques, and the grave concern regarding their consequences for child and parent–child relationships,[1] identifying the best "scientifically proved" ways to discipline kids is a bit challenging. This challenge is driven by at least three factors: (1) We are not able to randomly assign parents and children to specific discipline groups (see question 14 for further discussion of the importance of random assignment), (2) the effectiveness of specific discipline tactics often varies in different cultural contexts,[2] and (3) studies often lump together many discipline techniques, making it hard to isolate the effects of any specific technique.[3] Thus, this response reviews two of the more common discipline tactics—corporal punishment and time-outs—and closes with some general guidelines for how to approach discipline. To begin, however, it's probably a good idea to clarify exactly what is meant by the term *discipline.*

What is discipline?

When most people hear the word *discipline* in the context of parenting, they often think of *punishment,* which generally involves the application of some negative stimulus (e.g., physical pain, like spanking) or removal of something positive (e.g., removal from a rewarding activity, like a time-out from play) in hopes of changing a child's behavior. Researchers, however, conceptualize the term *discipline* far more broadly; it turns out that a lot of what parents might do when their children misbehave is considered discipline. For example, recent research by Elizabeth Gershoff and colleagues,[2] assessed how eleven different parental responses (or, as researchers refer to them, *discipline techniques*) in six different countries were associated with 8- to 12-year-old kids' future aggressive and anxious behaviors. Researchers asked parents how frequently they performed eleven behaviors after their kids misbehaved (kids also indicated how often their parents did these things). So what were these discipline techniques? Those techniques/behaviors included: (1) talking to the child about good and bad behavior (i.e., defining acceptable and unacceptable behavior); (2) asking the child to apologize; (3) putting the child in a time-out (more on this tactic later); (4) taking away privileges; (5) spanking or using other forms of corporal punishment; (6) expressing disappointment in the child; (7) telling the child he or she should be ashamed; (8) scolding the child in a loud voice; (9) telling the child that the parent will no longer love the child if the kid does it again; (10) threatening some punishment if the child performs the behavior again; and (11) promising to give the child something rewarding, such as a treat, if the kid behaves appropriately (i.e., a bribe). As you can see, these tactics view discipline very broadly in that they all attempt to change the child's behavior, but don't all involve punishment per se.

What did the researchers find? It turns out that most of the reported discipline techniques had little to no effect on kids' aggressive behaviors or anxiety. Which ones were effective? Use of corporal punishment, expressing disappointment in the child, loudly scolding, putting in time-out, and shaming the kid were all effective—effective at making the kids either more aggressive or anxious! That's right, none of the discipline techniques were effective in any true sense of the word, unless you're trying to raise a bully with mental health issues. Interestingly, when a specific discipline tactic is considered more *normal* or typical in a particular country, the negative effect of the tactic on aggression or anxiety was still negative, but slightly less so. In other words, for example, if you live in a community or culture where shaming a kid is considered normal or appropriate, your child may become less anxious than a kid who is shamed in a context where the culture considers shaming unacceptable, but your kid will still become more anxious than if you never shamed him or her.

It's important to note that findings such as these generally replicate what is seen in American samples. In a nutshell, *harsh parenting*, or being critical, yelling, or using physical punishment, will jack your kids up,[4-6] making them more aggressive, disobedient, anxious, and depressed (among other negative outcomes). So, does that mean you just shouldn't discipline your child? Not at all—*permissive* parenting (i.e., parents who don't use any discipline techniques) is bad too.[7] It's all about finding that right balance—one that teaches kids how to think for themselves and make appropriate decisions without being so heavy-handed they grow up resenting you or themselves. Sounds simple, huh? If it does, just wait until your three-old-year throws himself or herself down in the aisle of the supermarket screaming because you won't buy some ice cream. For those who are already afraid, and you should be, keep reading for some general guidelines for how to go about raising a healthy, well-behaved (eventually) child.

More on spanking

Admittedly, the vast majority of the research on discipline has focused on physical punishment, or, most commonly, spanking. Researchers define *physical punishment* as "the use of physical force with the intention of causing the child to experience bodily pain or discomfort so as to correct or punish the child's behavior."[8] Spanking, particularly within the United States, is remarkably common, with roughly 80% of parents reporting they have physically punished their child by the time he or she is in the fifth grade; 2- to 5-year-olds are the most likely targets.[8] As of 2008, however, 24 countries had banned physical punishment (the United States is not one of them), essentially viewing spanking as equivalent to striking or assaulting an adult (it is illegal to strike an adult in the United States, but until you're 18, you don't get such protections). Countries base these bans on moral rights or human rights arguments, and are in line with research findings that show spanking or corporal punishment is positively associated with many negative outcomes (e.g., stress, anxiety, aggressiveness).[1] Even in studies that look at "normal" levels of spanking (i.e., it is used as a last resort a few times a month), spanking is associated with, *at best*, no negative outcomes.[7]

Time-outs

Perhaps more important, there are far more effective means for disciplining a child than spanking, so you can shape their behaviors and avoid harming your kids to boot. Talk about a win–win! One strategy that parents employ quite frequently is the *time-out*, which generally involves removing a child from an enjoyable activity because he or she was behaving inappropriately. Unfortunately, many parents misuse time-outs, often putting a child in social isolation as a punishment (yours truly can remember spending a good chunk of time with his nose in a corner, becoming intimately acquainted with the subtle nuances of the walls). However, if you treat a timeout as an opportunity to have the child take a break from the activity, reach some acceptable level of composure that you define in advance (e.g., sit quietly for 2 minutes), and also use the time-out as an opportunity to have a conversation with your child about the circumstances that led to the time-out, then it can be a very effective strategy. (Note that it does require actually engaging with your kid and does not rely on social isolation as the primary mechanism.[9])

Basic principles of effective discipline

One of the things that can make time-outs effective is when the parent or caregiver focuses on the child's behavior and not the child's character. For example, coloring the wall with all 64 of Crayola's finest colors is an undesirable behavior, but doesn't make the child a bad kid, especially when you consider the fact that you actually praised your child for coloring just a few hours prior. How is your 2-year-old supposed to just spontaneously know that paper = good; walls = bad?[9] Focusing on the child's character (i.e., "bad boy/girl") starts to look a lot like shaming, whereas focusing on the kid's behavior implies the child has a sense of control or agency over their behavior (after all, we want the child to feel like they can control what they do, right?). Focusing on the behavior is a good rule of thumb. Here are a few other rules of thumb worth keeping in mind:

First, you should not dole out attention to your child only under certain conditions. Specifically, showing your children you love them only when they are good, or withdrawing your love when they are bad, can lead to resentment, a desire to do things only to please the parents, and poor academic performance. Rather, viewing the world through your child's eyes and helping him or her understand why doing "good" things or desired behaviors is advantageous (without linking it to external rewards) increases the desire to achieve and try new things *"All by myself,"* which is pretty much the pinnacle of toddlerdom.[10]

Second, do not underestimate the power and importance of a preemptive strike. Specifically, rewarding a positive behavior (e.g., praising the child for doing things you like) decreases the likelihood that unwanted behaviors rear their ugly heads in the first place. You should let your kids know when they are doing something good (otherwise they're liable to seek your attention in some other less desirable way). This shouldn't be shocking; We all like a thank-you or a little recognition now and then from the people we love.

Third, and this taps into the second point—many times simply ignoring a behavior is enough to make it go away. It is your reaction, or the reaction of those around you that a child keys onto, and letting kids know you don't like something by giving a negative reaction only gives them ammunition for the future. (This is analogous to the way a child might fall and then cry only if others react to the fall—attention is a powerful motivator.) Of course, you can't ignore everything (like when your son puts the cat in the freezer; this may or may not be based on actual events), but when the little one starts singing "S-H-I-T" (again, this may or may not be based on actual events) you might simply turn a blind eye and keep from giving the behavior any attention at all. (Forgoing the behavior yourself and setting a good example also helps.)

Fourth, and this is by no means an exhaustive list, the best parents monitor their kids, whether it's watching their every move when crawling begins or asking about the friends with whom your teenager hangs out. Monitored kids feel like valued kids. Valued kids feel better about themselves and are less likely to act like idiots.[11,12] More important, when you monitor, you create opportunities to redirect behavior (i.e., guide your child to more appropriate behaviors without drawing attention to the unwanted behavior) or reward acceptable behavior. If you're not watching, then you're not parenting. It is important to point out, however, that there is the possibility of "too much of a good thing." Monitoring your child is positive, but doing so at an overly high level may not allow him or her to feel independent or have the chance to learn from mistakes.

Conclusions

The most important idea to take away from this is to educate yourself about what your kid is and is not capable of. We read a manual to learn how to operate a blender (or should), but most people spend little time actually reading about or seeking assistance for how to parent. For example, don't ask your 2-year-old daughter to sit in a 5 minute time-out. You know what 5 minutes is to a 2 year-old? *Eternity!* (It is the toddler equivalent to an adult's trip to the DMV!) You're only setting her up for failure, because unless she falls asleep, there's no way she'll achieve a quiet 5 minutes. The punishment should fit the crime *in a developmentally appropriate way*. It's the last part of the previous sentence that makes it very hard to identify the best ways to discipline a child; what is best very much depends on the specific kid. But, hopefully, you now have a few more tools in your toolbox, and maybe realize you might need to throw a few out.

TAKE-HOME POINTS

- ♡ There are certainly a lot of wrong ways to discipline a kid, but identifying what is most effective has proved to be challenging.
- ♡ Some basic rules should guide your chosen discipline techniques, and what works for one kid may not work for another.
- ♡ Ideally, take a proactive stance by monitoring your kid, which allows you to shape appropriate behavior from the beginning. Yet, even the most well-behaved children are going to push your buttons from time to time (or every minute).
- ♡ Stay calm, focus on the behavior, choose a developmentally appropriate strategy, and stick to your guns.
- ♡ And don't forget: The goal is for your child to behave appropriately when you are not around, so the more you can talk to your kid and help him or her internalize why some behavior is appropriate, whereas other behaviors are not, the better.

References

1. Gershoff, E. T. 2002. "Corporal Punishment by Parents and Associated Child Behaviors and Experiences: A Meta-Analytic and Theoretical Review." *Psychological Bulletin* 128 (4): 539–579.
2. Gershoff, E. T., A. Grogan-Kaylor, J. E. Lansford, L. Chang, A. Zelli, K. Deater-Deckard, and K. A. Dodge. 2010. "Parent Discipline Practices in an International Sample: Associations with Child Behaviors and Moderation by Perceived Normativeness." *Child Development* 81 (2): 487–502.
3. Bosmans, G., C. Braet, W. Beyers, K. Van Leeuwen, and L. Van Vlierberghe. 2011. "Parents' Power Assertive Discipline and Internalizing Problems in Adolescents: The Role of Attachment." *Parenting: Science and Practice* 11 (1): 34–55.
4. Fletcher, A. C., J. K. Walls, E. C. Cook, K. J. Madison, and T. H. Bridges. 2008. "Parenting Style as a Moderator of Associations between Maternal Disciplinary Strategies and Child Well-Being." *Journal of Family Issues* 29 (12): 1724–1744.
5. McKee, L., E. Roland, N. Coffelt, A. Olson, R. Forehand, C. Massari, D. Jones, C. Gaffney, and M. Zens. 2007. "Harsh Discipline and Child Problem Behaviors: The Roles of Positive Parenting and Gender." *Journal of Family Violence* 22 (4): 187–196.
6. Rhoades, K. A., L. D. Leve, G. T. Harold, J. M. Neiderhiser, D. S. Shaw, and D. Reiss. 2011. "Longitudinal Pathways from Marital Hostility to Child Anger during Toddlerhood: Genetic Susceptibility and Indirect Effects via Harsh Parenting." *Journal of Family Psychology* 25 (2): 282–291.
7. Baumrind, D., R. E. Larzelere, and E. B. Owens. 2010. "Effects of Preschool Parents' Power Assertive Patterns and Practices on Adolescent Development." *Parenting: Science and Practice* 10(3): 157–201.
8. Gershoff, E. T. 2008. *Report on Physical Punishment in the United States: What Research Tells Us about Its Effects on Children.* Columbus OH: Center for Effective Discipline.
9. Morawska, A., and M. Sanders. 2011. "Parental Use of Time Out Revisited: A Useful or Harmful Parenting Strategy?" *Journal of Child and Family Studies* 20 (1): 1–8.
10. Roth, G., A. Assor, C. P. Niemiec, R. M. Ryan, and E. L. Deci. 2009. "The Emotional and Academic Consequences of Parental Conditional Regard: Comparing Conditional Positive Regard, Conditional Negative Regard, and Autonomy Support as Parenting Practices." *Developmental Psychology* 45 (4): 1119–1142.
11. Bumpus, M. F., and K. B. Rodgers. 2009. "Parental Knowledge and Its Sources." *Journal of Family Issues* 30 (10): 1356–1378.
12. Gaertner, A., J. Rathert, P. Fite, M. Vitulano, P. Wynn, and J. Harber 2010. "Sources of Parental Knowledge as Moderators of the Relation between Parental Psychological Control and Relational and Physical/Verbal Aggression." *Journal of Child and Family Studies* 19 (5): 607–616.

Dig Deeper

Bailey, J. A., K. G. Hill, S. Oesterle, and J. D. Hawkins. 2009. "Parenting Practices and Problem Behavior across Three Generations: Monitoring, Harsh Discipline, and Drug Use in the Intergenerational Transmission of Externalizing Behavior." *Developmental Psychology* 45 (5): 1214–1226.

Dix, T., and L. N. Meunier. 2009. "Depressive Symptoms and Parenting Competence: An Analysis of 13 Regulatory Processes." *Developmental Review* 29 (1): 45–68.

Dix, T., A. D. Stewart, E. T. Gershoff, and W. H. Day. 2007. "Autonomy and Children's Reactions to Being Controlled: Evidence That Both Compliance and Defiance May Be Positive Markers in Early Development." *Child Development* 78 (4): 1204–1221.

Q40: AM I A BAD PARENT FOR PUTTING MY CHILD IN CHILDCARE?

M. Minda Oriña

First, let's set the record straight. Bad parents forget their kid's birthday, never give their child ice cream, and take family vacations to Neverland instead of Disneyland. Bad parents exist; absolutely perfect parents do not. The question about childcare is one that many mothers and fathers ask, worried that they might be harming their kid by staying home with him or her. Fundamentally, every parent wants to do what is best for his or her child. But when it comes to childcare, knowing what is "best" for kids is a bit unclear. Often, parents may not have much of a choice—money pays the bills. Yet, needing to work and using childcare to make that possible often leads to an avalanche of questions and concerns: Will working hurt my ability to bond with my child? Will it affect my child's ability to develop language, or focus attention, or regulate their behavior? Will my child have more social problems if I put my child in childcare? Will my children learn aggressive behaviors from their peers and become more aggressive because of childcare? Instead of asking if it is bad or good for parents to work, researchers instead ask about the conditions under which employment affects child development (either good or bad), and how employment may affect child development socially, emotionally, academically, and cognitively? We can condense all of these questions into two central questions: (1) How does maternal employment affect child development, and (2) what are the effects of childcare on child development? (Note: The vast majority of research has focused on *maternal* employment, which is why the question at the top of this page could read *Mom* rather than *Parent*. But just because research has ignored the Paternal side of the question does not mean it should continue to be ignored.)

Is it bad for the child if mom works?

Maternal employment is not necessarily detrimental for child outcomes. In fact, the more important question is whether mothers *want* to work and how that matches up with whether they *do* work. When mothers work, and want to work, their children fare just as well as mothers who want to stay at home and do stay at home.[1]

However, children are worse off when mom works when she would prefer to stay home or when mom stays at home when she wants to be working outside the home. The bottom line is that the best work situation for mom is the one she truly wants, not the one she feels obligated to do. So if you want to return to the field, classroom, cubicle farm, or your corner office—go right ahead! You'll be doing your child a favor, and he or she will fare much better than if you stay at home when you'd rather be working outside of the home.[2]

If I work, how will that influence my relationship with my child?

Many mothers also worry that working will impair the quality of their relationship with their child. Working mothers: Do not worry! There is little evidence that working undermines the quality of the mother–child relationship.[2] Whereas working may detract from the amount of time mothers spend with their children, many working mothers tend to prioritize their time to ensure that they spend time with their children when they are not working. In other words, quality trumps quantity, and it is the *quality* of mother–child interactions that is associated with positive outcomes. Mothers who are sensitive, responsive, and attentive (but not smothering!) to their children tend to have children who fare well, both socially and cognitively. In short, it's the quality of your interactions, not the quantity, with your children that leads them to have good relationships with you and to be smart and popular with their peers.

Is all childcare created equal?

If you are going to place your child in childcare, be it in your own home (i.e., relatives or caregivers come to your home to care for your child), at a caregiver's house, or at a daycare center, it is important that you look for *high-quality* care. Unfortunately, there isn't a Zagat guide to help parents identify high-quality care in their neighborhoods. Fortunately, thanks to the NICHD Study of Early Child Care and Youth Development (SECCYD), a nationally representative, longitudinal study conducted in the United States that has been studying the effects of early childcare on children's emotional, social, cognitive, and physical development, we know what features of childcare lead to the best possible outcomes.[3] Ideally, your childcare providers should be warm, positive, sensitive, and responsive to your child's needs and behaviors. They should model positive behaviors to your child and should encourage positive behaviors from your child. For example, they should actively share toys and activities with others, while also encouraging the children to share toys with each other. Sort of like a cross between Mr. Rogers and Barney. Caring is sharing, neighbor. Furthermore, the size of the group and the adult-to-child ratio should be small (and ideally smaller than most state laws mandate). This is particularly important when the child is very young, when having small group sizes is especially associated with positive outcomes. The American Academy of Pediatrics recommends the following: at age 6 months to 1.5 years, 3 children to 1 staff member; at age 1.5 to 2 years, 4 children to 1 staff member; from 2 to 7 years, 7 children to 1 staff member. Finally, the caregivers should provide an environment that promotes curiosity and exploration of the children's world, which benefits children's cognitive and emotional development.

What are the potential benefits of childcare?

On the whole, findings from SECCYD suggest that there actually may be benefits to placing your child in *high-quality* childcare. Most of the research that examined the associations between childcare and cognitive development (including language development and later academic achievement) strongly suggests that placing your child in a high-quality childcare setting does have beneficial effects. For example, children who are placed in higher-quality care show greater school readiness prior to kindergarten. Furthermore, some argue that children develop important social skills by interacting with their peers when placed in center-based care.[4] Cognitively, socially, and academically, high-quality care is beneficial! Although it is important to note that these are not large differences, the effects of childcare are above and beyond the influences of parents and family. High-quality childcare really can help.

What are the potential problems with childcare?

However, there may be some downsides to placing your child in childcare. The NICHD study also provides some evidence that children who are placed in childcare early in life and spend long hours during the day in center-based childcare display more aggressive and disobedient behavior. More "extensive" childcare is also associated with internalizing problems, like anxiety.[5,6]

Notably, these findings do not apply to children in very low-income families. In fact, for disadvantaged children, longer hours in childcare (provided those long hours are in high-quality care) are associated with favorable adjustment.[7] Moreover, children who participate in programs such as Head Start show better social and emotional adjustment and fewer conduct problems. It is important to note that even large-scale studies such as the NICHD study cannot state that having high-quality care *causes* children to develop positively, or negatively, because in these studies the researchers merely measured children over time. In an ideal world (at least for researchers), we would take a large sample of children and then randomly place them in childcare or at home with their parents, then see who fares better. Unfortunately, such a design isn't practical or ethical. Instead, we can measure and observe children in differing childcare environments and then discuss the kinds of outcomes that tend to be associated with these environments.

Conclusions

The bottom line? Having your child in childcare because you want to work doesn't make you a bad parent. Just be sure you do your homework and find sensitive and responsive caregivers for your child. Your child will directly benefit from *good* childcare experiences. In addition, your kid is likely to benefit indirectly because of the happiness and sense of fulfillment you achieve through your work, whether it be managing play dates or managing the office.

TAKE-HOME POINTS

♡ Child outcomes are best when mothers are satisfied with their roles. If mothers prefer to work, then work! If mothers prefer to stay at home, then stay home!

♡ Your relationship with your child will not necessarily be harmed if you do work. Quality of interaction with your children trumps quantity of interaction.

♡ If you do place your child in childcare, look for places offering high-quality care. Your child will benefit cognitively, socially, and emotionally.

References

1. Kalil, A., and K. Ziol-Guest. 2005. "Single Mothers' Employment Dynamics and Adolescent Well-Being." *Child Development* 76: 196–211.
2. Gottfried, A. E., A. W. Gottfried, and K. Bathhurst. 2002. "Maternal and Dual-Earner Employment Status and Parenting." In *Handbook of Parenting*, 2nd ed. Vol. 2: *Biology and Ecology of Parenting*, edited by M. H. Bornstein, 207–229. Mahwah NJ: Erlbaum.
3. NICHD Early Child Care Research Network Ed. 2005. *Child Care and Child Development: Results of the NICHD Study of Early Child Care and Youth Development.* New York: Guilford Press.
4. Volling, B. L., and L. V. Feagan. 1995. "Infant Day Care and Children's Social Competence." *Infant Behavior and Development* 18: 177–188.
5. NICHD Early Child Care Research Network. 1998. "Early Child Care and Self-Control, Compliance, and Problem Behavior at Twenty-Four and Thirty-Six Months." *Child Development* 69: 1145–1170.
6. NICHD Early Child Care Research Network. 2003. "Does Amount of Time Spent in Child Care Predict Socioemotional Adjustment during the Transition to Kindergarten?" *Child Development* 74: 976–1005.
7. Votruba-Drzal, E., R. L. Coley, and P. L. Chase-Lansdale. 2004. "Child Care and Low-Income Children's Development: Direct and Moderated Effects." *Child Development* 75: 296–312.

Dig Deeper

Eunice Kennedy Shriver National Institute of Child Health and Human Development, NIH, DHHS. 2006. *The NICHD Study of Early Child Care and Youth Development (SECCYD): Findings for Children up to Age 4 1/2 Years (05-4318).* Washington DC: U.S. Government Printing Office.

NICHD Early Child Care Research Network, editors. 2005. *Child Care and Child Development: Results of the NICHD Study of Early Child Care and Youth Development.* New York: Guilford Press.

EPILOGUE

Parting Thoughts and a Thank You

As we mentioned in the introduction, the idea for this book came to life on a snowy June night in Breckenridge, Colorado. Now, almost exactly seven years later, *The Science of Relationships* has finally come to fruition. In many ways, the completion of the book is a testament to persistence (and more than just a little stubbornness) and the fundamental belief that people value their lives enough to want to learn about what science has to say about how relationships develop and function. We also believe strongly, based on our experiences in and out of college classrooms and from dealing with the popular press, that consumers (i.e., you) care about and want to know how knowledge about relationships is gained. In fact, with any luck, our book has increased the value you place on research-based information.

We hope that the 40 questions addressed in these pages have laid the foundation for your interest in relationship science. Admittedly, it is likely that you felt our selection left some things unanswered. We couldn't agree more; we left *a lot* of things unanswered. Such is the nature of any "Top XX List" or compilation of "Greatest Hits." If you'd like to learn more about what science has to say about relationships, the editors of this book have created a website (http://www.ScienceOfRelationships.com) dedicated to disseminating high-quality information about relationships in an engaging, informative, and often humorous way. Feel free to drop by the site; it will further help you learn about your own relationships and why, more generally, people feel and behave the way they do in their dealings with others. And if you have a question we didn't answer here, maybe we'll address it on the site.

We believe passionately in the mission to pull the science of our field out of academic journals and present it in a way that most people can appreciate. The amount of research published in academic journals has increased dramatically since the turn of the millenium.[1] Yet, an astonishingly small amount of that research (less than 0.005% of publications in psychology) finds its way into mass media (e.g., books, magazines, websites, talk shows), where people can learn and benefit from the research findings and their implications. Science is fundamentally about contributing to humans' knowledge, but if relationship science continues to be confined to academic journals that are primarily read by other academics, the potential impact of this knowledge cannot be fully realized. So, please, by all means, share this book, check out the website, and don't hesitate to pass on your newfound knowledge to others.

Most important: *Thank you.* Thank you for investing your time and money in our book. We hope you have enjoyed reading it as much as we enjoyed writing it. Best of luck in the future, and may your relationships continue to benefit from science.

Reference

1. Suleski, J., and M. Ibaraki. 2010. "Scientists Are Talking, but Mostly to Each Other: A Quantitative Analysis of Research Represented in Mass Media." *Public Understanding of Science* 19: 115–125.

INDEX

ABOUT
...the Authors and Contributors

Lorne Campbell, Ph.D.
University of Western Ontario

Dr. Campbell earned his Ph.D. in Social Psychology from Texas A&M University in 2001 and is currently an Associate Professor of psychology at the University of Western Ontario. He is a recognized expert in the fields of interpersonal relationships, research design and data analysis, and evolutionary psychology. Lorne's work includes an impressive list of published research articles and chapters, and he has been the recipient of many research grants and awards. From 2008-09 Lorne was a Harrington Faculty Fellow at the University of Texas at Austin. He is on the editorial board of *Journal of Personality and Social Psychology* and *Personality and Social Psychology Bulletin*, and is currently the editor of the journal *Personal Relationships*. Dr. Campbell has also discussed research regarding interpersonal relationships with many media outlets, including print media, national and local radio programs, and national and local television programs.

Jody Davis, Ph.D.
Virginia Commonwealth University

Dr. Davis earned her Ph.D. in Social Psychology from the University of North Carolina in 2000 and is currently an Associate Professor of psychology at Virginia Commonwealth University, where she teaches courses on interpersonal relationships, social psychology, and the teaching of psychology. Her research examines close relationship processes such as attitude alignment, forgiveness, and sacrifice. She also is interested in non-interpersonal relationships such as interdependence with the natural world.

Robin S. Edelstein, Ph.D.
University of Michigan

Dr. Edelstein is an Assistant Professor of Psychology at the University of Michigan. She received her Ph.D. in Social/Personality Psychology from the University of California, Davis, in 2005, and completed a postdoctoral fellowship in the Department of Psychology and Social Behavior at the University of California, Irvine. Her research focuses on close relationships in adulthood, particularly individual differences in the way that people regulate their emotions and behavior in close relationships and the physiological implications of these differences. Robin teaches graduate and undergraduate courses in close relationships, and she is currently serving on the editorial board of *Personal Relationships* and *Social Psychological and Personality Science.*

Nancy Frye, Ph.D.
Long Island University Post

Dr. Frye received her Ph.D. in Social Psychology from the University of Florida in 2002 and is currently an Associate Professor at Long Island University Post. Her research interests include factors related to the use of physical aggression within romantic relationships, and while at the University of Florida she contributed to the design and management of two four-year longitudinal studies of newlywed marriage. Nancy has published articles on marital processes and development in journals such as *Journal of Personality and Social Psychology* and *Personality and Social Psychology Bulletin.*

Marci Gleason, Ph.D.
The University of Texas at Austin

Dr. Gleason received her Ph.D. at New York University in Social and Organizational Psychology in 2004 and is currently an assistant professor in Human Development and Family Sciences at the University of Texas at Austin. Her research focuses on how couples navigate stressful circumstances such a chronic illness and the transition to parenthood. She is currently teaching a senior level course on how families navigate important transitions such as marriage, parenthood, divorce, and bereavement.

Jennifer Harman, Ph.D.
Colorado State University

Dr. Harman received her Ph.D. at the University of Connecticut in Social Psychology in 2005, and is currently an Assistant Professor of psychology at Colorado State University. In addition, she has graduate training in psychological counseling at Teacher's College, Columbia University, and post-graduate training in Gestalt psychotherapy. She worked for several years as a counselor and counseling supervisor before finishing her doctorate, and she now studies interpersonal processes in intimate relationships. Specifically, Jennifer examines relationship behaviors (e.g., sexual risk taking, communication problems) that put people at risk for physical and psychological health problems.

Benjamin Le, Ph.D.
Haverford College

Dr. Le earned his Ph.D. in Social Psychology from Purdue University in 2003, and is currently an Associate Professor of psychology at Haverford College. He has been doing research on close relationships since 1996, and his current work involves commitment, the experience of geographic separation in relationships, and relationship maintenance, as well as how social networks influence dating relationships. Currently, he is a member of the editorial board for the journal *Personal Relationships* and a co-founder of www.ScienceOfRelationships.com

Gary Lewandowski, Ph.D.
Monmouth University

Dr. Lewandowski received his Ph.D. in Social/Health Psychology from the State University of New York at Stony Brook in 2002. Gary is an Associate Professor at Monmouth University, where he teaches courses in Intimate Relationships and Research Methodology, and he is a co-founder of www.ScienceOfRelationships.com. Currently, he is a member of the editorial board for the *Journal of Social and Personal Relationships*. His research has been published in a number of scholarly journals and focuses on romantic relationships, including interpersonal attraction, relationship maintenance, infidelity, and break-ups. His research has been featured in a number of media outlets including: local newspapers, *The New York Times, CNN, Science Daily, United Press International, Woman's World, Marie Claire, WebMD, Self Magazine, Woman's Day, Cosmopolitan Magazine, Ladies Home Journal, Women's Health, Men's Health,* and *USA Today.*

Timothy Loving, Ph.D.
The University of Texas at Austin

Dr. Loving received his Ph.D. in Social Psychology from Purdue University in 2001. He is currently an Associate Professor in The University of Texas at Austin's Department of Human Development and Family Sciences. Prior to arriving at Texas, he received Post-doctoral training at The Ohio State University College of Medicine in Psychoneuroimmunology. Dr. Loving's research addresses the mental and physical health impact of relationship transitions, with a particular focus on affectively positive transitions (e.g., falling in love) and the role network members serve as relationship partners adapt to these transitions. He is currently an Associate Editor of Personal Relationships and a member of the editorial board for the Journal of Personality and Social Psychology and is a co-founder of www. ScienceOfRelationships.com. His work has been published in the Journal of Personality and Social Psychology, Personal Relationships, Psychosomatic Medicine, Psychoneuroendocrinology, and Archives of General Psychiatry. In addition, he teaches a large introductory course on family relationships and has received numerous teaching awards for his teaching excellence.

Debra Mashek, Ph.D.
Harvey Mudd College

Dr. Mashek earned her Ph.D. in Social/Health Psychology from the State University of New York at Stony Brook in 2002, and is currently an Associate Professor of Psychology at Harvey Mudd college. Her research interests include the experience of feeling too close to intimate others, processes involved in confusing the self with close others, and extending close relationship theory to the community domain. Her research has been highlighted in high-profile media outlets including *The New York Times, Time Magazine,* and *USA Today.* Deb is an award-winning teacher and regularly contributes to psychology textbook projects. Her edited volume, *Empirical Research in Teaching and Learning,* blends her research interests with her passion for teaching.

Lisa Neff, Ph.D.
The University of Texas at Austin

Dr. Neff received her Ph.D. in Social Psychology from the University of Florida in 2002, and is currently an Assistant Professor in the Department of Human Development and Family Sciences at the University of Texas at Austin. She is an expert on marital relationships and her research focuses on identifying the factors that contribute to marital well-being and dissolution. She currently has funding from National Science Foundation to examine how stressors outside the marriage (e.g. work stress, financial strains) may influence relationship processes and outcomes during the early years of marriage.

M. Minda Oriña, Ph.D.
St. Olaf College

Dr. Oriña is a developmental social psychologist whose program of research examines processes that help individuals maintain and enhance the quality of their adult romantic relationships. Currently, she is on the editorial board of Psychological Science, Journal of Personality and Social Psychology, Personality and Social Psychology Bulletin, and Personal Relationships. Her primary interests involve studying romantic relationships within a developmental context. By understanding prior developmental history in conjunction with proximal factors, she believes that we will achieve a deeper and more nuanced understanding of current relationship functioning and dynamics. Additional research interests include social influence in romantic relationships, attachment theory, interdependence theory, empathic accuracy, power, and trust.

Eshkol Rafaeli, Ph.D.

Dr. Rafaeli received his Ph.D. from Northwestern University in Clinical and Personality Psychology in 2001. He is currently the head of the adult clinical psychology program at Bar-Ilan University, and serves as a research scientist at Barnard College, Columbia University. Eshkol's research addresses affective and relational processes in typical individuals as well as in ones suffering from psychopathology – primarily personality disorders. His clinical training was predominantly cognitive behavioral, with an internship at McLean Hospital/Harvard Medical School, and additional training in structural family therapy at the Minuchin Center for Family Therapy. He is a founder of the Israeli Institute of Schema Therapy, and co-authored the book *Schema Therapy: Distinctive Features* with Jeffrey Young and David Bernstein.